Evolving Jewish Identities in German Culture

Evolving Jewish Identities in German Culture

Borders and Crossings

Edited by
Linda E. Feldman and Diana Orendi
Foreword by Sander L. Gilman

PRAEGER

Westport, Connecticut
London

Library of Congress Cataloging-in-Publication Data

Evolving Jewish identities in German culture : borders and crossings /
   edited by Linda E. Feldman and Diana Orendi ; foreword by Sander L.
   Gilman.
      p. cm.
   Includes bibliographical references and index.
   ISBN 0–275–95557–5 (alk. paper)
    1. German literature—20th century—History and criticism.
  2. German literature—Jewish authors—History and criticism.
  3. Jews in literature. 4. Antisemitism in literature. 5. Germany—
Ethnic relations. 6. Germany—Civilization—Jewish influences.
  7. Jews—Germany—Intellectual life. I. Feldman, Linda E.
  II. Orendi, Diana.
  PT405.E83 2000
  830.9′352924—dc21   97–18194

British Library Cataloguing in Publication Data is available.

Library of Congress Catalog Card Number: 97–18194
ISBN: 0–275–95557–5

First published in 2000

Praeger Publishers, 88 Post Road West, Westport, CT 06881
An imprint of Greenwood Publishing Group, Inc.
www.praeger.com

Printed in the United States of America

The paper used in this book complies with the
Permanent Paper Standard issued by the National
Information Standards Organization (Z39.48–1984).

10 9 8 7 6 5 4 3 2 1

Contents

Foreword

Sander L. Gilman

The scholarly work on the history and the culture of the Jews in Germany has taken a new turning in the past decade. No longer memorialization or martyrology, the new arena of Jewish Cultural Studies has taken the vicissitudes and triumphs of German Jewry (in all its complexity) as one of the models for itself. This volume is a major contribution to this new Jewish Cultural Studies as it looks at the German-speaking world.

Dealing with the wide sweep of Jewish cultural presence in Germany (and the representation of that presence), the authors encompass but do not stop at the Shoah. The living tradition of post-Shoah German/Jewish cultural life is represented in all its complexities and difficulties. It is the "negative symbiose" incarnate that Dan Diner presented in the first volume of the Jewish German journal *Babylon*. The authors of this volume undertake a sophisticated and intelligent approach to aspects of Jewish life in nineteenth- and twentieth-century German culture—and ask difficult questions about them.

I am pleased about the turn that this volume took. It grew directly out of the first joint National Endowment for the Humanities/German Academic Exchange Service summer seminars for college teachers, which I directed in the summer of 1994. The topic was Franz Kafka and post-Shoah Jewish writing in Germany. The contributors were all members of that seminar. This purposeful connection of the complex and self-contradictory world of Kafka's Jewish experience in the Pragues in which he lived and the equally (but also very different) contemporary world of writers such as Esther Dischereit or Maxim Biller seemed to me a means of stressing both the continuities and the radical differences of what it meant to write and feel as a "Jew" (however defined) in the world of German letters.

The scope of this volume helps set the broader agenda. No longer is it possible (or necessary) to stop Jewish history as if the Nazis were indeed victorious. The rebirth of a Jewish culture in a Germany still dealing with its multiple pasts as it deals with its futures makes this project most timely.

Sander L. Gilman,
Henry Luce Professor of the
Liberal Arts in Human Biology,
The University of Chicago

Introduction

Linda E. Feldman
Diana Orendi

> The road led through the wintry night in the Eifel, on smugglers'
> routes to Belgium, whose custom officials and policemen would have
> refused us a legal crossing of the border, for we were coming into the
> country as refugees, without passport and visa, without any valid na-
> tional identity. It was a long way through the night.
> —Jean Améry, *At the Mind's Limits,* 41

In January 1939, a young man by the name of Hans Maier furtively slipped over the German border into Belgium, accompanied by his young wife. On the German side of the border, the clauses of the Nuremberg race laws threatened to constrain and eventually strangle the young intellectual's existence. On the far side of the border, in a strange land and language, lay the comparative freedom, but also the uncertainty, of life as a bureaucratic nonentity. In wavering French, the man who would later become known as Jean Améry telegraphed a safe arrival. The finality of his arrival, however, would prove to be a delusion, for in the war years to come, Améry would illegally cross many more frontiers. Crossing, in this life of exile, entailed slipping from one uncertainty to another, from one illusory identity to another. Améry's description of his nocturnal escape from the textual "legality" of life in Germany, where his every movement was literally circumscribed, to the "illegality" of life in Belgium, where he lived outside the letter of the law, marks the border as a textually symbolic site. But in Améry's case, the border is more than just the meeting place of judicial codes encrypting differing constructions of civic reality. The border also serves as a site of ambiguity, transition, and danger, a living membrane that keeps in and lock out, that exudes and absorbs, that validates and invalidates individual and group identity. It does not surprise, then, that in later life, armed with sufficient documentation, Améry nonetheless cannot escape the frisson of terror whenever his identity comes under bureaucratic scrutiny at the frontier.

A generation later, many of Améry's experiences and responses are uncannily echoed in *Joëmis Tisch* (*Joëmi's Table*), a "Jewish" story written by the Jewish German writer Esther Dischereit:

> At the border, I draw a breath of relief. Made it, got through. My heart pounding, I had held the passport, had forced my hands to be still. My ears still expecting a "Stop!", they sense the dogs at my back, see the border gate already lifted, hesitate. Of course, my papers are valid, and I carry no contraband. But if they were to demand that I get—why would they?—if they were to demand I get undressed, and I got undressed.—And the star could be seen through my clothes—it can't be seen—through my clothes, burnt into my skin —it isn't burnt, have never been there—burnt into my skin, and the dogs were drawing close. (35)

For this post-Holocaust Jewish writer, a 1988 border crossing from West Germany into France is anything but routine. History, like the star, shimmers through the present: the border of today echoes the border of yesterday; the fragility of identity is all too apparent, despite and because of the failure of the French official to doubt the narrator's identity or suspect the presence of her existential contraband. What once was now becomes a moment of potential, extending the reach of the past into the present and on to the future. For the narrator, the experience of her mother, a Holocaust survivor, is literally and figuratively embodied in her sense of Jewish identity. The vulnerability of this construction becomes most apparent at the border. To cross borders for this young writer is to leave danger in order to face unknown perils. There is no safety beyond the borders. "Prophylactically, I learn many languages and other things" (35).

While the foregoing discussion of the semantic multiplicity of the border is restricted to Améry's and Dischereit's confrontations with the geopolitical frontier, it is clear that borders, boundaries, perimeters, limits, demarcations, and crossings find multiple applications in our intercourse with the outside world. Common daily experiences with borders include, for example, the body as the membrane between inside and outside, or ritual as the boundary between inclusion in and exclusion from the group. Every day, discourse serves as the tool assigning subject or object status to individuals and collectivities, while age functions as a generational divide, enabling or disabling the sharing of wisdom and experience in the formulation of self-identity. The border may serve as a barrier or a bridge, it may rupture or connect, or it may shift, allowing whatever is behind it or before it to assume new definitional contours.

In cognizance of the impossibility of assigning permanent meaning to this term, this volume presumes the mutable quality of the frontier, and examines the role of the border in the construction of twentieth-century Jewish identity in German culture. The title of the anthology, *Evolving Jewish Identities in Ger-*

man Culture: Borders and Crossings, is thus intended to point not just to the delimiting and transcending possibilities of the border, but also to the processes underlying multiple and fluid formations of Jewish identity. The first section, entitled "Drawing Borders: Cutting and Binding Communities," examines the ambiguity of dividing lines between the Jewish and non-Jewish worlds before the Holocaust. In contributions by Christopher D. Kenway and Sonja M. Hedgepeth, the construction of Jewish difference is viewed from the perspective of dynamics and discourses issuing outside the Jewish community.

The ambiguity of the *Körperkultur* (physical culture) movement, as reflected in little-studied journals of the first two decades of this century, is Kenway's focus in his chapter "Regeneration of the *Volkskörper* and the Jew's Body: The German *Körperkultur* Movement at the Turn of the Century." Recent research has tended to emphasize how the Nazis were able to appropriate *Körperkultur* theories of degeneration to advocate the special degeneracy of the Jews. Kenway approaches this phenomenon from a different angle by suggesting that this elision was not a foregone conclusion. As a counterbalance, he argues that the movement's belief in the capacity for regeneration of the *Volkskörper* (national body) often provided for the inclusion of Jewish as well as non-Jewish bodies. This reading of *Körperkultur* reveals a quintessential duality expressed in its ability to throw bridges between Jewish and non-Jewish Germans, and subsequently tear them down.

While *Körperkultur* theory represents the use of a modern, "scientific" discourse for anti-Semitic purposes, premodern critiques of Jewish identity serve as the point of departure for Hedgepeth's discussion of selected examples of German *Notgeld* (emergency money) from the Weimar Republic. In her contribution, "The Palimpsestic Identity: Residual Discourses on Jews Exemplified by German *Notgeld*," Hedgepeth demonstrates how traditional and dormant anti-Semitic discourses are restored to common ideological currency by superimposing on them contemporary discourses on Jews. The result of these palimpsestic layers is not merely the vilification of historical and contemporary Jewry. Rather, objectified on currency, Jews are exchanged, and exchangeable, in commodity transactions that link but separate them from the majority community. This dual process of what contributor Steven Taubeneck would term "cutting and binding" is discussed more fully in his article later in this section.

While Kenway and Hedgepeth anchor their investigations in discourses formulated outside the Jewish community, David Brenner and Steven Taubeneck study processes of boundary drawing initiating within the Jewish community. Brenner's discussion of the theme of reconciliation, as portrayed in two serialized novels carried by the popular weekly *Israelitisches Familienblatt*, points to the acute uncertainty with which Jewish authors and readers defined and redefined their social relationships to non-Jews in the political tumult of 1923–1924. While the now largely forgotten author Meta Opet-Fuß advocates an increasingly hesitant rapprochement between the two communities, her fellow contributor, Rabbi Martin Salomonski, chooses in his novel to erect barriers and keep them stable in the face of an encroaching and increasingly hostile world. Brenner argues that in simultaneously proposing reconciliation *and* differentiation, the *Familienblatt* concretizes the growing ambivalence experienced by many Jews in their relations with the non-Jewish world.

The relational implications of cutting and binding also reveal paradoxical features in Taubeneck's broad analysis of the function of circumcision in Jewish and non-Jewish culture, inside and outside Germany. Taubeneck draws on lines of inquiry deployed in cultural studies to show that while circumcision has traditionally engendered group coherence and distinctiveness in all their positive and negative ramifications, the onslaught of assimilation undermines and erodes the cohering function of the ritual among German Jews. Citing examples from the Bible, Franz Kafka, and Edgar Hilsenrath, Taubeneck demonstrates that where rituals fail to cohere—where, as in the case of circumcision, there is absence of bonding through cutting—communities and their texts fall apart. Under such circumstances, group formation becomes dependent on patchwork seaming, a phenomenon reflected in literary production as in life.

Taken together, the contributions by Kenway, Hedgepeth, Brenner, and Taubeneck suggest the multiple ambiguities associated with the act of drawing borders between the Jewish and non-Jewish worlds. In contrast, polarization rather than ambiguity underlies the construction of intergenerational relations in much Jewish writing in German. Must the generational, and hence experiential, divisiveness of age in a time of crises be an insurmountable gap, or can bridges be thrown to link the generations? In the second section of this volume, "Bridges and Gulfs: Intergenerational Ruptures and Connections," contributions by Scott Spector, Iris M. Bruce, Diana Orendi, and Linda E. Feldman enumerate the possibilities.

By analyzing the strategy underlying tropes of size in Kafka's writing, Spector approaches the well-known conflictive relationship between Kafka and his father from an innovative perspective. In his chapter, "From Big Daddy to Small Literature: On Taking Kafka at His Word," Spector argues that conventional readings that contrast paternal strength with filial weakness are in fact victims of a trap reading. Equating the father's bulk with the majority discourse of assimilating Jewry, Spector argues that the son's retaliatory extolling of smallness and weakness in his life and texts is not capitulation, but a means to escape from the father's ponderously materialistic value system. What is weak is light, and what is light can soar and aspire to the spirituality of aesthetic realms. By extension, minor literature, as a metaphorical lightweight, can also subversively transcend the onerous value system seeking to suppress it. In this context, the maintenance of the generational breach between father and son becomes a moral imperative, in life as in literature.

The necessity to maintain the generational gulf is also advocated in Iris M. Bruce's contribution, "'A Frosty Hall of Mirrors': *Father Knows Best* in Franz Kafka and Nadine Gordimer." By juxtaposing Kafka's accusatory letter to his father with Gordimer's fictitious response by the elder Kafka, the explosive dynamics within the turn-of-the-century Prague Jewish minority are exposed. In the process, the father's—and by extension the older generation's—values are shown to be defined by complicit prejudice, racism, and petty middle-class morality. By contrast, Gordimer's construction of Kafka—and his youthful contemporaries—reveals a rebellious generation bent on fighting assimilation, preoccupied with self-hatred, and in search of escapist artistry. The reflections of this "frosty hall of mirrors" reach backward as well as forward in time and space, inviting the reader to read Gordimer's South African homeland against the backdrop of Kafka's Prague.

If generational rupture is a moral imperative in Spector's and Bruce's contributions, it is reformulated as a moral crisis in Diana Orendi's chapter, "Narrative Strategies to Disclose Pious Lies in the Works of Irene Dische." What is the correct stance for the child to assume when Kafka's assimilatory monster two generations later becomes the traumatized Shoah survivor and, for his estranged child, a moribund monster? American-born Dische's angry and agonizing search for Jewish self-definition despite Catholic roots entails rejecting not just the pious lies shrouding her father's, and hence her own, past but grotesquely and compulsively enacting a "final solution" upon the father himself. As Orendi demonstrates, compulsive and repeated literary parricide serves as the recurring vehicle by which the narrative alter ego expiates an ever-quelling anger. This assumption of textual guilt is paradoxically the first step in Dische's literary process of Jewish self-affirmation.

For her part, Linda E. Feldman, in her contribution "Through a Distant Lens: Cultural Displacement, Connection, and Disconnection in the Writing of Maxim Biller," uncovers a very different and evolving negotiation of the post-Shoah generational breach. Biller's Eastern European background, she argues, enables him, in contrast to Jews of exclusively German background, to defer Jewish German identity issues by displacing them in literature onto non-German milieus. This strategy, by elucidating the possibilities of Jewish life and death, serves to counteract the asphyxiating "oblivion" that Biller perceives as engulfing Germany. In the five years extending from *Wenn ich einmal reich und tot bin* (*One day, when I'm Rich and Dead*) through *Land der Väter und Verräter* (*Land of the Fathers and Traitors*), Biller gradually redefines the Jews as *amchu*—Hebrew/Yiddish for "the common people,"—attaining a sense of cultural and multicultural contiguity by erecting what might seem to be barriers between Jews and the German non-Jewish world. However, the diversity modeled in texts written for a German public places into question, resists, and subverts conventional notions of German cultural homogeneity.

While intergenerational rupture, as we have suggested, is one of the main problems besetting post-Shoah Jewish youth, another is the erosion of traditional religious values, which in the past provided a central pillar of Jewish self-understanding, even for the nonobservant. With nonobservance, assimilation, and acculturation escalating sharply, especially in the last quarter century, the value and essence of Jewish difference has come increasingly under scrutiny. Accordingly, the last section of the book, "Redrawing Borders: Redefining Jewish Identity," explores how younger writers seek to retain and redefine their concept of Jewish identity, in the process transcending or obliterating traditional parameters.

The process—and impossibility—of crossing over from "Unjew" to "Jew" is the central problem examined in Sabine Gölz's chapter, " 'My Ears Repeat': Interpretive Supplementarity in Esther Dischereit's Novel *Joëmis Tisch: Eine jüdi-sche Geschichte (Joëmi's Table: A Jewish Story)*. Gölz skillfully identifies and interweaves key metaphors underlying diffuse and variegated narrative strands. In the process, she shows how, for the narrator, Jewishness is a swiveling posi-tionality rather than an attainment of fixed identity, a consequence of the semi-otic blindspot to which her female gender and her leftist politics have consigned her. Subsumed neither by religious tradition nor by the "representative" function of Jews in the German body politic, the search for self-definition entails sub-merging below the surface of a "Dead Sea" of conventional meaning, in search of articulatory and existential being and legitimation.

If Gölz's rendering of *Joëmis Tisch* interprets the narrator's Jewishness as being a no-woman's-land between non-negotiable frontiers, Feldman argues for the elision of the boundaries between Jewishness and Turkishness in "Zapping Jews, Zapping Turks: Microchip Murder and Identity Slippage in a Neo-Nazi Hate Game." Her analysis of KZ Manager reveals a postmodern aesthetic cen-tered on a diffuse and weak (male) centrist ego, and a genocidal program that slips between past, present, and future in its programmatic annihilation of Jews a.k.a. Turks. Overlapping constructions of Turkish and Jewish ethnicity, com-bined with temporal polyvalence, allow the player to relegate, delegate, or abro-gate responsibility for his actions, while at the same time observing and/or re-jecting West German liberal democratic traditions. As a recruiting vehicle, KZ Manager derives its effectiveness from a strategy of temporal, spatial, and iden-tity slippage, which allows the player simultaneously to adhere to and transgress political and social conventions.

On the other hand, in her study "The New Expatriates: Three American-Jewish Writers in Germany Today," Orendi examines the construction of boundaries as exemplified in the evolving identity politics of three expatriate American women intellectuals in Germany, namely, Jane Gilbert, Jeanette Lander, and Susan Neiman. Drawing on Isaac Deutscher's analysis of non-Jewish Jews and the applicability of this construction to the past lives of the three subjects under study, Orendi demonstrates their marked retreat from as-similationist secularism in Germany, an evolution that Orendi attributes to their experiences in a more hostile and ethnocentric milieu. She shows that under the onslaught of increased anti-Semitism and xenophobia in Germany in the 1980s, the three writers cross over backwards, moving into a more traditional, more observant practice of Jewishness. This marks the reversion of Jewish identity to a religious nexus, a particularly surprising development given the women's feminist and left-liberal leanings.

The most extensive and radical reworking of Jewish identity is to be found in the last chapter of this section, Denis M. Sweet's "An Entrepreneur of Victim-hood: Jewish Identity in the Confessions of a *Stasi* Informant." In his analysis of Andreas Sinakowski's confessional memoirs *Das Verhör (The Interrogation)*, Sweet demonstrates how the gay, East German secret service collaborator rede-fines Jewish identity so that it functions as a category devoid of any cultural, religious, or philosophical signification. Instead, Sinakowski's purportedly Jew-ish background is called upon to explain, signify, and also subsume all forms of abuse and suffering that he claims to have endured at the hands of his family, schoolmates, and state authorities. In this way, Jewish identity becomes a semantically blank term, a literary device and conceptual artifice that helps the narrator avoid a coming-to-terms with history, be it his own, or that of any of the German states in which he has lived.

Taken together, the contributions in all three sections suggest that the construction of Jewish identity in majority German culture is in a critical state of flux. Indeed, the ongoing disappearance of the pre-Shoah generation has merely exacerbated the need of the post-Shoah cohorts to wrestle with the temporal, religious, and social distortions incurred by the Holocaust. If the highly differing analyses of the contributors are any indication, this process has not yet reached its apogee. Instead, the years ahead can only escalate the centrifugal and centripetal forces seeking to define new borders and new frontiers for Jewish identity in Germany. Coincidentally, the offices of both editors of this volume overlook international bodies of water. One vista, in Cleveland, reveals the expanses of Lake Erie coursing seamlessly to the horizon. The other, in Windsor, overlooks the taut flanks of the Ambassador Bridge linking two cities and two nations. They serve to remind us that bridges and gaps, borders and crossings, as well as multiple vantage points, solicit sooner or later the determinism of choice, chance, or imposition.

Linda E. Feldman, University of Windsor
Diana Orendi, Cleveland State University

WORKS CITED

Améry, Jean. "How Much Home Does a Person Need?," *At the Mind's Limits*. Trans. Sidney Rosenfeld and Stella P. Rosenfeld. New York: Schocken, 1986.
Dischereit, Esther. *Joëmis Tisch*. Frankfurt am Main: Suhrkamp, 1988.

Part 1

Drawing Borders: Cutting and Binding Communities

Chapter 1

Regeneration of the *Volkskörper* and the Jew's Body: The German *Körperkultur* Movement at the Turn of the Century

Christopher D. Kenway

In his book *The Jew's Body* (1991), Sander Gilman critiques anti-Semitic, antimodern discourse in late nineteenth-century Germany. He argues that Jewish bodies were made to symbolize the unwholesome effects of urbanization and modernization. Christopher D. Kenway's chapter examines the other side of this diagnostic coin, the so-called Regeneration Movement. Referring to hitherto neglected popular and scientific journals, Kenway explores the argumentations used to advance *Körperkultur* goals, namely, the development and maintenance of a healthy, fit, and beautiful body, both on an individual and a national level. Unexpectedly, however, the author concludes, in slight disagreement with Gilman, that from 1890 to 1920 these publications stressed regeneration over racial recrimination, even though potentially racist and exclusionary elements of *Körperkultur* ideology found their way into later Nazi thought.

In reaction to widespread fears that the process of individual, national, and racial degeneration was gaining a hold in Germany as a result of the rapid transformation to urban industrial society, the turn of the century saw the beginnings of a movement for the regeneration of society founded in a revival of *Körperkultur* (physical culture). This broad-based popular movement aimed at the almost literal resurrection of the body from what was widely viewed as its interment in an *einseitige Gehirnkultur* (one-sidedly cerebral culture). The reassertion of the physical in German life amounted, in effect, to the popularization of eugenic ideas and their wide dissemination among the educated middle classes.[1] It emphasized "rational cultivation of the self" as a harmonious entity composed equally of physical and mental spheres.[2]

It is the aim of this chapter to analyze the racial goals of the *Körperkultur* movement, as they were expressed in the first half of the first decade of the twentieth century, and the position of the Jews of Germany in relation to these goals. The *Körperkultur* movement drew its members predominantly from the middle and upper-middle classes, and may be described as both liberal and nationalist in philosophy. The discussion will locate these goals and ideas along the political spectrum squarely to the left of exclusionary, conservative, racial anti-Semitism, and equally, to the right of internationalist, class-based socialism. Finally, the chapter will consider briefly the relationship between the racial ideas of the *Körperkultur* movement and National Socialist racial ideology. It will be shown that the racial ideas underlying the *Körperkultur* movement can be regarded on two levels: first, in general terms, the "typical" European racial consciousness of the day, an outlook complacently assured of white European racial superiority. Second, on a more detailed, specifically German level, the educated, liberal-*völkisch*[3] racial consciousness found in the *Körperkultur* movement provided a bridge to the later National Socialist ideology.

I am using the term *Körperkultur*[4] to distinguish the literature and movement I am dealing with from the larger *Deutsche Turnerschaft* (German Gymnastics Association), founded in 1861. This is by no means a clear-cut distinction, since the two tendencies did share basic goals and activities and merged in many important ways—especially with the outbreak of war. However, the *Körperkultur* movement brought with it many new ideas, such as *Nacktkultur* (nudist culture), a tendency to abstain from alcohol, and, more generally, an emphasis upon regeneration. The *Körperkultur* movement sought reforms within the gymnastics movement, too, and this was not at first welcomed by the more conservative *Turnerschaft*.

My sources are the popular journals that were concerned with regeneration through the revival of *Körperkultur*. This literature first surfaced in the 1890s, focusing, on the one hand, upon sexuality as the cause of degeneration and, on the other hand, upon the drive by educators and doctors to implement physical education in schools.[5] *Körperkultur* literature became popular in the first decade of the twentieth century as *Körperkultur* programs combined with eugenic ideas to facilitate the formulation of a regenerate response to degeneration. Although the *Körperkultur* movement continued through the First World War and the Weimar Republic, it is not necessary to go beyond the first decade of the twentieth century in order to present a discussion of the nature of the racial aims and beliefs that informed the movement at its birth.

The subject matter of the literature falls into such diverse categories as popular medicine and hygiene, physical education, exercise, gymnastics and sports, beauty care, and overall lifestyle reform, as well as smatterings of history and *volkstümliche* (nationalistic) ideology. Contributors and editors came from the fields of medicine, education, art, and aesthetics, with some of the principal writers designating themselves as both aestheticians and doctors. Judging from the standard of the writing and the subject matter discussed, the general literature was directed at a highly educated, middle-class lay readership, with specialized journals aimed at schoolteachers and university students.[6] The journals address both males and females, and direct their readership in the pursuit of an ideal human being who combines physical strength and beauty in equal harmony with intellectual and spiritual qualities.

The *Körperkultur* movement carried eugenic ideas into the homes of educated Germans, who might then strive to put them into effect in their own lives. Where eugenics aimed to solve social problems and strengthen the German nation through the rational management of its genetic resources, the *Körperkultur* movement worked toward the same goal via a regeneration of the self founded in the cultivation of qualities ascribed to the race. Eugenics provided a concrete scientific grounding to the pursuit of these sometimes nebulous "racial" qualities, which were, in turn, individualized expressions of what eugenicists called the nation's "genetic resources."

Although the movement's underlying impulse called for the redefinition of the Germanic racial element in the heterogeneous German national character, nowhere in this literature is responsibility for German degeneration assigned to the Jews and their influence on German society.[7] The need for regeneration was consistently presented as an urgent universal concern in which the individual and collective responsibility of all Germans was stressed. The regenerate self would be composed of qualities ascribed to the German racial type, but in delineating this racial type, there was no call for the exclusion of a racially incompatible "other." Purity of race was not seen as a practical option.

However, like those of eugenics, *Körperkultur* ideas did possess a compatibility with racist thought, and, as in the eugenics movement, some of its major figures were anti-Semitic—but this was not apparent from their writings in the *Körperkultur* journals. For example, Heinrich Pudor, a founder of *Nacktkultur*, was a committed anti-Semite whose work was later espoused by the National Socialist regime, as was that of Emil Peters, editor of two prominent journals. Another example was the educator Otto H. Jäger, a frequent contributor to *Körperkultur* literature. In the field of eugenics, Alfred Ploetz is, of course, the prime example of a seminal thinker who started out in rational contempt of anti-Semites, only to join their camp later.

It may certainly be said that in the first decade and a half of this century, the *Körperkultur* movement did not embrace anti-Semitism, and its literature showed no trace of the anti-Semitic campaigning of such journals as *Der Hammer* (The Hammer). This is not to say that fault is not freely found with the character of the Jews and other "races." It is taken for granted that the superior German racial character should dominate, not only within Germany, but as the keynote in European culture as a whole. The undesirability of European civilization taking on the distinctive tone lent by, for example, Romance or Slav racial character is a recurrent theme. What *Körperkultur* literature does contain, although limited to the *Rassenheft* (issue on race), are matter-of-fact references to, for example, the Jew's "inborn talent for calculating" (Häberlin 1) and to the Jewish youth as a prime example of a dietary-based degeneration of the upper body, which inhibits arm movement to the extent that the individual cannot perform true physical labor but can only reach forward to pick up the fruits of the labors of others (Siemens 23)! These comments pinpoint flaws in the Jewish "racial character," but it may well be more appropriate to situate them in the broad context of European racial chauvinism than to zero in on them as specifically anti-Semitic propaganda,[8] especially since other groups besides the Jews, such as the Chinese,[9] are also the objects of this type of casual deprecation.[10]

RACE AND RACIAL MIXING

Heinrich Driesmans, writing in the *Kraft und Schönheit* (*Strength and Beauty*) *Rassenheft*,[11] provides a useful definition of race: "race" is the typical, established inner nature of a people ("Rassenhygiene" 20), the expression of the strongest racial element of the *Volk* (people), which is made up of *Rassen* (races, breeds). People who "have race" have a native character that is settled and whole, and will not allow any challenge or temptation to change their inborn outlook upon life ("Rassenhygiene" 21). In his view, it was that which remained of the original Germanic race in both the Germans and the English that had given them their preeminence among the peoples of Europe and had enabled the German race to develop social systems founded upon freedom, law, and social justice ("Rassenhygiene" 19). He described the German racial mission as being not to allow the Germans to be overcome by inferior, decadent, foreign, racial elements, but to become more conscious, as individuals and as a race, of what was most valuable in themselves and push vigorously upwards and onwards in the development of these strengths ("Rassenhygiene" 20). From Driesmans, we understand the quality of "race" as something that the individual should strive to conserve and foster, since it determined both the content of character and the qualities represented by the state in which the individual lived.

In "Der Segen der reinen Rasse" ("The Blessings of a Pure Race"),[12] physician Dr. Häberlin presents an example of the strengths embodied in a racial type still predominantly composed of that superior Germanic element that had so advantageously imprinted the culture and institutions of Europe. He does not claim that racial mixing had given rise to an inferior degenerate race, rather that, as a consequence of racial mixing over the centuries, mental and physical racial distinctions had become blurred, and Germans had lost awareness of the significance of race. His elaboration of the German racial ideal includes a program of positive steps to be taken to restore the strength and vitality of Germans. His account is a paean to the virtues of the Frisian Islanders, who, "since the Ice Ages," had inhabited the land of which their islands represented the sole remainder. They had remained in clear possession of their racial character. From Häberlin's account we receive the impression of a group who now possessed such virtues as were more usually found in Homeric heroes and their gods than in the citizens of a modern industrial state. They were clearly superior to their fellow Germans in every respect.

The superiority of the pure racial strain is, in this view, incontrovertible; the qualities of the Frisians, which have evolved unmixed through centuries of relentless struggle against a threatening environment, are the expression of essential

"Germanness." After Häberlin's tribute to the purity of the Frisians and their physical, moral, and intellectual excellence, it might be expected that a return to a pure strain of a blue-eyed, blond-haired Germanic racial type would be advocated. That this is not the case in the *Körperkultur* literature, where the matter of German racial composition was not so straightforward, is illustrated by an excerpt from Dr. Hans Meyer's book, *Das Deutsche Volkstum* (*The German Nation*).

Meyer points out that, far from being solely an indication of Germanic racial extraction, the light coloring may also be possessed by Latvians, Kurds, Poles, Finns, and Jews. In a highly detailed account of the Germanic tribes' wanderings and settlements, mixings and nonmixings, Meyer presents as equally Germanic the southern dark-haired and dark-eyed type who has intermixed with Slav, Romany, Roman, and Celtic elements. He finds skull and facial shape to be more reliable distinguishing features of the original Germanic race than coloration. Meyer contrasts the long face and long skull of the original Germanic tribes with the broad face and skull of the Slav, with which the German race is now widely intermixed. He concludes that even despite this multiplicity of races, "After a process of development extending over thousands of years, the tribes have coalesced into a great unilingual nation, but the descent out of two distinct groups, the German and the non-German, is still clearly recognizable in their physical appearance. The original, primitive physical type is uncommonly tough and vigorous; it remains dominant through continued hereditary transmission" (Meyer 15).

This physical type was underpinned by the particular psychic *Eigenart* (character) of the German race, which, despite the intercourse, the somatic mixing, and the exchange of *Weltanschauungen* and feelings with other groups, had spread throughout the population and had had a unifying effect. The analogy Meyer draws is that of a harmony in which the German element should be the keynote, with the power to assimilate all the foreign tones. "It is this power of the Germanic *Volkskraft* [a nation's vitality] that has made German *Volksleben* [national life] so rich, capable as hardly any other of great and diverse cultural accomplishment" (Meyer 15), he finally concludes.

The German racial condition was therefore not one of purity. In fact, "Germanness" was so thoroughly mixed with foreign racial characteristics that only its native strength and tenacity had enabled it to survive as the element that gave the German peoples their characteristic stamp. That it was a quality worth preserving was demonstrated by the Frisians' calm immovable courage; their moral integrity, and their physical grace. Perhaps the dawning of the age of modern transportation, combined with the ever-present specter of social and racial degeneration inherent in urban industrial society, gave rise at this time to fears of an even greater mixing of races and the loss of this tenuous position of dominance. In any case, the time was now ripe for a reversal of prevailing trends, and the qualities associated with racial purity emerged as an ideal, an important ingredient in the antidote to a degenerative modernity.

THE SOCIAL AND POLITICAL SIGNIFICANCE OF RACE

The question of whether race was an important factor in the lives of nations and individuals was a controversial one in the first decade of the twentieth century. Heinrich Driesmans remarks:

> The press is full of considerations of the value of racial purity, racial in-
> terbreeding, racial hygiene, and so on . . . [E]verything to do with the
> idea of race has gained the kind of significance that would not have been
> dreamt of ten years ago. Racial biology stands in the foreground of
> popular interest. Historians and sociologists, natural scientists, theologi-
> ans and philosophers are arguing about this new, growing scientific dis-
> cipline. ("Rassenhygiene"16)

Some, according to Driesmans, saw *Rassenkunde* (racial science) underlying the history of all civilizations, and others denied it any role at all due to its inaccessibility to scientific investigation. But, he asserted, even those "opponents of the racial question" would not go so far as to deny the existence of the difference between races and claim, for instance, that the Negro or the Mongol would ever be in a position to construct a civilization like that of the Caucasian and the Aryan. Driesmans himself, however, did not accept the claims of Arthur, comte de Gobineau; Houston Stewart Chamberlain; and others that modern states and social systems, in fact, the whole of modern civilization, were the product of the superior Germanic racial elements alone ("Rassenhygiene"16).

Driesmans's viewpoint, and by extension, that of the *Körperkultur* movement, emerges as he enters into the disagreement between sociologists and racial hygienists, socialists and conservatives, concerning the social and historical significance of race. He argues against the sociologists who objected to the premises of racial science on the grounds that it was not, in fact, a science, and the socialists who viewed history as the operation of anonymous forces and class interests that transcended racial and national boundaries. In Driesmans's view, race preceded politics in determining the nature of social and political systems. In this light, regeneration of the "human material" was a more pressing concern than attempts to reform social institutions, because changes in social conditions would be effected through changes in the human material rather than in the system itself. The racial question would therefore logically influence and inform political philosophies, a view congruent with the principles of the *Körperkultur* movement, which viewed the placing of political loyalties before the regeneration of the individual and *Volk* as counterproductive. Even the conservative *Deutsche Turnerschaft* stipulated that political and confessional preference were matters of individual conscience that should not be allowed to interfere with the primary task at hand. On these constitutional grounds, the Lower Austrian section of the *Deutsche Turnerschaft* was expelled from the *Turnerschaft* in 1887, following the exclusion of Jews from its *Vereine* (associations).

Driesmans's analysis of the race issue contains a discernibly middle-class, social political agenda that seems to be a blend of both liberal and conservative outlooks. He continues: if the social system depends ultimately upon the psychological character of the race, then "it [the social system] must be borne by those individuals in whom the racial factors upon which it is founded are most strongly imprinted" ("Rassenhygiene"19). Thus, he argues, to be strongly racially identifiable is to be capable of exerting the most energetic, productive, and forceful effect upon social conditions. Driesmans is advancing a racially based individualism intended to undermine the Marxian materialist conception of history by asserting that it is the individual rather than the collective or anonymous sociohistorical processes that carries the burden of historical development. Driesmans thereby "transfers the focal point of historical development from collectivism to individualism to prove that it is personalities, and not the masses, who make history, and that it is the people of the race and not the people of the herd who are the bearers of history" ("Rassenhygiene" 21).

This thesis of culture-carrying individuals and races undergirds the thinking of Gobineau and Chamberlain. Driesmans does not, however, concur with Chamberlain's Manichaean view of the relationship between races. For Driesmans, the enemy is internal degeneration, not the intrusion of a malevolent "other." Driesmans also attacks the upper classes, accusing them of decadence and of squandering their noble birthright by entering into unsuitable marriages dictated by conventional or material considerations. He claims that inbreeding was the undoing of the aristocracy, leading to their psychological impoverishment and idiocy. Unfortunately, the plutocracy replacing them was following their example and was, as a result, also on the path to rapid degeneration.

Despite claims to impartiality and higher motivation, Driesmans's analysis leaves only the middle classes unindicted. Although he does not specifically name them, it fell to them, by process of elimination, to lead the fight against degeneration. It is clear from Driesmans's social analysis that he was addressing the bourgeoisie: it was surely they who had to "cultivate their bodies and souls to pile capital upon capital which will bear interest for all eternity" ("Rassenhygiene" 21). Appealing to bourgeois individualism, Driesmans gets to the core of the *Körperkultur* movement when he argues that, as with nations, so it was even more necessary for individuals to shepherd and preserve their vital, creative energies: "Racial hygiene should sharpen their awareness that they must preserve and acquire anew that which they have inherited from their fathers as psychologically good and wholesome, and, wherever possible, transmit this in increased measure to their offspring out of a sense of responsibility to the 'holiness of generation'" ("Rassenhygiene" 20).

These clear expressions of a capitalist ethic applied to racial assets indicate that the *Körperkultur* movement formed part of an educated middle-class response to the constraints placed upon the social and political position of this class within the Second Reich. Frustrated by the political limitations imposed upon them by the Wilhelmine state on the one hand, the middle classes felt besieged by the rising tide of socialism on the other. They were also highly ambivalent about the materialism of modern society, feeling revulsion at its dominance while at the same time gladly accepting the prosperity it afforded them. Regeneration through *Körperkultur* was, then, a middle-class initiative, which bypassed the political system but attempted to render ideals of proletarian solidarity ineffectual, and presented the élites of birth and wealth as unfit to govern. It provided the middle classes with an ostensibly apolitical avenue by which to pursue social ascendancy while sublimating their political frustrations. The program of national rebirth entailed in regeneration transcended the day-to-day, factional concerns of politics. Its significance, in contrast, extended into future generations, and it was presented as being of critical import for the life of the nation as a whole. It relied on "social and self-selection in the sense of a cultivation of the body and soul which affords one's descendants an easier, freer, happier existence" (Driesmans, "Rassenhygiene" 20).

OF RACEHORSES AND HUMAN RACES:
THE PROCESS OF RENEWED RACIAL CULTIVATION

"Civilized man, who can rear fine, fast, powerful animal stock, and surround himself with beauty, has made an exception of himself and has, in consequence of an excessively intellectual *Kultur*, arrived at the nadir of his own physical development" ("Was wir wollen!" ["What we want!"] 3).

Having established race as a critical factor in national, social, and political life, the theoreticians of the *Körperkultur* movement outlined in the *Rassenheft* their racial ideal, offering a kind of programmatic goal toward which the movement should work. The notion of applying the same principles that govern the breeding of thoroughbred horses to the regeneration of the German *Volk*, with the erasure it implies of the dividing line between animals and humans, was encountered frequently in the regeneration literature. In racial consciousness, one of the advantages of the practice of rearing animal stock was the attention devoted to ancestry. In a brief discussion of the value of lineage, Ferdinand Puetz pointed out that whereas the successful animal breeder would not think of operating without the *Zuchtbücher* (lineage books), which enabled him to combine or exclude the exact characteristics he wished to cultivate in a horse, the average human being did not even know the name of his or her own grandparents (32–33). Puetz criticized the conventional respect afforded to lineage, which, he said, took the form of a misguided deference to the traditional nobility, a class he considered to be seriously degenerate. In Puetz's view, the value of lineage was inextricably tied to the accomplishments of the individual possessing it. In the animal realm, even those of the highest pedigree were not brought to breed if their performance was not also superior, but with human beings, the worst criminal had the right to perpetuate his line "even though a number of prominent scholars have recognized and demonstrated that criminality is inheritable" (Puetz 33). Taking a negative eugenic line, Puetz demanded that "the State should render reproduction by these enemies of society impossible; the eradication of criminality would be better served by castration than by the punishments which have lately been so warmly recommended" (33).

Gustav Möckel, the editor of *Kraft und Schönheit*, saw the process of rearing a fine strain of horses as one that involved the systematic cultivation of inner qualities by means of rigorous training and repeated peak performance. He applauded the emphasis upon inner qualities as a challenge to the materialist values that were both abhorred and embraced by German cultured society. It seemed to Möckel that the pursuit of external happiness in the form of wealth dominated the minds of the vast majority of his contemporaries ("Leibeszucht" [Body Cultivation] 33). Along with many others in the *Körperkultur* movement, he maintained that the body and health of the individual, as well as the strength of the entire nation, had suffered as a consequence of this and other imbalances inherent in German *Kultur* ("Leibeszucht" 33). Möckel found it ironic that modern man, who had so little regard for himself, his body, and his family, and who was ignorant of even the simplest rules of hygiene and health, had in fact had so much success in the field of horse breeding, a practice that he now endorsed as a model for the cultivation of the human body ("Leibeszucht" 34).

For instance, the breeder first ensured that the temperament and characteristics of the stallion and mare were compatible, and that they possessed the characteristics he desired in their offspring. Möckel believed this was the ideal way to proceed with human marriages. Like Puetz, Möckel held the second major aspect of horse-breeding programs, that of training and performance, to be as important as the act of breeding. Without a standard of performance in keeping with the inherited excellence, combining talents at the breeding stage was, for all practical purposes, meaningless. The training and running of the racehorse was the essential test of its value. Only through a rigorous training program that tested the animal's entire constitution to its highest level could the highest quality be reached and maintained. Möckel concludes that the results of two centuries of horse breeding prove that

> [w]ith rational cultivation of their physical as well as their mental characteristics we can improve and ennoble every creature on earth. What has been shown to be possible with horses is, analogously, equally attainable with human beings. Where there exists the will, the means and the methods are available. But where the will is absent the physical and moral degeneration of the individual as well as the *Volk* will slowly but surely ensue. ("Leibeszucht" 40)

There remained a major drawback to this plan. Although "both Darwin and the Darwinian school" had accepted that natural selection governed human as well as animal existence, Möckel freely allowed that controlled breeding, which for the racehorses represented an intensified, goal-oriented process of "natural" selection, was not feasible for human beings ("Leibeszucht" 37). He therefore sought an alternative agency to perform the role of selection. Möckel's surprising conclusion was that love should begin in humans what the horse breeder and natural selection achieved in horses ("Leibeszucht" 38).

This, of course, raises certain problems for those who wanted the development of human races to proceed along rational lines. If it took two centuries to produce a strain of thoroughbred horses with the aid of controlled breeding, lineage books, and all the accoutrements, how long would it take for humans to reach a comparable level with only love to guide the blending of their hereditary characteristics?

This question is answered only by the implication that if love were to replace material grounds for marriage, the German race would find itself upon the right track toward regeneration.

GERMAN REGENERATION AND THE JEWS OF GERMANY

In order to illustrate the diversity of views toward the Jews in the *Körperkultur* movement, it is necessary to consider the social realities of Jewish participation in the movement as well as theories about Jewish race and assimilation. The *Körperkultur* movement may be seen as emblematic of German middle-class society; in terms of racial consciousness, the critical questions are whether Jewish participation in its activities and associations was accepted and whether Jewish assimilation into the larger German society was viewed as either possible or desirable. It was, as we have seen, the official policy of the *Deutsche Turnerschaft* that confessional and party political matters were the private concerns of individual members alone. But this was always a difficult rule to enforce, and despite official policy, the participation of Jews was a controversial matter within the *Turnerschaft*. Gershom Scholem has characterized the Berlin gymnastics association as "[p]robably the most characteristic organization of the petite bourgeoisie. Until the eighties [it] was decidedly liberal in character, but from 1890 on [it] was increasingly open to anti-Semitic tendencies" (9).

In practice then, Jews had to face anti-Semitism and sometimes exclusion from the *Turnvereine*. As stated earlier, in 1887 the Lower Austrian *Vereine*, which had begun to exclude Jews from their clubs, were expelled on this account from the *Deutsche Turnerschaft* and established their own *Deutscher Turnerbund* (German Gymnastics League), an avowedly *völkisch* organization, in 1889.

Thus, the situation facing Jews as they participated in *Turnvereine* and sports clubs was fraught with uncertainty, mirroring their general predicament in post-Emancipation Germany. In theory and in law they possessed equal rights, but in practice they were subject to prejudice that diminished their equal standing. Jewish reaction to these tendencies varied from remaining within the non-Jewish *Turnvereine*, where they were often "merely tolerated," in the hope that this would help toward their eventual integration within German society, to their forming their own gymnastics association, with its own governing body, the *Jüdische Turnerschaft* (Jewish Gymnastics Association).

In October 1898, Zionist Jews in Berlin founded the Bar Kochba *Turnverein*, named after the warrior hero who had fought the Romans in 130–133 C.E.[13] By 1903, there was a *Jüdische Turnerschaft* espousing principles that paralleled those of the *Deutsche Turnerschaft*. The primary goals outlined in the *Jüdische Turnzeitung* (Jewish Gymnastics Newspaper) were the regeneration of the Jewish body, this to be carried out within a Jewish association in order to counter assimilationist tendencies and raise Jewish self-consciousness and a sense of solidarity. The *Turnerschaft* also sought to overcome the "one-sided training of the mind, which is the cause of our nervousness and mental slackness" and, as we have seen, a universal goal of the regeneration movement; to resurrect the old Jewish ideals, which Jewish youth no longer seemed to understand; to bravely and energetically fight anti-Semitism, which, if less unruly than it had been, was gaining in intensity; and, last but not least, to foster a nonchauvinistic national feeling, not intended to exclude the ideal of working on behalf of humanity as a whole (*Jüdische Turnzeitung*, May 1900, 1).

However, the membership of these new *Vereine* was very small since, according to one contemporary, most Jews in fact viewed sport as an integrational tool and participated in non-Jewish *Turnvereine* and sports clubs (Jalowicz 58). In order to broaden their appeal, the Jewish *Vereine* adopted a Jewish-national rather than a single-mindedly Zionist inclination, elaborated as follows:

> The Jews are a community which is in no way confined to shared relig-
> ious convictions, but is founded in common origins and history, pos-
> sessing a common intellectual and spiritual character, and a strong sense
> of belonging together, which has held it together until the present day.
> Next to the encouragement of gymnastics we hold the cultivation of this
> national consciousness as our highest responsibility. (*Jüdische Turnzei-
> tung*, May 1900, 5)

In 1901 there appeared an influential opinion on Jewish self-determination within the *Körperkultur* movement. The *Jüdische Turnzeitung* reported with enthusiasm the appearance of a piece concerning itself and the Jewish gymnastics movement in *Kraft und Schönheit*, "a highly regarded, non-Jewish specialized journal" (April 1902, 68). Usually, according to the *Jüdische Turnzeitung*, such articles were not worthy of comment because of their lack of originality, or their vulgarity.[14] This one was, however, particularly worthwhile due both to the prestige of the publication,[15] and to the "fine powers of observation" of its author Karl Mann, a renowned figure in the sports and gymnastics world as well as one of the founders of *Kraft und Schönheit*.[16]

The *Jüdische Turnzeitung* praised Mann for having "grasped the idea at the heart of the Jewish gymnastics movement, and not allowing racial considerations to enter into his assessment of it" (April 1902, 68). Mann accepted that, although Jews were supposed to have equal rights within the *Deutsche Turnerschaft*, this was often not the case, and they found themselves "merely tolerated" within the *Turnvereine*. As a result of the prejudice they experienced, many Jews avoided the *Turnvereine* (April 1902, 68). Mann found this regrettable since he viewed the Jews as precisely the group who most needed to reap the benefits of *Turnen*:

> The great majority of those civilized Jews involved in the struggle for
> survival suffer acutely from the consequences of their premature and
> one-sided intellectual education. Contemporary *Kulturjuden*, with their
> physical and nervous degeneration, should serve as an earnest warning
> to the dominant intellectual races not to take their intelligence and their
> intellectual culture, together with the neglect of their spiritual nature,
> further than the body can bear without harm. (April 1902, 69)

Mann's statement of Jewish degeneration was not accusatory, and was not received as such, since he made no distinction between Jewish and non-Jewish degeneration. In its comments on the article, the *Jüdische Turnzeitung* asserted with satisfaction that it showed that their faith in the "intelligence and character of the German gymnasts" had been justified (April 1902, 69). Mann had not described degeneration as a fixed characteristic of the Jewish race, any more than of the German: the revival of *Körperkultur* would be an effective countermeasure in both cases. Whether or not the Jews were regarded as a race—and clearly they were—is secondary to the question of the fixity of such "racial" characteristics as degeneration.

The eager, repeated reporting of Mann's article in the *Jüdische Turnzeitung* shows that the question of Jewish degeneration and regeneration was appropriate for discussion by both Jew and non-Jew. Jewish physical degeneration, as framed along these lines, was an accepted fact in the Jewish gymnastics literature. It mirrored the German condition just as Jewish regeneration paralleled the German program in its fundamental aspects. Mann supported the Jewish *Turnvereine* as a logical response to the prejudice that met Jews in the *Turnvereine* and the degree to which this hindered Jewish gymnasts from attaining their regenerative goals.

Three years later the subject arose again in the pages of *Kraft und Schönheit*. Gustav Möckel, then the journal's editor, addressed the question of the Jews' place in Germany in May 1904. The article may be viewed as an editorial statement on the "Jewish question" by *Kraft und Schönheit*, especially since it appeared one month after the publication of the *Rassenheft*, and is indicative of the attitude of the *Körperkultur* movement in general on the subject. "Deutschland und die Juden" ("Germany and the Jews") is a strongly reasoned statement of Möckel's own "nonpartisan German-nationalist position with regard to the Jews" ("Deutschland" 160). Analyzing current anti-Semitism, he presents a complex picture of certain aspects of German-Jewish relations in which he finds neither side without virtue or fault. He is clearly without respect for anti-Semites, yet he does not champion Jewry.

Möckel sees prejudice based on racial differences as the lesser of two grounds for anti-Semitism. He does find that differences in blood and in historical and geographical origins render the Jews an irreversibly foreign element in the German *Volkskörper*, but points out that the German racial character is already a mixture of at least five different groups. The degree of difference represented by the Jews would be about the same as that of the already assimilated Romance element ("Deutschland" 159). Based on their numbers alone, Möckel argues that the racial influence of the Jew can only be minor. Implying that Jewish influence would, in any case, be positive, he cites such authorities on race as Driesmans, Ammon, and Ranke, who have judged the absorption of external elements such as the Celtic and the Slav to have been racially beneficial ("Deutschland" 160–61).

Möckel therefore finds it illogical that such a low level of racial difference should result in the fanatical hatred so often displayed against Jews. He argues that, even though some Germans were angered by the small minority of Jews who held on to their own customs and seemed to want to become a "foreign body in the German nation" ("Deutschland" 160), the more virulent strains of popular anti-

Semitism were rooted not in questions of race, but in economic relations between the two groups ("Deutschland" 161). These relations were given their stamp by "the indisputable economic ascendancy of the Jews over a great many of the German people" ("Deutschland" 160).

Möckel attributes Jewish economic "ascendancy" to the historical consequences of the religious anti-Semitism, which had forced Jews into certain commercial positions such as peddler and trader, from which they rose, "through a thriftiness bordering on avarice," to become professional merchants and "the dominant commercial group in Germany." With "typical intelligence" they then became the decisive power in banking and finance, the areas of the greatest concentration of wealth ("Deutschland" 160). Their commercial success bred fear and envy among certain sectors of the German population, particularly those sections of the middle classes and artisans who felt they had gained least in the transformation to modernity, and who blamed Jewish capital for their decline, and the rural population. Intense anti-Semitism was evident in areas like Upper Hessia and Lower Silesia, where "Jewish cattle and wheat dealers exploit the mostly stupid and inexperienced local populace in a way that naturally produces an extreme reaction in the form of a fanatical hatred of Jews" ("Deutschland" 160). In the cities, where Germans were "intelligent, enlightened, and intellectually superior, as well as schooled in matters of business, such a situation, with its accompanying anti-Semitism, would never arise" ("Deutschland" 161).

Möckel's reference to the Jew as exploiter is not a wholly disapproving one; he shows little sympathy for his rural compatriots, whom he appears to view as backward peasants. It seems that as far as he is concerned, the rural peasantry is fair game for the more sophisticated Jewish merchants. Möckel's stance on economic anti-Semitism is intended to demonstrate that economic reasons do in fact underlie the anti-Semitism of certain groups and that such groups are either ignorant and fearful, like the peasants, or simply casualties of modernity, like the artisans. In a somewhat self-satisfied manner, Möckel argues that the Jews' role in the misfortunes of these groups was a minor one; after all, he and his cosmopolitan peers in the cities had no reason to fear Jews nor, therefore, to hate them.

The analysis Möckel presents is mixed and, perhaps for that reason, credible. His picture of Jewish-German relations is one in which both sides are flawed, and, like an arbitrator trying to bring both sides of a dispute together through the exercise of reason and unbiased analysis, he makes demands of both. Overall, Möckel judges in favor of the Jews rather than the anti-Semites. He sees much in the "Jewish character" that he respects as far as the successful negotiation of modern economic and social life is concerned, but draws attention to mean, self-interested elements among the Jews. This, he feels, accounts for the concentration of capital in Jewish hands, the prominence of Jews in the theater, the press, and literature, and the fact that no new enterprise ever appeared without it soon needing the support of Jewish capital ("Deutschland" 161). On the other hand, the Jew possessed gifts that Germans often lacked: intelligence, frugality, and particularly sobriety, as well as the drive toward education, strength of will, tenacity, and energy. These are qualities Möckel very much wanted to see incorporated into the German *Volkskörper*.

Möckel concludes that in the modern world the Jew possessed a temporary advantage over the German by virtue of his more materialistic, less scrupulous character, but that the greater idealism, inwardness, and basic disposition of the German would necessarily win out in the long run ("Deutschland" 161). This confidence in the strength of the German character is underlined by his advocacy of racial blending; he believed that "the tens of thousands of Jews in Germany should be absorbed and digested by the giant German *Volkskörper* with ease, just as it absorbed Celtic and Slavic elements in the past" ("Deutschland" 161). This assimilation must be as a part of the *Volkskörper*; Jews could not, in Möckel's view, be allowed to form a separate faction within the state as the Bar Kochba and other Zionist-inclined Jewish *Turnvereine* desired.

Although he accepted that anti-Semitism had driven the Jews in this direction, Möckel demanded that they drop their particularist pretensions and allow their "undisputed intelligence, sobriety, and moderation, which Germans so often lack," to become integrated into the German racial character. Otherwise, they would remain a foreign element in the homogeneous German *Volkskörper*, unlike the long-assimilated Celtic, Slav, and Romance elements. If they tried to form a "state within a state," as recent tendencies like "the founding of Jewish-only *Turnvereine* implied, the opposition to them would be as great as it would be to greater-Polish factions on German soil" ("Deutschland" 161). Thus, for Möckel, the total and mutually advantageous assimilation of the Jewish race into the German *Volkskörper* was essential.

To alleviate the anti-Semitism that drove Jews to take a separatist tack, he calls for a campaign to enlighten the German population that would, presumably, enable it to understand its own position in the modern world, alleviate its fears, and eradicate its anti-Semitism. If only they *knew* better, he seems to be saying of the rural population, the artisans, and the anti-Semitic members of the middle class. Such a campaign would also educate the Germans in sobriety, an accepted "Jewish quality," the lack of which had, according to Möckel, claimed many more victims among Germans than Jewry ever could ("Deutschland" 161).

Möckel's rationalist liberal position, his absolute faith in the power of enlightenment to eradicate anti-Semitism, sits uncomfortably beside his rigidity in requiring that the Jews assimilate to the point of absorption by the German *Volkskörper*. This dichotomy illustrates a problem facing Liberal Protestants and Jews alike at the turn of the century, described by Uriel Tal as "the impotence of the Enlightenment to answer the question of freedom from the standpoint of self-determination within the sphere of human reality" (Tal 180). Assimilation appeared to be a way out of the impasse, but for liberals like Möckel it necessarily entailed the disappearance of the Jews as a distinct group, a solution not acceptable to many Jews.

Despite points of disagreement between Möckel and Mann, it is clear that *Kraft und Schönheit*'s position, as stated by its two principal writers, was a nonracist one. Taking *Kraft und Schönheit* as the central voice of the *Körperkultur* movement, it can be seen that the movement was opposed to anti-Semitism in the *Turnvereine* and in German society as a whole and embraced a more liberal, inclusive vision of the national community and its regeneration. The Jews are straightforwardly identified as a racial group, but, as Möckel's article shows, in a positive way. In their racial character, they possessed something of value to contribute to the larger *Volkskörper*.

Elsewhere, Driesmans argued that anthropologists viewed the Jews, in racial terms, as "a model example" and countered the liberal Jewish contention that the Jews formed a religious and not a racial community with the admonition that they should proudly recognize their racial assets:

> If you were even slightly acquainted with [the field of anthropology] then you would not defend yourself against the "typical characteristics" of your race and attempt to deny them. . . . [Y]ou would be proud in general of having typical characteristics and would find the pride of your race in them. For a *Volk* or tribe lifts itself out of the mass, out of the general *Völkerbrei* [tribal porridge], precisely through its racial individuality, of which the characteristics offer external witness.[17]

The designation of the Jews as a race was, in this sense, a highly positive one, lifting them out of the amorphous masses of modern urban industrial society and designating the fullness of their identity. The movement's mission was to enable the cultivation of the qualities that composed this racial identity. Karl Mann accepted the formation of a separate Jewish identity in the face of German anti-Semitism, but Gustav Möckel, his successor as editor of *Kraft und Schönheit*, demanded Jews be incorporated into the *Volkskörper*, since, if they were to remain outside of the national body, they would constitute a foreign, implicitly hostile entity.

From Möckel's analysis of anti-Semitism, it is clear that the distance between his conditional acceptance of the Jews and their designation as racial enemy was not great.[18] If they attempted to remain outside the *Volkskörper*, he felt that action would need to be taken against them. Remove the barrier of reason, in which Möckel placed an exaggerated, complacent faith, and the way would be left open to prejudice, resentment, and fear for the formation of another Jewish identity, that of the malignant racial "other." Within liberal, middle-class consciousness, the *Körperkultur* helped lay the foundation, and the later National Socialist ideology had only to raise it to another level in order for Nazi policies to be executed without demur.

NOTES

1. The year 1895 saw the publication of seminal works in both movements: in eugenics, Alfred Ploetz's *Die Tüchtigkeit unsrer Rasse und der Schutz der Schwachen* (*The Fitness of our Race and the Protection of the Weak*), and in the physical culture movement the appearance of the journal *Regeneration*, edited by Dr. Alfred Damm.

2. Programs for the "intelligent self-cultivation of the body" and, thereby, the mind, were central to the *Regeneration-Körperkultur* movement. Through such programs, which were informed by eugenic thought and a pseudo-Darwinian belief in the struggle of all against all, the *Regeneration-Körperkulturists* advocated a "return to Nature" without forsaking the comforts and material benefits of urban life.

3. *Völkisch* thought was especially influential in Germany, where it permeated the right. It may be viewed as a form of romantic and mystical nationalism that emphasized race, the influence of nature upon the characteristics of the individual and race, and a rejection of modern urban, industrial social and political forms. Often anti-Semitic, it was especially influential in Germany. Of particular interest here is that the *Körperkultur* movement employs both *völkisch* and modern rationalistic ideas in the drive to regenerate individual, nation, and race. See George Mosse, *The Crisis of German Ideology*, particularly 1–10, for an account of the influence of *völkisch* ideas in twentieth-century German history.

4. The terms *Regeneration* and *Körperkultur* are, practically speaking, interchangeable, and I will be using *Körperkultur* for both (this avoids alternation of terms or awkward hyphenation). The German *Regeneration* movement, founded by Alfred Damm in 1895, formed the first wave of what is here referred to as the *Körperkultur* movement. Damm believed that all degeneration, individual and national, was caused by "unnatural sensuality," meaning any use of the sexual function for purposes other than reproduction. He also campaigned for the revival of the physical in German *Kultur*. The emphasis upon a purification of sexuality is less sharply focused in the broader *Körperkultur* movement, where there is a general emphasis upon a return to more natural and healthy patterns of life as a counter to the degenerative effects of modern urban, industrial civilization.

5. For instance: Dr. Alfred Damm's journals, *Die Wiedergeburt der Völker* (*Rebirth of the Nations*), 1892–95, and *Regeneration*, 1896–1901. Damm's journal merged into *Volkskraft* (*Strength of the Nation*) in 1902. The principle journal of the *Körperkultur* movement, *Kraft und Schönheit* (*Strength and Beauty*), 1901–1927, included *Volkskraft* as a supplement for some time. Teachers' journals such as *Körper und Geist* (*Body and Mind*), 1883–86; *Monatsschrift für das Turnwesen* (*Gymnastics Monthly*), 1890–1920; and *Zeitschrift für Turnen und Jugendspiel* (*Journal for Gymnastics and Youth Games*), 1892–1901; campaigned for the revival of physical education and the introduction of games and gymnastics in schools. The literature of the gymnastics movement, the *Deutsche Turnzeitung* (*German Gymnastics Journal*), 1861–1943, and the *Akademische Turnzeitung* (*Academic Gymnastics Journal*), 1891–1916, also carried this campaign forward, but tended to take a more stridently nationalist and conservative stance (particularly the *Akademische Turnzeitung*).

6. Wolfgang Krabbe notes that the membership of the *Deutscher Verein für Vernünftige Leibeszucht* (German Society for Rational Care of the Body), of which *Kraft und Schönheit* was the official organ, was predominantly middle-class in composition, with business people, members of artistic professions, officials, clerks, and students among its members. The *Jugendstil* artist Fidus was a member of its board, and Chief of General Staff von Moltke an honorary board member (Krabbe 94).

7. It is not until the second half of 1915 that the Jews are charged with an assault upon the nation via control of the economy, opposition to the war, and manipulation of public opinion, as well as with instigating Germany's enemies to take up arms against her. This isolated outburst passes, however, and, in contrast to the outcry raised on the right, is not repeated at the end of the war, when, for the *Körperkulturists*, the priorities of national reconstruction appear to outweigh those of recrimination.

8. In "Ein Nichtjude über die jüdische Turnerei," *Jüdische Turnzeitung*, Aug. 1903, 148–53, the Jewish commentator on an article by Karl Mann (see page 46 ff.) says that Jewish regeneration will require, apart from gymnastics and the like, adherence to a simple diet and standard of life. Mann's article appeared in the first year of publication of *Kraft und Schönheit*, which is now unavailable. The bulk of it was reprinted in the *Jüdische Turnzeitung* in April 1902 and again in August 1903.

9. For instance, the use of human fertilizers in Chinese agriculture is taken to explain both Chinese skin coloring—the fertilizers deposit more toxins in the produce grown than the human liver can eliminate—and the "fact" that the aroma issuing from Chinese cooking pots resembles that of human excrement. Thus, the characteristic yellow pigmentation of the Chinese is seen as a symptom of a jaundiced condition, an overburdened liver caused by faulty agricultural techniques (Siemens 23).

10. Donald E. Niewyk says of Germans: "Most continued to harbor unflattering stereotypes of Jews and to regard them as unassimilated outsiders, but rarely was any of this translated into overt hostility. Indifference was in far greater supply than antagonism." *The Jews in Weimar Germany* (Baton Rouge : Louisiana State University Press, 1980) 9.

11. From 1904–1907 *Kraft und Schönheit* published five special issues on the subjects of strength (*Sandow Heft*), beauty, race, clothing, and the *Sportluftlichtbad* (a type of open air sports and gymnastics arena). Driesmans's contribution to the *Rassenheft* was an article entitled "Über Rasse und Rassenhygiene" (On Race and Racial Hygiene).

12. Häberlin's work appears in other journals (*Der Kulturmensch, Körperkultur*), where he writes also as an aesthetician on the subject of beauty and its benefits.

13. For Zionists, Bar Kochba was a symbol of Jewish military force and empowerment.

14. For instance, in its Apr.–May 1904 issue, the *Jüdische Turnzeitung* presents a range of press reactions to the exclusion of the Lower Austrian Vereine from the 1904 *Deutscher Turnertag* because of their "Aryan paragraph." It concludes with the comment: "We have no desire to involve ourselves in this dispute."

15. *Kraft und Schönheit* ran from 1901 to 1927 and can be regarded as the central and most influential organ of the *Körperkultur* movement.

16. Mann, along with well-known Berlin gymnast Fritz Hoffmann, founded *Kraft und Schönheit* in 1901, after observing the "physical culture" school in England. Its founding coincided with the opening of the first German *Lichtluftbad* on the Kurfürstendamm in Berlin.

17. *Die Welt*, Dec. 1902, 5–6. Cited in Ragins 149.

18. This distance was traversed in 1915; see also note 7.

WORKS CITED

Primary Sources

Journals

Akademische Turnzeitung [*Academic Gymnastics Journal*]. Berlin, 1892–1916.
Deutsche Turnzeitung [*German Gymnastics Journal*]. Berlin, 1861–1943.
Jüdische Turnzeitung [*Jewish Gymnastics Journal*]. Berlin, 1900–1914.
Körper und Geist [*Body and Mind*]. Düsseldorf, 1883–1886.
Körper und Geist [*Body and Mind*]. Berlin, 1902–1918.
Körperkultur, Zeitschrift für körperliche Vervollkommenheit [*Physical Culture, Journal for Physical Perfection*]. Berlin, 1906–1914.
Kraft und Schönheit [*Strength and Beauty*]. Berlin, 1902–1927.
Der Kulturmensch [*The Civilized Human Being*]. Berlin, 1904–1905.
Monatsschrift für das Turnwesen [*Gymnastics Monthly*]. Berlin, 1890–1920.
Regeneration. Berlin, 1896–1901.

Volkskraft [*Strength of the Nation*]. Berlin, 1908–1909.
Die Wiedergeburt der Völker [*Rebirth of the Nations*]. Berlin, 1892–1895.
Zeitschrift für Turnen und Jugendspiel [*Journal for Gymnastics and Youth Games*]. Berlin, 1892–1901.

Articles

Driesmans, Heinrich. "Über Rasse und Rassenhygiene" ["On Race and Racial Hygiene"]. *Kraft und Schönheit Rassenheft*, May 1904, 16–21.

"Ein Nichtjude über die jüdische Turnerei" ["A Non-Jew on Jewish Gymnastics"]. *Jüdische Turnzeitung*, Apr. 1903, 148–53.

Häberlin, Dr.med. "Der Segen der reinen Rasse" ["The Blessings of the Pure Race"]. *Kraft und Schönheit Rassenheft* [*Strength and Beauty Race Issue*]. Special issue of *Kraft und Schönheit*, May 1904, 1–8.

Jalowicz, Hermann. "Die körperliche Entartung der Juden, ihre Ursachen und ihre Bekämpfung" ["The Physical Degeneration of the Jews: Causes and Countermeasures"]. *Jüdische Turnzeitung*, May 1902, 57–65.

Meyer, Hans. "Die Rassenmischung im Deutschtum" ["Racial Mixing among the Germans"]. *Das deutsche Volkstum* [*The German Nation*], ed. Meyer (Berlin: Bibliographisches Institut, 1898), excerpted in *Kraft und Schönheit Rassenheft*, May 1904, 9–15.

Möckel, Gustav. "Rassen- und Leibeszucht bei Menschen und Tieren" ["Race and Body Cultivation in Humans and Animals"]. *Kraft und Schönheit Rassenheft*, May 1904, 33–40.

———."Deutschland und die Juden" ["Germany and the Jews"]. *Kraft und Schönheit Rassenheft*, May 1904, 159–61.

Puetz, Ferdinand. "Der Wert einer guten Abstammung" ["The Value of a Good Descent"]. *Kraft und Schönheit Rassenheft*, May 1904, 32–33.

Siemens, Gustav. "Rasse und Ernährung" ["Race and Nutrition"]. *Kraft und Schönheit Rassenheft*, May 1904, 21–24.

"Was wir wollen!" ["What we want!"]. *Körperkultur*, Oct. 1906, 3.

Books

Carus, Carl Gustav. *Symbolik der Menschlichen Gestalt: Ein Handbuch zur Menschenkenntnis* [*Symbolism of the Human Form: A Handbook for the Understanding of Human Beings*] 1853. Reprint, Celle: Kampmann, 1925.

Chamberlain, Houston Stewart. *Foundations of the Nineteenth Century*. 2 vols. 1899. Reprint, New York: Howard Fertig, 1968.

Driesmans, Heinrich. *Rasse und Milieu* [*Race and Environment*]. Berlin: Räde, 1902.

Gobineau, Arthur, comte de. *The Inequality of Human Races*. 1853. Reprint, New York: Howard Fertig, 1967.

Meyer, Hans, ed. *Das Deutsche Volkstum* [*The German Nation*]. Berlin: Bibliographisches Institut, 1898.

Ploetz, Alfred. *Die Tüchtigkeit unsrer Rasse und der Schutz der Schwachen* [*The Fitness of Our Race and the Protection of the Weak*]. Berlin: S. Fischer, 1895.

Schallmayer, Wilhelm. *Vererbung und Auslese im Lebenslauf der Völker: Eine Staatswissenschaftliche Studie auf Grund der neueren Biologie* [*Heredity and Selection in the*

  Life Cycle of Peoples: A Political-Scientific Study Based upon Modern Biology]. Jena: Fischer, 1903.

Scholem, Gershom. *From Berlin to Jerusalem: Memories of My Youth.* New York: Schocken, 1980.

Secondary Sources

Gilman, Sander L. *Difference and Pathology: Stereotypes of Sexuality, Race, and Madness.* Ithaca: Cornell University Press, 1985.

———. *Franz Kafka, the Jewish Patient.* New York: Routledge, 1995.

———. *The Jew's Body.* New York: Routledge, 1991.

Krabbe, Wolfgang. *Gesellschaftsveränderung durch Lebensreform* [*Changing Society through Lifestyle Reform*]. Göttingen: Vandenhoeck & Ruprecht, 1974.

Mosse, George L. *The Crisis of German Ideology: Intellectual Origins of the Third Reich.* 1964. Reprint, New York: Schocken, 1981.

———. *Nationalism and Sexuality: Middle-Class Morality and Sexual Norms in Modern Europe.* Madison: University of Wisconsin Press, 1985.

———. *Towards the Final Solution: A History of European Racism.* Madison: University of Wisconsin Press, 1978.

Niewyk, Donald E. *The Jews in Weimar Germany.* Baton Rouge: Louisiana State University Press, 1980.

Ragins, Sanford. *Jewish Responses to Antisemitism in Germany, 1870–1914.* Cincinnati: Hebrew Union College Press, 1980.

Tal, Uriel. *Christians and Jews in Germany: Religion, Politics and Ideology in the Second Reich, 1870–1914.* Trans. Noah J. Jacobs. Ithaca: Cornell University Press, 1974.

Theweleit, Klaus. *Male Fantasies.* 2 vols. Trans. Stephen Conway. Minneapolis: University of Minnesota Press, 1987.

Weiss, Sheila Faith. *Race, Hygiene and National Efficiency: The Eugenics of Wilhelm Schallmayer.* Berkeley: University of California Press, 1987.

Chapter 2

The Palimpsestic Identity: Residual Discourses on Jews Exemplified by German *Notgeld*

Sonja M. Hedgepeth

Numismatists aside, few people today are aware of the existence of emergency money—*Notgeld*—issued by fiscally beleaguered municipalities in the Weimar Republic during the inflationary years of 1919 through 1923. The messages conveyed on *Notgeld* printed by the communities reveal particular views held by those people, including their beliefs about Jews. In an examination of anti-Semitic notes issued by two towns—Sternberg in Mecklenburg and Brakel in Westphalia—Sonja M. Hedgepeth shows how this currency raises questions regarding German notions about Jews after World War I, and queries how identification with the past is made via the mutable identity of the Jew. Hedgepeth investigates how the adaptation of myth reflects a process to categorize Jews during the early chaotic years of the Weimar Republic. She shows how early modern discourses on the Jews are retold and elaborated in a series of three notes from the town of Sternberg, while a note from Brakel likewise reaches back into early modern local history to retell the crime—and punishment—of a Jew for his perceived lack of decorum. Hedgepeth argues that lurid anti-Semitic portrayals on money not only imply on a subliminal level that the then-current German economic emergency is linked to the Jews but also offer definitive "solutions" to a particular "Jewish problem" or "problem Jew."

During the period of hyperinflation that followed World War I, the German *Reichsbank* was not the only institution printing emergency money known as *Notgeld*. Between 1919 and 1923, cities, towns, and small communities flooded the local markets with their own, sometimes illegal, issues of *Notgeld*. While official emergency money printed by the government tended, perhaps for pragmatic reasons, to be visually dull, *Notgeld* created locally was colorful and graphically interesting, and varied widely in composition and design. The clever juxtaposition of picture and text provided commentary on the difficult economic times, though many towns used *Notgeld* to celebrate the singular qualities of their locale. Community history and culture presented in pictorial and anecdotal form made each piece of such emergency money unique. This attractive local emergency money quickly became a desired collectible, and the ensuing trade in *Notgeld* extended well beyond regional boundaries.

The messages conveyed on *Notgeld* printed by communities reveal particular views held by those people, including their beliefs about Jews. The appeal of specific pieces issued in 1921–1922 by two small German towns, Sternberg in Mecklenburg and Brakel in Westphalia, lies in their notable depiction of Jews. An examination of anti-Semitic *Notgeld* from Sternberg and Brakel raises questions regarding German notions about Jews after World War I and queries how identification with the past was made via the mutable identity of the Jew. Other German municipalities, including Bockenem, Beverungen, Tostedt, Bremen, Hamburg, and Rudolstadt, also printed anti-Semitic emergency money.[1] However, the anti-Semitic *Notgeld* created for Sternberg and Brakel was embellished, either to unveil a fiery outcome for a group of Jews or to cloak the castigation of an individual Jew. We will investigate how the adaptation of myths on emergency money circulated by Sternberg and Brakel reflects a process to categorize Jews during the chaotic early years of the Weimar Republic.

Jews had officially attained emancipation in Germany during the nineteenth century and had become increasingly assimilated.[2] Yet it was not until the establishment of the Weimar Republic that they could become real participants in the governance of the Fatherland. Unfortunately, recognition of Jewish participation in the German democratic experiment of the Weimar years was often registered in pejorative terms. The sentiment "[W]e don't need a Jewish Republic, phooey on that Jew-Republic" (Megerle 215)[3] was shared by those who resented Germany's loss of the monarchy and those who wanted revenge for the humiliating peace terms dictated by the Treaty of Versailles: "Germany, these fanatics insisted, had not lost the war fairly on the battlefield; rather, it had been stabbed in the back, at home. Nor did they have any trouble 'proving,' naturally without evidence, that those who had held the treacherous knife were Jews" (Gay 243).

It was not only rabid fanatics who were ready to blame Jews for the dire economic conditions that prevailed in Germany after World War I. From politician to commoner, Judeophobia had infected many a citizen of Weimar Germany. Evidence of this affliction is not only found in overt allusions to a "Jewish problem," but can also be detected in subtle insinuations of "problem Jews." Such is the case even in a seemingly objective contemporaneous treatise on the German economy. In his 1922 essay "Gegenwartsfragen des deutschen Wirtschaftslebens" ("Current Questions of German Economic Life"), Goetz Briefs ends with a backhanded reference to the cliché of the Jewish usurer. In assessing the excessive demands for reparations made by England and France, this scholar likens the victors' unjust claims and merciless behavior to that of the cruel Jewish moneylender: "One only sees billions in gold, which must be extorted with the justice of Shylock, but one does not see the pitfalls which lie before them" (303).[4] As Donald L. Niewyk points out, not all Germans blamed the Jews for their misfortunes, yet he notes, "By 1919 the 'mythical Jew' was already an established figure in the minds of those who chose to believe in him. Had the Jews succeeded in attaining perfection itself, they would have been denounced for yet another demonic plot" (46). Many had chosen to believe the myth that vast amounts of money were in Jewish hands and that blame for Germany's financial woes and humiliation rested with the Jews. Even in small communities, there were those who saw the Jews as a nuisance, if not as a threat to their way of life. The negative images of Jews on *Notgeld* from Sternberg and Brakel illustrate far more than a simple narrative from town chronicles. Lurid anti-Semitic portrayals on money reminded the populace to identify Jews with the practice of usury. These pieces of *Notgeld* not only implied, albeit on a subliminal level, that the current German economic emergency was linked to the Jews, but offered solutions to a particular "Jewish problem" or "problem Jew."

A proposed solution to the recovery of Germany after World War I was the expulsion of the Jews. Some Germans imagined their defeated and friendless country to be poised at the edge of an abyss that threatened to devour the nation and all that was truly German. In 1921 Bernhard Funck emphatically reminded his compatriots in *Der jüdische Einfluß in Deutschland* (*Jewish Influence in Germany*) that in order to straddle the gaping rift left by the Great War, they would have to negotiate the lingering "Jewish question": "The Jewish question is the gateway through which we must go, whether we want to or not, for to the left and the right lies the yawning chasm into which everything that was once called German will slip slowly, but irremediably!" (34).[5] He suggested that Germans look to Egypt, Rome, and Spain, which had expelled Jews in the past, and likewise rid their country of, and literally "cut out" the Jewish cancerous growth that tormented and threatened to kill its host: "And in the same manner as these people were able to rid their suffering bodies of the consumptive cancerous growth through a ruthlessly painful, yet redeeming incision, so, too, a new dawn that finds our people free of spiritual and social chains must one day break over Germany's fields" (Funck 4).[6]

The question whether Jews had a right to assume a significant role in determining the moral, legal, and financial structure or strictures of the newly fashioned nation was completely alien to any German who held on to the belief that Jews were foreigners merely to be tolerated in the Weimar Republic. Should they become superfluous or onerous, then displacement and even death were viable solutions to the "Jewish question." However, justification for such a permanent solution to a perceived "Jewish problem" in Weimar Germany did not require a look to other countries for examples. One had only to turn to past German history to find models for the disposal of Jews.

Notgeld issued by Sternberg in 1922 relates events of 1492 that led to the removal of Jews from Mecklenburg. In three sequential pieces this particular set of *Notgeld* presents a famous fifteenth-century case in which the Jews of Stern-berg allegedly desecrated the Eucharist. According to Jack H. Haymond, a paper packet wrapped around some sets of Sternberg *Notgeld* provided a more complete story of the "Holy Blood of Sternberg as portrayed on the City Bank notes of the City of Sternberg" (6). His translation of the German text on the envelope merits a close reading, because it renders the morbid tale as disseminated in 1922:

> The mass priest Peter Dane [*sic*] was a poor slob [shuckler] who had pawned his cooking utensils to the Jew Eleasar because of his own financial embarrassment. Eleasar wanted to get hold of the god of the Christians in the form of the sacred host in order to play his sacrile-gious game. Eleasar had managed to get a number of Jews from the cities of Mecklenburg interested in his devilish game and had ob-tained money from them for the procurement of the host. . . . Peter Dane [*sic*] entered into this terrible bargain because of his avarice needs and on the 10th of July 1492, he turned over to Eleasar two sa-cred loaves which he had wrapped up into a silken altar cloth. . . .
>
> They wanted to liven up the wedding day of Eleasar's daughter (20 July 1492) through the frivolous game of ridiculing the Christian god. . . . At eight o'clock on the morning of the wedding everyone as-sembled in the garden of the house and five men started to work on the Sternberg hosts with needles. In the evening of the same day the same was done with the other hosts with knives. And O wonder, both times streams of blood flowed from the wounds. The news of the event quickly spread through the Jewish community and brought them joy and satisfaction. But as a result of the flowing blood, fear gripped the culprits. Eleasar himself fled and took along two hosts. His wife kept the other two but she wanted to get rid of this horrible guest and took them wrapped in the silk cloth back to the priest say-ing, "[T]here you have your god." The priest buried the hosts in the year [*sic*] of the princely residence. where he just happened to be be-cause he was miraculously unable to take them from there. (Hay-mond 6, 20)

The wrapper then relates how after discovery of the alleged sacrilege twenty-five Jews and two Jewesses were burnt alive on October 24, 1492 at what later became known as the *Judenberg* (Jew Mountain). On March 13, 1493, the priest suffered his punishment. A further consequence was the expulsion of all Jews from Mecklenburg. The Jews, in turn, put a ban on Mecklenburg that remained in effect for almost two centuries (Haymond 6, 20).

Thus, the town of Sternberg retold and sold the account of the desecration of the host, with all of its medieval anti-Semitic trappings, to interested *Notgeld* collectors in the early years of the Weimar Republic.

However, most pieces of this anti-Semitic *Notgeld* series from Sternberg cir-culated without the printed wrapper described by Haymond. Even without the printed propaganda (as the set came into my collection), the story of the blas-phemous evildoers of Sternberg is effectively told in "three easy pieces" using explicit and provocative illustrations (see figs. 2.1, 2.2, and 2.3). Conveyed through images, an anti-Semitic conversation begun in the Middle Ages continues into the time of Weimar Germany.

The reproduction of the well-known 1492 woodcut (fig. 2.2) depicting the Sternberg Jews stabbing the host and watching holy blood flow from it perpetuated the medieval notion of Jews as sorcerers and killers of Christ. As the Church became established in Europe during the Middle Ages, the belief that the Jew represented all that was anti-Christian developed and took hold among the faithful. Attacks against Jews not only served to distance and sever Christian doctrine from its Jewish roots but, as we shall see, had practical economic applications as well. Religious anti-Semitism secured material interests as well as the spiritual welfare of Christians, while affording them control over the so-called infidels.

A charge commonly leveled at the Jewish "heathens" was that they continued to defile the body of Christ in form of the host. Particularly after the Fourth Lateran Council in 1215, which ruled that transubstantiation took place during the consecration of the host at mass, Jews were increasingly accused of desecrating the Eucharist. Supposedly, Jews were compelled to murder the Nazarene again and again, and therefore sought to procure the actual body of Christ embodied in the host. By stabbing the host until blood flowed, they allegedly reenacted the crucifixion. Belief in this nefarious act promulgated the idea that Jews were sorcerers:

> The magical reputation of Jews was already firmly established before the Christianization of the Roman Empire. But in medieval Christianity Jewish magic came to be seen as essentially demonic. . . .
> The remarkable development in the century between 1450 and 1550 was that the medieval ambivalence concerning Jews as magicians eventually gave rise to a new view of German Jews which dissolved the medieval foundations of pogroms but established simultaneously the basis of modern anti-Semitism. (Hsia, "Jews," 116)

The association of Jews with the supernatural would not be wiped from German cultural memory. Myths surrounding fear of the demonic fostered distrust between Christian and Jewish neighbor and by extension made it possible to disempower and persecute those perceived as a threat to the burgeoning society of the late Middle Ages.

Superstitions about the magical powers of the Jewish people could easily be transferred to accuse others of heretical practices. Especially the desecration of the host was related to witches, who presumably burned, stabbed, or cut the communion bread during the Black Mass, or used the consecrated wafer to make

Figure 2.1
Priest Peter Dane Selling Consecrated Hosts to the Jews

Figure 2.2
The Caption Reads, "The Desecration of the Host by the Jews of Sternberg on July 20, 1492"

Figure 2.3
Depicts the Fiery Death of the Sternberg "Blasphemers of the Host" on October 24, 1492

the ointment that enabled them to fly (Trachtenberg 212). Only six years before the purported desecration of the host in Sternberg took place, the *Malleus Malificarum* (*Hammer of the Witches*), published in 1486, declared that witches exist as a matter of faith, and outlined the procedures to deal with "heretics with ancient beliefs in a Devil, in the power of the supernatural, the magical, and women's special powers" (Anderson and Zinsser 165). Though he incorrectly cites a later date for the *Malleus Malificarum*, Adolph Kohut reminds his Jewish readers in his *Geschichte der deutschen Juden: Ein Hausbuch für die jüdische Familie* (*History of German Jewry: A Home Companion for the Jewish Family* [1898?]) that the witch-hunts of the fifteenth century were part of the same persecution that sought to quell Jewish knowledge:

> In due course, the clergy became aware of the danger conveyed by books, which through the art of printing were becoming increasingly available, namely [the danger] of Hebrew and Jewish writings. Therefore, Pope Alexander VI, who otherwise looked kindly upon Humanism, introduced censorship and the proscription of non-ecclesiastical writing, and therefore the process of religious inquisition was established in order to hold down seekers of freedom and to exorcise them of the thrill of independent thought. It is noteworthy

that two years after the discovery of America, in 1494, the *Hammer of the Witches* was written, and in Catholic as well as in Protestant areas gave rise to the most horrific witch hunts, which trampled the honor of human dignity into the dust, lasting well into the eighteenth century. (Kohut 479) [7]

After approximately 250 years, however, the sinister witch trials did cease, but the oppression of Jews continued.[8]

The conviction that Jews were magicians coupled with the false notion that they desired to harm the Eucharist encouraged Christian regulation of Jewish life. So great was the fear of their supposed power that Jews were saddled with what Ernest A. Rappaport termed the "Lady Godiva Injunction," meaning that Jews were prohibited from appearing on the streets or at their windows when the host was carried in a procession (Rappaport 333). Jews were implicated as a group in cases concerning the profanation of the host, and pogroms ensued as penalty upon all of them for their inherent guilt. Though they were dealt with differently and as individuals, it is interesting to note that Christian sorcerers convicted of using the Eucharist in magic were often forced to wear distinctive round yellow badges, similar to the Jew badge. Joshua Trachtenberg remarks that "[a] more telling identification of sorcerer and host-desecrating Jew could hardly have been invented. Indeed . . . the circular Jew badge may have been intended to 'represent the host, emblem of the Christian religion which they denied'" (116). The same Lateran Council that had formulated the doctrine of transubstantiation in 1215 also decreed that all Jews must wear a distinctive emblem on their clothing to avoid any case of mistaken identity. However, it was not until the fifteenth century that this dictate took effect in Germany and Jews were forced to display the round yellow ring on their garments (Gay 20).

In light of Mosaic law, which explicitly proscribes the consumption of blood, the desecration of the host appears to be a particularly ridiculous allegation made against the Jewish people. Jewish "sorcerers" seemingly performed a miracle when blood flowed from the tormented wafer, a mysterious act that mirrored the belief that Jews killed and made blood flow from innocent Christian children, using their vital life fluid to make unleavened bread for Passover. In the flat shape of the host, the Eucharist mimicked the form of matzo, the unleavened bread, which led to the inane deduction that the Jews ate Christ at the celebration of Passover: "[T]he Messiah was placed on the Seder plate as the totem God Jesus and the Jews were accused of having killed Him and of eating Him. The red wine on the Seder table was turned into the blood, and the matzo into the body of Jesus Christ, who thus was eaten in two manifestations, as the lamb and as the unleavened bread, the Eucharist" (Rappaport 330–31).

By focusing on alleged Jewish reenactments of killing Christ, attention could be shifted from the cannibalistic aspect of consuming the body and blood of Christ at mass. The process of blaming Jews of "ritual murder" and host desecration is described by Alan Dundes as "projective inversion," a psychological process whereby another is accused of carrying out an act which one wants to commit oneself, saying in this case, "[I]t is not we Christians who are guilty of murdering an individual in order to use his blood for ritual religious purposes (the Eucharist), but rather it is you Jews who are guilty of murdering an individual in order to use his or her blood for ritual religious purposes, making matzo" (Dundes 354). The absurdity of the fable that Jewish bloodletting cannibals needed the host in order to act out their hatred of the Christian god is apparent when viewed from the vantage point of Jewish doctrine: "A Jew, who believes neither in the divinity of Christ nor in the fact that the wafer screens his invisible presence, is not apt from mere curiosity to pierce that wafer in order to see if blood will flow from it. Such sacrilege could originate only in a Christian brain" (Leroy-Beaulieu 36).

During the late fifteenth century, as German medieval society was expanding and poised on the threshold of the Reformation, pogroms against Jews dramatically increased. For example, Jews were expelled from Würzburg in 1489, from Mecklenburg in 1492, from Magdeburg in 1493, from Nuremberg in 1498, and from Ulm in 1499.[9] German civilization was at a stage of its cultural development when collective memory underwent tremendous synthesis and crystallization. Superstitions about Jews had become accepted as concrete facts, and religious anti-Semitism could be used for political ends by creating a shared history and common cultural values pernicious to the Jewish outsiders: "[T]he consolidation of a unified discourse on ritual murder and Host desecrations created a moment of synthesis between past memory and present experience; tradition acquired the aura of historical truth" (Hsia, *Myth*, 42). With the development of printing, cultural transmission had become more immediate and permanent. In numerous chapbooks, printed broadsheets, and printed woodcuts, ritual murders and host desecrations by Jews were depicted, so that the populace could "see" and "know" these evil deeds for themselves. R. Po-chia Hsia emphasizes the commercial aspect of the popular printing of the time:

> Folklore was meant to be marketed. Written by clerics and literate laymen, produced by printers in the larger cities, and peddled by hawkers and booksellers along the pilgrimage routes, broadsheets, chapbooks, and poems of Host desecrations and ritual murders depended on pilgrimage sites as primary points of marketing. The physical appearance of this genre of popular print reflects their character as mass commodities: usually printed in small, octavo "pocket" size, the products often featured woodcuts to enhance their aesthetic appeal, and they had such catchy titles as "A Miraculous Tale" or "A Pretty Song" to arouse the curiosity of potential customers. (*Myth* 48–59)

Christian religious folklore in the form of printed propaganda accelerated the permutation of superstition into truth, further enabling and justifying the persecution of Jews.

The renewed outbreak of anti-Semitic sentiment and the many trials involving Jews in late fifteenth-century Germany must also be viewed against the backdrop of an evolving mercantile system. Though they were often reviled for the practice of usury, Jews nevertheless had filled an economic gap in medieval society until the advent of the fifteenth century. However, with the establishment of banking houses (1402 in Frankfurt, 1421 in Lübeck) and the rise of the Fugger and Welser dynasties, currency loans no longer had to be procured solely from Jews (Liebe 32–33). The end of a Jewish monopoly in the realm of moneylending took away the primary function of Jews in medieval society. The leverage some Jews may have enjoyed vis-à-vis the dominant culture vanished. Trials of the now superfluous Jewish lenders abounded, working in favor of Christian borrowers, since all loans were made null and void if Jews were found guilty of the charges brought against them. In addition, Jewish property was confiscated and redistributed. The Jews of Sternberg were convicted of desecrating the host precisely for monetary gain. Germans had outlived the economic need for them as usurers in Mecklenburg: "Frequently expulsion was motivated by the old accusations, such as the unusually persistent charge of 1492 in Mecklenburg, concerning an alleged stabbing of the host in the small town of Sternberg. . . . But that is only a pretense, which one thought one could use to conceal the economic levers controlling such activity."[10] Under the guise of religious anti-Semitism, German lords and clergymen were able to rid the land of Jews as a modern banking system was introduced. The newfound relationship with non-Jewish bankers must have ostensibly infused debtors with a sense of financial independence, until it was time to pay the new creditors.

It appears that in Weimar Germany medieval prejudices against Jews were revived and used in a new context, ultimately serving as commentary on the hard times that had befallen the German people. It is extremely curious that in 1922 the town of Sternberg issued *Notgeld* featuring the expulsion of the Jews from Mecklenburg in the late Middle Ages. Why did the town elders choose to dust off and circulate the old woodcut depicting the alleged desecration of the host in 1492? Jack H. Haymond reports that the *Notgeld* set was intended as an inducement to attract tourist trade to Sternberg, as well as to raise badly needed local revenue directly through the sale of the notes! (6). Drawing on fifteenth-century tactics, the woodcut was marketed for commercial gain by invoking the same anti-Semitic sentiment and curiosity that sold chapbooks and broadsides in the late Middle Ages and drew pilgrims to Christian holy sites. In a time of an extreme shift in the German economy at the beginning of the Weimar Republic, Sternberg propagandists intimated that as in the late fifteenth century, financial improvement would be found in the displacement of the Jews as the nation's "bankers." Local currency deficits could once again be remedied at the expense of the Jews. The originators of the Sternberg emergency notes not only reprinted the 1492 woodcut in order to awaken latent anti-Semitism for profit, but also added two illustrations to augment the medieval woodcut image.

The first illustration, showing the priest bringing the host to the Jews (see fig. 2.1), and the last illustration, depicting the execution of the Sternberg Jews (fig. 2.3), are not woodcuts of medieval origin, but representations executed in a similar style by the twentieth-century artist Josef Dominicus.[11] The artist's imitation of medieval design is so skillful that all three images of the *Notgeld* set seem to have originated in the same era. Only upon close scrutiny can the eye discern the initials "JD" in the first and last illustrations, confirming that Dominicus was indeed the creator of both. These additions suggest that the three *Notgeld* pieces were designed to convey the grisly tale of the Jews of Sternberg at a glance, from beginning to end. The suggestion that a scarlet fungoid organism (*Micrococcus prodigiosus*), which forms on stale food kept in a dry place, may actually account for the appearance of red spots on hosts, did little to arrest the belief that Jews could draw blood from the wafers.[12] In fact, Josef Dominicus added dripping blood to the centerpiece of the Sternberg *Notgeld* set—the original woodcut of 1492 did not display blood flowing from the loaves on the table!

The notes' tacit message might be that, as in the past, Jews of Weimar Germany continued to dupe Germans into serving them for their own evil purposes, only to scorn what is sacred to non-Jews. However, flowing blood frightens the Jews (in the case of the corpus christi, it is flowing Jewish blood) and causes them to flee. The Jew who did not escape in time or who was too slow to understand the possible consequences of the allegations brought against the Jewish people was tortured and burned. These Sternberg *Notgeld* pieces suggest a truly frightening scenario, particularly when viewed from our post-Holocaust perspective. Did the Sternbergers want to remark on the alleged innate mendacity of all Jews? Did they intend to divulge to others how in the past they were able to "control" the Jews of their locale and get rid of them? The selection of illustrations for Sternberg's *Notgeld* issued in 1922 was by no means haphazard, nor was the anti-Semitic message incidental, for the story and image of Sternberg Jews allegedly desecrating the host was widely known: "The most often cited and also satirically portrayed desecration of the host is that of Sternberg in Pomerania in the year 1492" (Fuchs 158).[13] In his 1921 analysis of caricature and Jews, Eduard Fuchs points out the power of the medieval Sternberg woodcut to prompt actions against Jews, not only among the populace of the Middle Ages, but also in devout Christians of his day: "[T]angible representations of the supposed incident were meant to arouse latent Jew-hatred and provoke corresponding behavior. It is without a doubt credible that also in this case, under identical circumstances, the desired results were occasionally attained, for even today a strictly devout Christian soul would consider a desecration of the host to be one of the most frightful crimes" (Fuchs 159).[14] The Sternberg zealots not only promoted anti-Semitic discourse by choice of the medieval woodcut, but in order to increase local revenue they commissioned supplemental visuals, thus rousing distrust, hatred, and fear in a period of extreme economic and political instability in Germany.

Political anti-Jewish discourse in Weimar Germany made use of medieval religious conceptions of the Jew as evil "Other." Familiar Jewish stereotypes enabled anti-Semites to heap blame and shame for national defeat and cultural turmoil upon the perceived "enemy within," that is, their Jewish neighbors dwelling inside the borders of the German Fatherland. Portrayals of Jews as foreign interlopers resonated with those Germans frightened by the precarious condition of their nation, which was no longer led by a monarch, but was truly a German experiment in democracy. In the early years of the Weimar Republic, some locally issued *Notgeld* skillfully propagated the notion of the Jew as Other, portraying Jews as ugly undesirables. It is no surprise that Jews were rendered in a negative manner during a time of perceived chaos, for as Sander Gilman notes, "Stereotypes arise when the integration of self is threatened. They are therefore part of our manner of dealing with the instabilities of our perception of the world" (*Inscribing* 13). In his analysis of the process of differentiation between self and Other, Gilman describes stereotyping as a means by which reality is understood or explained in dichotomies, such as "good" and "bad," or "us" and "them": "Stereotypes reflect a crude set of mental representations of the world. They are palimpsests on which the initial bipolar representations are still vaguely legible" (*Inscribing* 12). On anti-Semitic *Notgeld*, the contrast of good and evil is redefined as the conflict between German and foreigner, referring simultaneously to the practice of distinguishing Christian from Jew. Anti-Semitic *Notgeld* from Sternberg certainly reveals the palimpsestic identity of the Jewish Other, the "infidel," "outsider," and "thief," redrawn and enhanced for popular consumption in 1922.

Local emergency money printed in Germany between 1919 and 1923 extolled virtues surrounding "hearth and home" and promoted pride in regional culture and community history. While the Weimar government was preoccupied with the renewal of international alliances, many German towns focused on restoring connections to locale. *Notgeld* documents that in many villages and towns across Germany, citizens turned inward, gazing back to a time before World War I, when the homeland, their German *Heimat*, was not a source of embarrassment. This seemingly innocent emergency money did more than only provide municipal coffers with additional revenue—*Notgeld*, using motifs from legends, folklore, and local history, often alluded to the limitations of the Weimar government, while surreptitiously offering old solutions to new problems. Much *Notgeld* bemoaned inflation and lamented that only profiteers (*Schieber*) could make a decent living. Though sometimes stated in doggerel, reproof was more often conveyed by the *Notgeld* images themselves. In view of the capacity of *Notgeld* design to transmit nonverbal cues, representations of Jews on *Notgeld* were not simply friendly criticisms or amusing witticisms. As Eduard Fuchs points out, caricatures have long been used to attack and oppress Jews: "Because caricature has never been, and still is, anything other than an attack upon the Jews, one therefore sees in the anti-Jewish caricatures of a time nothing more than one of the forms of that era's general persecution of Jews" (Fuchs 105).[15] Furthermore, the image of a Jew on emergency money itself points to the insipid belief that Jews are merely usurers, that is, profiteering *Schieber*. Anti-Semitic *Notgeld* portrays these outsiders as a nuisance, disturbing the tranquil German way of life that ordinary folk were striving to recapture.

A *Notgeld* piece issued by the small Westphalian town of Brakel in 1921 illustrates that a simple tale of disrupted harmony, taken from local history, could become a vehicle for anti-Semitic propaganda. The illustration and stanza in local dialect on the reverse of Brakel's *Notgeld* recount an ostensibly momentous event of 1655—a man held a defecating baby out the window just as a prominent citizen of the town walked by, who thus became the target of the infant's falling excrement (see fig. 2.4). The text, which is followed by an assurance that this story is indeed true, states: "We didn't have a better chamber, that is why the youngest one shat out the window. However, oh dear, an accident took place: just then a councilman went by, he mistook the treatment, and I was the one hit by shit."[16] In return for his horrible deed, the offender, the adult, that is, was chained to an obelisk in the town square, as shown on the obverse of the same *Notgeld* piece (fig. 2.5). The perpetrator is hook-nosed, wears a skullcap, and has long earlocks. It is obvious that this is a Jew who must be punished for his lack of decorum.

Which elements imply that the caricature featured on Brakel's *Notgeld* is indeed that of a Jew? In his 1988 publication on Brakel, Herbert Engemann notes the distinct Jewish quality of the likeness, basing his identification on the clothes, perhaps in reference to Eastern European garb: "The Brakel *Notgeld* of 1923 shows a man in Jewish attire at the pillory" (97).[17] Dr. Engemann, however, avoids any mention of the hook-nosed countenance of the depicted individual. Certainly the profile of the face is meant to leave no doubt in the beholder's mind that the figure is Jewish, for the exaggerated nose alone is "one of the central loci of difference in seeing the Jew" (Gilman, *Body*, 180). It is well known that in caricatures Jews are characterized by an elongated and enlarged curve for a nose:

> The unusually large and often hook-shaped nose, which is undeniably to be found among the mass of Jews, had to naturally become the primary aid of the Jewish caricature. It had to, so to speak, become the focal point of each caricature of a Jew, when the development of caricature reached a point when psychological features were no longer depicted by objective symbols (such as a sack of money), but attempted above all to depict physical appearance using specific lines. The nose not only primarily gives the face its character, but also determines the whole demeanor, and alone through an accentuated Jewish nose the caricaturist can, in the most simple and at the same time most direct manner, define a person, whether male or female, as a Jew. It is of equal importance to note that even the slightest exaggeration of the nose is enough to evoke a comical impression in the viewer. For this reason alone, the so-called Jewish nose eventually became the preferred playground of all humoristic and satirical artists of caricature all over the world. (Gilman, *Body*, 180)

The representation of "Jewish nostrility" on the *Notgeld* piece is visually underscored by the beak of the raven perched upon the obelisk, linking the bird and Jew to each other. The crafty raven, which is said to be attracted to shiny objects and which in myth often functions as the familiar of sorcerers and witches, becomes associated with the supposed Jewish fascination for sparkling coins, at

Figure 2.4
1921 *Notgeld* Illustration and Text Recounting the Incident that Took Place in Brakel in 1655

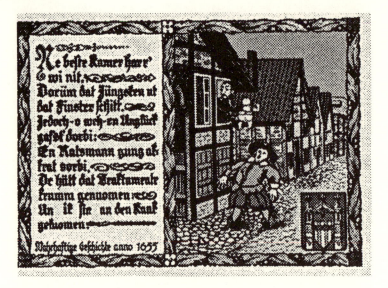

Figure 2.5
Original Obverse of Figure 2.4 Depicts a Jew Chained to a Pillar

Figure 2.6
**Later Overprint of Obverse in Figure 2.5 Includes Buildings Around the Town
Square to Conceal the Semitic Features of the Figure**

the same glance reminding viewers of the medieval notion that Jews possess magic powers. Anti-Semitic discourse in 1921 is again linked to old beliefs about money and religion: "Anti-Semitism in Brakel, as in other places, was nurtured by two sources—religious difference and, above all in economically difficult times, the sense of competition in commerce and trade" (Engemann 97).[18]

The choice of anecdote on the *Notgeld* reverse reflects yet another anti-Semitic view conceived in the Middle Ages. The scene with the man holding the baby out the window implies that Jews have filthy habits and their smell may stick to the most innocent of bystanders. The medieval concept of the *foetor judaicus*, which was invented by Church fathers to "enlighten" followers and which asserts that Jews emit a foul odor because they are nonbelievers, while Christians radiate the sweet smell of their true religion, is at the root of the notion of the "dirty Jew." Edith Wenzel points out that the offensive smell of onions and garlic is linked with Jews in perpetuation of the *foetor judaicus* myth, and foul odor eventually comes to be seen as a physical attribute identifying them:

> Already in the fourth century, this metaphor appears robbed of its
> spiritual and redemptive message, and instead the "foetor judaicus" is
> connected to the consumption of onions and garlic and attributed to

the Jews as a distinguishing feature. The labels of foreignness and otherness assigned to Jews, which are explained chiefly by their religious separateness, become understood, above all in the literature of the late Middle Ages, as concrete physical peculiarities of the Jewish people. (30)[19]

The idea of a discernible Jewish stench became ingrained in German culture, as evidenced by the "Alphabet of Natural History," created by the famous nineteenth-century satirist Wilhelm Busch, who is still widely read by Germans of all ages. In his illustrated and rhyming alphabet, Wilhelm Busch constructs a silly verse for the letter "Z," using the idea that Jews eat onions: "The onion is the food of the Jew,/One sees the zebra in places few" (298).[20] It is interesting to note that the Jew in the picture drawn by Busch for the letter "Z" has a pronounced hooked nose and wears the same kind of long coat and boots with tucked-in trousers as the Jew depicted on the obverse of the *Notgeld* piece from Brakel! Just as the zebra cannot change its stripes, Jews were still not able to rid themselves of negative stereotyping in early Weimar Germany.

The proliferation of anti-Jewish posters in public places, as described by Eduard Fuchs in 1921, especially must have made anti-Semitic caricature seem commonplace in post–World War I Germany:

> The most significant documents of the flood of anti-Semitism in the conquered countries since the November days of the year 1918 are not the . . . pamphlets containing anti-Semitic jokes, but, moreover, the anti-Semitic posters which, since this time, one encounters again and again on the walls of most towns and villages in Germany, Austria, Hungary, and Poland. These posters constitute. as it were, the height of modern anti-Semitic caricature. (Fuchs 273)[21]

In this postwar period of rising overt German anti-Semitism, the veil of small-town history very thinly disguised the suggestion that methods used against a Jew in 1655 be remembered when dealing with Jews in the Weimar Republic. Coupled with the image of a Jewish figure shackled to a pillar in the town square, the illustration and stanza describing the appalling act committed against a town magistrate by a "dirty" seventeenth-century Jew seem to imply that Jews who continue to sully German life with their filth must be punished in 1921, as in the past. The representation of a Jew chained to a pillory was later taken up in the thirties by Streicher in the Nazi tabloid *Der Stürmer* and came to personify Jewry itself (Siemsen 23–24), substantiating the pernicious nature of the message conveyed by Brakel's seemingly innocuous *Notgeld*: "The nationalistic *Stürmer* used the same symbols to smear Jewish compatriots. A fatal 'tradition,' indeed" (Engemann 97).[22]

However, Jews of Brakel did not mistake the virulent subplot of the *Notgeld* narrative marketed by their town. According to numismatist Herbert A. Friedman, "a complaint from the Jewish citizens of the town led to a redesign"(42). *Notgeld* collector Carl Siemsen adds to this that "the city of Brakel was forced by government authorities to make these [design] changes" (24). The obverse of the two-mark piece was altered to obscure the Semitic features of the fettered figure.[23] Once overprinted on the original note, the same *Notgeld* currency evidently lost its objectionable meaning and satisfied the demands of Brakel's Jews. The redesigned obverse shows additional buildings in the background, which disguise and shorten the nose; the filled-in hair hides the skullcap and earlocks (fig. 2.6). However, the old ink bleeds through, and the outlines of the original drawing are still visible upon close viewing of the actual overprint. Just as in painting or drawing, an earlier or underlying part of an image might show through, usually with age, revealing a conceptual process, so, too, Brakel's *Notgeld* obverse is a "pentimento" that has become even more transparent in our time, inscribed by the memory of the Holocaust. This pentimento undoubtedly divulges an underlying wish to castigate Jewish individuals for the financial ills of a nation. The subsequent modification of the *Notgeld* image attests to Jewish reaction to overt anti-Semitism and government intervention in at least one small Westphalian town in Weimar Germany.

The messages conveyed by the anti-Semitic *Notgeld* pieces from Sternberg and Brakel are not just reflections of forgotten notions about Jews. An anti-Semitic conversation begun out of religious animosity in the Middle Ages, which was reframed and amplified in the course of German history to serve a political purpose when needed, still continues well into the twentieth century. Notable vestiges of religious anti-Semitism certainly still abound in church art and commemoration, such as the "Deggendorfer Gnad," which into the late 1960s celebrated an alleged fourteenth-century desecration of the host in the Bavarian town of Deggendorf.[24] We are reminded that it was not until Vatican II in 1965 that the Catholic Church exonerated Jews of killing Christ. Latent anti-Semitism has again been resurrected to serve the needs of East German youth affected by the extreme political and economic shift in their country. With German reunification, anti-Semitic sentiment in the guise of xenophobic aggression again found expression not far from Sternberg in Mecklenburg. In the city of Schwerin, only thirty kilometers from Sternberg, young right-wing radicals launched attacks against foreigners in 1992. Citizens of Schwerin, such as Margot Schnelle, were at a loss to explain the revival of Third Reich slogans used by angry youth: "Up to a certain point I can understand their aggression, because they are unemployed and feel inferior to youth in the West. But where the Nazi slogans come from, I don't know" (*Gemischte* 19).[25] However, it should be no surprise that Nazi slogans, which anti-Semites used in a previous era to urge Germans to rid the land of Jews, are now used against foreigners deemed by some as undesirable—to xenophobes the alien element resembles the Jewish Other, and by extension is still the Jew.

Some Germans prefer to evade the question of anti-Semitism in their history altogether. In 1994 I visited Brakel and spoke with a self-appointed town historian and collector, who in his home has a museum dedicated to local events. There an enlarged image of the reverse of Brakel's 1921 *Notgeld* showing the man holding the baby out the window is on display. When asked about the anti-

Semitic nature of the emergency note, he categorically denied that any Jew had committed or was punished for the depicted atrocity. He vehemently stated, "This is not even what a Jew looks like." According to this community chronicler, only scholars have viewed this piece of Brakel's emergency money as anti-Semitic. In times of financial and political crisis, as in the period of the Weimar Republic and the Third Reich, some Germans continue to act on old anti-Semitic perceptions they have inherited or embraced. Others choose to deny any past anti-Jewish sentiment in their communal history. This is especially the case when difficult times have been relegated to distant memory.

The anti-Semitic emergency notes from Sternberg and Brakel reflect the fact that ambivalent attitudes toward Jews indeed prevailed in Germany after World War I and demonstrate how the image of the Jew could be shaped and amended to serve as a commentary on difficult times. Remnants of discourses on Jews exemplified by these *Notgeld* pieces are extant, particularly in recurring efforts to identify and inscribe the Other.

In closing, it is unfortunate that only numismatists and collectors have discussed the circulation of private *Notgeld* in Weimar Germany. While numerous books have been published on other ephemera, such as stamps or posters, to illustrate German cultural life, *Notgeld* has been completely ignored by scholars writing on the Weimar Republic. Most research focuses primarily on the Weimar culture of the cities, which defied the German bourgeoisie and rejected a *völkisch* tradition. Perhaps in future studies, some Germanists will weigh the notions espoused in rural and small town Weimar Germany and will critically evaluate *Notgeld* as a document of middle-class attitudes during that era of political turmoil. *Notgeld* certainly merits academic consideration—it delivers a pictorial and anecdotal account of Weimar culture and history that has been largely neglected. Even a few pieces of *Notgeld* can suggest certain solutions to puzzles surrounding the German past.

NOTES

1. See David Atsmony, "Antisemitic Paper Money," *The Shekel*, July–Aug. 1984, 19–21, and Carl Siemsen, "Anti-Semitic Emergency Notes: A Sequel," *The Shekel*, July–Aug. 1984, 22–27.

2. For a detailed history of Jewish emancipation see Ruth Gay, *The Jews of Germany: A Historical Portrait* (New Haven: Yale University Press, 1992), 118–59. Also: Leo Sievers, *Juden in Deutschland: Die Geschichte einer 2000jährigen Tragödie* (Hamburg: Stern, 1977), 207–34.

3. "Mit dem Vers 'Wir brauchen keine Judenrepublik, pfui Judenrepublik' wandten sich die Angeklagten gegen die 'gegenwärtige republikanische Staatsform des Reiches und des Landes Thüringen'."

4. "Man sieht nur Goldmilliarden, die mit dem Rechte Shylocks erpreßt werden müssen; aber man sieht nicht die Abgründe, die vor ihnen liegen."

5. "Die Judenfrage ist das Tor, durch das wir hindurch müssen, ob wir wollen oder nicht, denn links und rechts gähnt der Abgrund, in den langsam aber rettungslos das gleiten wird, was sich deutsch nannte!"

6. "Und wie diese Völker es vermochten, ihren leidenden Körper von dem zehrenden Krebsgeschwür durch einen rücksichtslosen schmerzhaften aber erlösenden Schnitt zu reinigen, so wird, so muß auch eines Tages über Deutschlands Fluren ein Morgenrot aufgehen, das unser Volk frei von geistigen und sozialen Fesseln findet."

7. "Der Klerus war sich rechtzeitig der Gefahr der durch die Buchdruckerkunst so sehr erleichterten Bücherverbreitung, namentlich des hebräischen und jüdischen Schrifttums, bewußt; deshalb führte der sonst dem Humanismus freundliche Papst Alexander VI. die Zensur und Proskription unkirchlicher Schriften ein und deshalb wurde der kirchliche Inquisitionsprozeß ins Leben gerufen, um die nach Freiheit ringenden Geister niederzuhalten und ihnen den Kitzel des unabhängigen Denkens auszutreiben. Es ist bezeichnend, daß zwei Jahre nach der Entdeckung Amerikas, 1494, der *Hexenhammer* verfaßt wurde und in katholischen wie protestantischen Ländern den Anlaß zu den scheußlichsten und die Ehre der Menschheit in den Staub tretenden, bis in das 18. Jahrhundert hineinreichenden, Hexenprozesse gegeben hat."

8. Rainer Erb extends the medieval notion of sorcery to include the Roma and Sinti: "Der Hexenwahn der Frühen Neuzeit trat in gewisser Weise die Nachfolge der mittelalterlichen Judenfeindschaft an. Aber die Judenfeindschaft blieb erhalten, als die Hexenverfolgung auslief. Auch den Zigeunern wurde der Vorwurf des Kindesraubes und der Menschenfresserei gemacht" (11).

9. For a more extensive list of the numerous pogroms in the late fifteenth century see Otto Stobbe, *Die Juden in Deutschland während des Mittelalters in politischer, socialer und rechtlicher Beziehung* (Berlin: Philo-Verlag, 1923), 291–92.

10. "Vielfach nahm die Austreibung die alten Anschuldigungen zum Anlaß, so die ungewöhnlich nachhaltige Meklenburger [*sic*] 1492 eine vorgebliche Durchstechung der Hostie in dem Städtchen Sternberg. . . . Aber das ist nur ein Mäntelchen, dessen man zu bedürfen glaubte, um die wirtschaftlichen Hebel der Bewegung zu verdecken."

11. For more on Josef Dominicus (1885—1973), see *Paderborner Künstlerlexikon,* ed. Friederike Steinmann, Karl Josef Schieters, and Michael Aßmann (Paderborn: Verein für Geschichte an der Universität, 1994), 60.

12. See "Host, Desecration of," *Encyclopedia Judaica*, 8:1043. Also see "Hostienschändung" in *Jüdisches Lexikon* (1928), 2: 1682: "Zu den vielfachen Beschuldigungen, Hostien geschändet zu haben, trat oft die Behauptung, die durchstochenen Hostien hätten geblutet. Die scheinbare Blutbildung erklärt sich durch die Ansiedlung von farbstofflichen Pilzen. Der an sich farblose Bacillus prodigiosus (= wunderwirkender Bacillus), der auf Brot, Kartoffeln, Agar, Nährgelatine und anderen Nährboden wächst, bildet, wenn der Sauerstoff der Luft zutritt hat, in seinen Kulturen einen blutroten Farbstoff."

13. "Die am häufigsten erwähnte und auch satirisch dargestellte Hostienschändung ist die zu Sternberg in Pommern im Jahre 1492."

14. "[M]it den handgreiflichen Darstellungen des angeblichen Vorganges sollte der latente Judenhaß zu entsprechenden Taten aufgeputscht werden. Daß es auch in diesem Fall bei den entsprechenden Voraussetzungen mitunter zu den gewünschten Folgen kam, ist ohne weiteres glaubhaft; denn eine Hostienschändung würde selbst heute noch für ein strenggläubiges christliches Gemüt zu den furchtbarsten Verbrechen gehören."

15. "Weil die Karikatur niemals etwas anderes als der Angreifer gegenüber den Juden war und ist, darum hat man in den antijüdischen Karikaturen einer Zeit schließlich nichts anderes vor sich, als eine der Formen der jeweiligen allgemeinen Judenverfolgungen."

16. This author's translation of "Ne besre Kamer harr' wi nit, Dorüm dat Jüngsten ut dat Finster schitt. Jedoch, o weh, en Unglück gafst' dorbi: En Ratsmann gung akkrat vorbi, De hätt dat Traktamente krumm genoumen: Un ik sin an den Kaak gekuomen." Compare to a translation of the same text by Herbert A. Friedman in "A Look at Anti-

Semitic Propaganda on German Inflation Money," *The Shekel*, July–Aug. 1984, 41: "Since he didn't have a toilet, the child defecates out the window. Unfortunately, a city magistrate walks beneath and gets covered with the waste."

17. "Das Brakeler Notgeld von 1923 [*sic*] zeigt eine [*sic*] Mann in jüdischer Kleidung am Pranger."

18. "Der Antisemitismus in Brakel wie auch woanders nährte sich aus zwei Wurzeln: Dem religiösen Anderssein und vor allem in wirtschaftlich schlechten Zeiten dem Konkurrenzverhalten in Handel und Gewerbe."

19. Edith Wenzel, *"Do worden die Judden alle geschant"*: *Rolle und Funktion der Juden in spätmittelalterlichen Spielen* (München: Fink, 1992), 30: "Schon im vierten Jahrhundert erscheint diese Metapher ihres heilsgeschichtlichen Aspektes beraubt, und statt dessen wird der foetor judaicus mit dem Verzehr von Zwiebeln und Knoblauch in Verbindung gebracht und den Juden als diskriminierendes Charakteristikum zugeschrieben. Die Zuschreibung von Fremdartigkeit und Andersartigkeit, die sich zunächst aus der religiösen Separation der Juden erklärt, wird vor allem in der Literatur des Spätmittelalters als konkrete physische Eigenart des jüdischen Volkes interpretiert."

20. Wilhelm Busch, "Naturgeschichtliches Alphabet," *Die schönsten Bildgeschichten für die Jugend* (München: Südwest, 1960), 298: "Die Zwiebel ist der Juden Speise,/ Das Zebra trifft man stellenweise."

21. Fuchs 273 : "Die bezeichnendsten Dokumente des [*sic*] die Länder der Besiegten seit den Novembertagen des Jahres 1918 überfluteten Antisemitismus sind nicht die . . . antisemitischen Witzblätter, sondern viel mehr die antisemitischen Plakate, denen man seit dieser Zeit in Deutschland, Österreich, Ungarn und Polen immer wieder an den Mauern der meisten Städte und Dörfer begegnet. Diese Plakate bilden sozusagen den Gipfel der modernen antisemitischen Karikatur."

22. "Der nationalistische 'Stürmer' bediente sich des gleichen Symbols zur Diffamierung der jüdischen Mitbürger. Eine verhängnisvolle 'Tradition'."

23. I wish to thank Dr. Charles Jansen, professor of art history at Middle Tennessee State University, for generously providing this piece of Notgeld from his private collection for this study.

24. "Eine eucharistische Verehrungsgeschichte ist jetzt ausführlich dokumentiert": Manfred Eder, *Die "Deggendorfer Gnad": Entstehung und Entwicklung einer Hostienwallfahrt im Kontext von Theologie und Geschichte*, Deggendorf: Stadt Deggendorf, 1992. Also see "Deggendorf," *Encyclopedia Judaica*, 5:1459–60: "[T]he last mass pilgrimage took place in 1843; the pictures in the church depicting the affair were covered up in 1967."

25. "Bis zu einem gewissen Grade kann ich die Aggressionen verstehen, weil sie arbeitslos sind, sich gegenüber Westjugendlichen zweitrangig fühlen. Aber woher die Nazi-Parolen kommen, weiß ich nicht."

WORKS CITED

Anderson, Bonnie S., and Judith P. Zinsser, *A History of Their Own: Women in Europe from Prehistory to the Present*. Volume I. New York: Harper & Row, 1988.

Atsmony, David. "Antisemitic Paper Money." *The Shekel*, July–Aug. 1984, 19–21.

Briefs, Goetz. "Gegenwartsfragen des deutschen Wirtschaftslebens." In *Deutsches Leben der Gegenwart*, ed. Philipp Witkop, 253–304. Berlin: Wegweiser-Verlag, 1922.

Busch, Wilhelm. "Naturgeschichtliches Alphabet." In *Die schönsten Bildgeschichten für die Jugend*. München [Munich]: Südwest, 1960.

"Deggendorf," *Encyclopedia Judaica*, 5:1459–60.

Dundes, Alan. "The Ritual Murder or Blood Libel Legend: A Study of Anti-Semitic Victimization through Projective Inversion." In *The Blood Libel Legend: A Casebook in Anti-Semitic Folklore*, ed. Alan Dundes, 335–75. Madison: University of Wisconsin Press, 1991.

Eder, Manfred. *Die "Deggendorfter Gnad": Entstehung und Entwicklung einer Hostienwallfahrt im Kontext von Theologie und Geschichte*. Deggendorf: Stadt Deggendorf, 1992.

Engemann, Herbert. *Nationalsozialismus und Verfolgung in Brakel*. Beverungen: Hillebrand, 1988.

Erb, Rainer. "Zur Erforschung der europäischen Ritualmordbeschuldigungen." In *Die Legende vom Ritualmord: Zur Geschichte der Blutbeschuldigung gegen Juden*, ed. Rainer Erb, 9–16. Berlin: Metropol, 1993.

Friedman, Herbert A. "A Look at Anti-Semitic Propaganda on German Inflation Money." *The Shekel*, July–Aug., 1984, 41ff.

Fuchs, Eduard. *Die Juden in der Karikatur*. München [Munich]: Albert Langen, 1921.

Funck, Bernhard. *Der jüdische Einfluß in Deutschland: Politisch, wirtschaftlich, geistig, in statistisch-bildlicher Darstellung*. München [Munich]: Sickingen-Verlag, 1921.

Gay, Ruth. *The Jews of Germany: A Historical Portrait*. New Haven: Yale University Press, 1992.

Gemischte Gefühle: Einheitsalltag in Mecklenburg-Vorpommern, ed. Rainer Busch. Bonn: Dietz, 1993.

Gilman, Sander L. *Inscribing the Other*. Lincoln: University of Nebraska Press, 1991.

———. *The Jew's Body*. New York: Routledge, 1991.

Haymond, Jack H. "Propaganda, Antisemitism and Tourism: The Case of the Sternberg City Notgeld." *Bank Note Reporter*, 11, 5, May 1983, 6 ff.

"Host, Desecration of." *Encyclopedia Judaica*. 1972.

"Hostienschändung." *Jüdisches Lexikon*. 1928.

Hsia, R. Po-chia. "Jews as Magicians in Reformation Germany." In *Antisemitism in Times of Crisis*, ed. Sander L. Gilman and Steven T. Katz, 115–39. New York: New York University Press, 1991.

———. *The Myth of Ritual Murder: Jews and Magic in Reformation Germany*. New Haven: Yale University Press, 1988.

"Josef Domenicus." In *Paderborner Künstlerlexikon*, ed. Friederike Steinmann, Karl Josef Schieters, and Michael Aßmann, 60–63. Paderborn: Verein für Geschichte an der Universität-GH-Paderborn, 1994.

Kohut, Adolph. *Geschichte der deutschen Juden: Ein Hausbuch für die jüdische Familie*. Berlin: Deutscher Verlag, 1898?.

Leroy-Beaulieu, Anatole. *Israel among the Nations: A Study of the Jews and Antisemitism*. New York: G.P. Putnam's, 1900.

Liebe, Georg. *Das Judentum in der deutschen Vergangenheit*. Leipzig: Eugen Diederichs, 1903.

Megerle, Klaus. "Verhaltensdispositionen und politische Orientierungen bei gesellschaftlichen Führungsgruppen: Richter und Großunternehmer in der Weimarer Republik." In *Pluralismus als Verfassungs- und Gesellschaftsmodell: Zur politischen Kultur in der Weimarer Republik*, ed. Detlef Lehnert and Klaus Megerle, 215—70. Opladen: Westdeutscher Verlag, 1993.

Niewyk, Donald L. *The Jews in Weimar Germany*. Baton Rouge: Louisiana State University Press, 1980.

Rappaport, Ernest A. "The Ritual Murder Accusation: The Persistence of Doubt and the Repetition Compulsion." In *The Blood Libel Legend: A Casebook in Anti-Semitic Folklore*, ed. Alan Dundes, 305–35. Madison: University of Wisconsin Press, 1991.

Siemsen, Carl. "Anti-Semitic Emergency Notes: A Sequel." *The Shekel* July-Aug. 1984, 22-27.

Sievers, Leo. *Juden in Deutschland: Die Geschichte einer 2000jährigen Tragödie*. Hamburg: Stern, 1977.

Stobbe, Otto. *Die Juden in Deutschland während des Mittelalters in politischer, socialer und rechtlicher Beziehung*. Berlin: Philo-Verlag, 1923.

Trachtenberg, Joshua. *The Devil and the Jews: The Medieval Conception of the Jew and Its Relation to Modern Antisemitism*. New Haven: Yale University Press, 1943.

Wenzel, Edith. *"Do worden die Judden alle geschant": Rolle und Funktion der Juden in spätmittelalterlichen Spielen*. München [Munich]: Fink, 1992.

Chapter 3

Reconciliation before Auschwitz: The Weimar Jewish Experience in Popular Fiction from the *Israelitisches Familienblatt*

David Brenner

David Brenner examines representations of German-Jewish life during the Weimar period as it was reflected in the most widely circulated weekly, the *Israelitisches Familienblatt*, during 1922–23. The *Familienblatt*, which reached approximately 15 percent of all German-Jewish readers of its time and was financed exclusively through advertisements and subscriptions, was a strenuously nonpartisan, assimilationist journal.

By exploring the installment novel as a genre that engaged dialectically and dialogically with the world of Weimar-era Jews, Brenner claims to arrive at a more realistic view of this minority's concerns than analyzing the products of high culture could possibly offer. Meta Opet-Fuß's *Versöhnung* (*Reconciliation*) and Martin Salomonski's *Die geborene Tugendreich* (*The Woman née Tugendreich*), as prototypical *Trivialliteratur*, reflect in paradigmatic form the middle-class values of the journal's target readership and—easily digested like all feuilleton fiction—offer readers survival strategies.

Coming upon the assassination of Walter Rathenau, Brenner sees the initial agenda for Opet-Fuß's *Versöhnung* to be just that: a warning not to descend into hatred but to remain conciliatory. The later *Tugendreich*, however, exhibits a greater resignation in the face of increased anti-Semitism and first signs of threats against the German-Jewish minority.

If one takes a cursory glance at the recent bibliographies in the yearbooks of the Leo Baeck Institute, one might think that all German-speaking Jews in pre-

Holocaust Europe preferred philosophy to popular culture, lyric to ladies' journals, the Jewish youth movement to joke books, and Schnitzler and Mahler to comic theater and cabaret. Yet the historical record shows that many favored Karl May over Kafka, Marlene Dietrich over Martin Buber, and the Prager Golem over Gershom Scholem. And many continue to do so today.

A diversity of entertainment forms—books, magazines, film, and theater—have influenced German-Jewish audiences since the midnineteenth century, yet they remain largely unstudied. Historians of Central Europe have tended to neglect popular culture as well as minority cultures. Researchers in ethnic history, for their part, are based largely in the United States and lack a transnational perspective. The field of Jewish studies continues to be focused on intellectual and political history at the expense of the history of mass culture, studies of which have been almost entirely limited to post-1945 America. Equally discouraging is the subdiscipline of German-Jewish history, where battles between Zionists and anti-Zionists still flare up.

The type of popular culture to be addressed in this chapter is the installment (or serial) novel. Serials appeared in 1922 and 1923 in the most widely circulated Jewish newspaper of Weimar Germany, the _Israelitisches Familienblatt_, a weekly published in Hamburg, Frankfurt, and Berlin (1898–1938). This and other periodicals, however, have rarely been analyzed in depth by historians. Their neglect is all the more surprising since the _Israelitisches Familienblatt_ was the best-selling Jewish publication in early twentieth-century Germany. It was especially representative for the following reasons:

- It considered itself a _Familienblatt_ (family journal), part of a tradition inaugurated by Ernst Keil's _Die Gartenlaube_ (_The Arbor_ [founded in 1853]), the most popular German-language periodical of the epoch (Belgum 91–92).
- It strove to be nonpartisan and to distance itself from political Jewish organizations, especially from the Zionists and, to a lesser extent, from the more assimilationist _Centralverein deutscher Staatsbürger jüdischen Glaubens_ (The Central Association of German Citizens of the Jewish Faith).
- The _Israelitisches Familienblatt_ was completely financed through advertising and subscriptions. It was thus imperative that it sell itself, and sell itself it did, finding a significant resonance in the German-Jewish community, and reaching at least 15 percent of the potential Jewish market in Germany (ca. 600,000)—a high figure for any mass publication.

While purporting to understand German-Jewish lives and mentalities between 1918 and 1933, scholars have ignored not only the periodicals most popular with Weimar Jewry, but also the installment novels and other fictions that appeared between their pages. Unlike memoirs, letters, and other more researched and more easily accessed sources, representative serialized fictions give us significant insight into the self-understanding of Jews since the nineteenth century. German-Jewish journal literature provided its targeted constituencies with the illusion of "community," that is, with a rhetorically constructed "ethnic" Jewish identity. In the fictional sphere of the feuilleton, an overarching consensus was achieved, a consensus that embraced the broad nature of Weimar Jewish social formations, which ranged from an established upper middle class to Jewish proletarians and migrants from Eastern Europe.

This chapter takes the installment novel seriously as a response to the social realities of Weimar-era Jews. No mere pulp fiction, stories in the *Israelitisches Familienblatt* engaged dialectically and dialogically with the world around them. That writers as disparate as Meta Opet-Fuß and Martin Salomonski felt compelled to address similar phenomena—class distinctions, refugees, prostitution, widows, and orphans—confirms as much. At the same time, these serial novels show that the public debates of German Jewry reflected their interior lives and experiences. In line with current research in cultural studies and ethnography, we can begin to see German-Jewish popular culture not as imposed from without or above, but as made from within and below.[1] Since serialized fictions mediate the range of attitudes and fantasies that are acceptable to a collective group at a certain time, they add significantly to our knowledge of the social and cultural history of that group. These and other texts found in popular magazines and newspapers reflect the myriad ways in which German Jews understood themselves both as Jews and as Germans.

Installment novels like those of Opet-Fuß and Salomonski are perhaps more "Jewish" than we are led to expect by the research on Weimar Jewry, where narratives of assimilation and of self-hatred predominate. Writing in response to this historiography of decline, Marion Kaplan has maintained: "What has become a paradox for historians appeared reasonable and consistent to the German Jews themselves: they were at one and the same time agents of acculturation and tradition and of integration and apartness" (Kaplan 11). Michael Brenner has also recently shown that Weimar Jews, even if they identified with neither the Zionist nor Orthodox communities, were not nearly as un-Jewish or a-Jewish as has been intimated in the work of other scholars such as Peter Gay. To be sure, fictions targeting Jewish middle-class readers and fictions directed at the non-Jewish middle class had much in common. But whereas German middle-class values were prevalent in the Jewish *Bildungs- und Besitzbürgertum* (educated and propertied bourgeoisie), the nexus of social interactions—running the gamut from daily tea and evening leisure to weddings and holidays—was mainly Jewish for Jews, even for those who were highly acculturated or even baptized. What the feuilleton fiction confirms for us is that Jews in the Weimar Republic developed independent ways of coping with the problems of everyday life. Their "survival strategies" were embodied in informal social structures and in symbolic cultural practices—like telling stories. It does not matter how closely the serialized stories were read. The fact is that they were constructed so that Jews would identify with them. As a result, the best clues we have for Jewish mentalities in this era are embedded in the stories that Jews told each other, in stories performed for a German-Jewish audience in a German-Jewish space.

ANALYSIS OF *VERSÖHNUNG*

Versöhnung, the first of the two novels to be discussed, was written by the Breslau-based Jewish female writer Meta Opet-Fuß, and dominated the feuilleton of the *Israelitisches Familienblatt* between October 12, 1922, and July 12, 1923. Little is known about Opet-Fuß or her works outside of standard bibliographies, which list only her publications after 1931. As we shall see, her Jewish-communal politics probably did not differ substantially from those of the *Israelitisches Familienblatt*. More significant, however, is the relationship of *Versöhnung* to the assassination of Walther Rathenau, perpetrated by anti-Semitic nationalists on June 24, 1922. The murder of Rathenau, the first foreign minister of the troubled Weimar Republic, may in part explain why the *Israelitisches Familienblatt* decided to go with an installment novel after running short stories in previous months. Nor would this be any ordinary installment novel. In a preview of October 5, 1922, the editors assure us that *Versöhnung* (writ in huge type) "will meet with appreciation and attention" in circles that read the newspaper since the novel "gives expression, in extremely vivid and inspiring fashion, to the idea of reconciliation [=*Versöhnung*] between Jews and Christians" (9).[2]

Indeed, the three months between the assassination of Rathenau and the appearance of *Versöhnung* suggest that the serial was specially commissioned for the *Israelitisches Familienblatt*, for *Versöhnung* is clearly the product of a particular cultural-historical configuration. (There is in fact no record that the novel was ever published in a separate edition.) The action takes place in a Berlin reeling from civil war and revolution in the early 1920s. The young protagonist, Adolf Thalheim, is a Jew, a writer, and a weakling; as such, he is very much a twentieth-century descendant of Bernhard Ehrenthal of Gustav Freytag's *Soll und Haben* (*Debit and Credit* [1856]). Adolf's best friend, Fritz Dietrich, is a blond-haired, blue-eyed student and *Turner* (gymnast). The young Jew's father pressures him to give up academics and become a businessman; Fritz's father, a well-known professor, preaches anti-Semitism at the dinner table. Whereas Adolf proves unfit for the *Wandervögel* movement, his "Aryan" friend leads a troop of hiking students. Yet Fritz is a philo-Semite, embroiled in conflict with his father. Indeed, he is secretly enamored of Adolf's sister, Eva, who here personifies the "beautiful Jewess" of lore. In part to be near her, he teams up with Adolf to establish an organization, the *Bund der Versöhnung* (Alliance of Reconciliation) which initiates gymnastic lessons for "physically challenged" Jewish males.[3] The integrity of the *Bund* is put to the test when Adolf confronts four closet anti-Semites in the group. Challenged to a duel, Adolf rises to the occasion. His courageous death in the ensuing shoot-out leads one of his enemies to renounce anti-Semitism. When the Christian German Fritz is denied the ultimate reconciliation, namely, intermarriage with Eva, he carries on the fight for civil rights in order to fulfill his friend's ideals and to right his father's wrongs.

In addition to having all the elements of a popular (or "genre") fiction, Opet-Fuß's *Versöhnung* was interested in creating consensus among its almost exclusively Jewish readership. Consensus was projected all the more urgently where there seemed to be few grounds for it: here, in the first major crisis years of Weimar Republic. The title itself speaks volumes: forging consensus through reconciliation forms the central moment of *Versöhnung*. What types of consensus take place here and in other serial novels published in the *Israelitisches Familienblatt*? While Jewish/non-Jewish reconciliation is often thematized, a reconciliation between Jews was more popular. In particular, the various extremes of the Jewish middle classes, which became even more extreme in the late *Kaiserreich*, are seen as in need of consensus. Such consensus is commonly brought about through marriage. Indeed, the largest source of *Israelitisches Familienblatt* revenues were the advertisements for marriage partners. And a careful examination of these *Heiratsannoncen* (marriage advertisements) suggests that social harmony—that is, a good dowry and a good match—was the primary motivation of advertisers and respondents. Trude Maurer, in an analysis of these "personals," estimates that the predominant group of readers were owners of retail stores, followed by *Angestellte* (white-collar employees) and traveling sales representatives. A smaller subgroup consisted of owners of large businesses. Rarer were manufacturers and factory owners—at least until the 1920s— as well as teachers, *Kultusbeamte* (Jewish communal officials), and academic professionals.

More microcosmic consensus takes place within fictional Jewish families, not only in leveling the gender gap, but also in leveling the generation gap between fathers and sons and mothers and daughters. Deviations from the family norm in fictions from the *Israelitisches Familienblatt* are the old maid aunt and the black sheep uncle, who is often an actor or an opera singer. Reconciliation of Jewish husbands and wives overcomes the threat of marital collapse. Finally, climaxes of the novels center around Yom Kippur, the Jewish day of atonement (in German, the *Versöhnungstag*). The type of reconciliation signified here is specifically and decidedly Jewish, and would have been understood as such by *Familienblatt* readers, allowing for differences in their level of Jewish literacy and observance.

RESPONSE TO HISTORICAL EVENTS IN VERSÖHNUNG

Just how precarious reconciliation actually was between Jews and non-Jews, Jews and other Jews, and Jewish men and Jewish women is underscored by the fault lines that emerge in *Versöhnung*. In this respect, the characters are—indeed, they had to be—more plausible than public Jewish figures like the late Rathenau. Also at stake in Opet-Fuß's novel is the female romance writer's wish for revenge as outlined in Tania Modleski's groundbreaking book, *Loving with a Vengeance*.[4] According to Modleski, "domestic novels" reveal a covert longing for power and revenge. Beneath highly orthodox plots, these and other mass-produced narratives for women contain elements of resistance to consensus and reconciliation. Modleski contends that "women writers of popular fiction have registered protest against the authority of fathers and husbands even while they appeared to give their wholehearted consent to it" (25). Opet-Fuß's foregrounding of the strong sister at the expense of the weak brother in *Versöhnung* may thus be read as protest against that authority and against the less domestic, more acculturated lives of middle-class German-Jewish males. It is no coincidence that the author "Meta" offers so many opportunities to identify with her artistic counterpart and near-namesake "Eva."

Contrary to expectation, male readers are not excluded from such identifications. This association is underlined when the Thalheim parents have a revealing fight over their children. At the climactic close of installment thirteen, Mr. Thalheim asks his wife: "'Do you think it's possible that Eva will get over this critical stage as easily as you did?'" (December 29, 1922, installment, 9). The answer comes at the start of the next episode:

> "I don't think so," rejoined Mrs. Thalheim. "As you know, she has a lot more energy than I do. If she has the same amount of talent—which of course remains to be seen—then she won't desist from the goals that she sets for herself."
> "Even if I had been more strict, it probably wouldn't have helped. You're probably right," added Mr. Thalheim.
> "If my parents had been more understanding of my poor brother, then maybe he'd still be living in our midst", said Mrs. Thalheim. What her daughter had said had made her think. (January 4, 1923, installment, 10)

Whereas the narrative perspective of this episode may privilege Eva, male readers, too, are invited to identify with her through the repeated associations with her uncle, a talented actor and thus role model. But above all, both sexes could be persuaded of the novel's plausibility insofar as the dialogue of women characters is almost without exception more convincing than that of men.

Thus, the fissures that appear in *Versöhnung* while at times undercutting social reconciliations, serve to make the plot more probable. For the forty installments of the novel are, among other things, a visible response to historical developments, and at least one major shift in the plot can be traced to current events. Throughout the first three-quarters of the novel there is little unevenness, and the flow of the narrative suggests that Adolf will become a successful writer, that Fritz will marry Eva, and that the extended family Thalheim will be reunited and live in harmony ever after. By all indications, a happy—if not so likely— end is on the way.

However, at this point the typeface changes abruptly, and the print size is reduced. Although it may only be a printer's error, it is possible that Opet-Fuß was compelled to rewrite and add new exposition. Whatever the case, the tragic deaths and near nonconsensus of the last quarter of the novel belie the positive expectations generated. This circumstance, however, makes *Versöhnung* more believable than comparable serial fictions from the *Israelitisches Familienblatt* (see the discussion of Salomonski's novel that follows). The final chapters also appear to be responding to a perceptible rise in anti-Semitism. As a result, they negotiate the possibilities of German-Jewish symbiosis with a high degree of ambivalence. Let us examine the second-to-last installment of June 28, 1923, where Adolf's sister Eva rejects Fritz's proposal to wed. Even though he has just declared his willingness to convert to Judaism in order to marry her, she replies:

> "It's not right to give up so much for me. . . . You'll find a more deserving woman. You see, we Jews want to . . . get along with everyone, but we don't want to give up our Jewishness and be absorbed into the world around us. Oh, I know there are lots of Jewish girls out there who would marry a Christian, even if he wasn't willing to become a Jew as you are. But I'm one of those who couldn't get over the contradiction involved in denying the existence of the Jewish people intellectually—somehow seeing being Jewish as just a religion—while at the same time feeling part of a national community [*Volksgemeinschaft*] deep in my heart. Jewish women are especially attached to the traditions handed down to us, traditions that in the seclusion of the ghetto, over the course of centuries, became flesh and blood. When you're brought up Jewish, there's simply something you have in common with other Jews that can't be put into words. It makes all Jews related to each other in some way, and makes most Jewish girls want to marry a fellow Jew. This of course doesn't prevent Jews and Christians from marrying, as is now so often the case, as long as—"
> "As long as the heart is in the right place," added Fritz.
> Eva was silent for a long, long time. Then she said, visibly moved, "I really didn't know that you were in love with me. Another man came first and won my heart. He is a Jew; he is actually the brother of my mother." (June 28, 1923, installment, 9)

The subtlety of Eva's own romantic ambivalence is remarkable for a feuilleton fiction. What began as antidefamation is rendered believable by recourse to a permissible variant of Jewish marriage, for Eva's near-incestuous engagement to her Uncle Karl is not as implausible as it may seem at first glance. We must remember that restrictions on marriage within the family were extended primarily to nuclear family members according to Leviticus. Cousin marriages of any type between Jews were allowed, and there was even a preference for patrilateral parallel cousin marriage, that is, a union between the children of two brothers, in some circumstances. Furthermore, there was no explicit rule against sexual relations or marriages between uncles and nieces despite aunt/nephew prohibitions (see Adolf's friendly but aloof relationship to his aunt). In fact, the Talmud and other rabbinical literature were predisposed to such marriages on the assumption that they would be more tender and loving (Boyarin). Such unions— at least in the realm of fiction—were not a far-fetched response to the increased anti-Jewish circumstances of 1923 Germany.

That even stronger responses would be required is evident from the final paragraph of *Versöhnung*, two installments later. Here, dialectic appears to give way to didacticism and social reality to social hygiene, as Fritz addresses his father and the Thalheims:

> "We Germans are strong in body and soul, and if you really want to be German Jews, then there shouldn't be any of you who think that training the body is unimportant. You're also going to have to integrate yourselves among our laborers, our artisans, and our farmers to the same extent you've done so among our learned men and business people. I have made this undertaking my life's goal, Herr Thalheim, and from now on I will work to bring about a reconciliation between Christians and Jews." The End (July 12, 1923, installment, 4)

To our ears in the post-Holocaust age, this rhetoric sounds dangerously racist. Moreover, as noted above, readers led to expect full-scale reconciliation might have been surprised by this discourse on occupational restructuring. Nonetheless, there are valid cultural and political grounds for the belated emphasis on the apologetics of physical fitness in *Versöhnung*. These grounds, in turn, confirm a striking correspondence between serial fiction and social reality. The notion that Jews should become farmers and artisans and/or improve their bodies had been around since the German Enlightenment. After *Versöhnung* had appeared, Opet-Fuß continued to be involved in anti-defamation, authoring essays, under variations of her family name, on Jewish sport and on Jews and pacifism, which appeared in liberal, acculturationist Jewish publications (Fuss-Opet, Opet-Fuß, "Jüdischer Sport," and Opet-Fuß, *Johann Reuchlin*). In fact, defending the faith (and the "race") became the most important agenda for Jewish media and thus for Jewish-directed fiction after 1918. Though most prevalent in the statements of the *Centralverein*, this ideology was quite nuanced and varied. To Zionists and their opponents alike, much immediate post-World War I activity was spent dispelling myths, the myth that Jews shirked military service and the myth of a Jewish, leftist stab in the back.[5]

The discourse of antidefamation took on a particular urgency amidst the historical events of 1922 and 1923, indicating a need for fantasies of reconciliation. Since 1918 Germans had experienced civil war, an inflation-fueled recovery, and other dislocations. In addition, Rathenau's assassination was one of several murders of leaders of Jewish descent—other victims were Rosa Luxemburg, Kurt Eisner, and Gustav Landauer—that did not go unmentioned in the Jewish press.[6] After *Versöhnung* had appeared for three months, French troops occupied the Rheinland and Ruhr. The response to the occupation was "a great upsurge in nationalist outrage which was sanctioned, inflamed and exploited by the Weimar government's declaration of a policy of 'passive resistance'" (Peukert 60). To ensure that the production goals prescribed in the Treaty of Versailles would not be achieved, the government of the Reich financed a general strike in the *Ruhrgebiet*, paying the wages and salaries of workers and public employees. Separatist violence and acts of terrorism were concurrently on the rise.

By the summer of 1923, it was clear that passive resistance in the Ruhr would fail, yet reactions to it may have already influenced the week-to-week composition of *Versöhnung*. The January 11, 1923, installment of the novel suggests such a condition: when Adolf proposes the idea of his *Bund der Versöhnung* to his Jewish bosses, they prove surprisingly blind and respond with ridicule. Their rejection moves the novel in a different direction, exacerbating Adolf's depression and *Lebensmüdigkeit*. This episode attempts to demonstrate that an overly commercial orientation among Germany's Jews was, at best, detrimental. The Jewish employers of Adolf, indifferent to their young charge's aesthetic bent, represent the old guard of the *Centralverein*. In contrast, Adolf proposes a new variant of *Centralverein* ideology in line with the need for anti-anti-Semitic agitation and propaganda.

Subsequent events further affected the composition of the next installments of *Versöhnung* and led to the complex, mediated close of the novel quoted above. In the summer following the Ruhr crisis of 1923, wage earners and those on fixed incomes were fighting a losing battle with hyperinflation. In addition to an alarming increase in cases of tuberculosis and rickets, a rise in anti-Republican disturbances culminated in emergency degrees in Bavaria in September 1923. Just two months after *Versöhnung* ended in the *Israelitisches Familienblatt*, attacks on Jewish-looking passersby took place in Beuthen. By October, East European Jews were being expelled from Bavaria, and in the second week of November 1923, the notorious *Scheunenviertel* pogrom was staged in Berlin.

ANALYSIS OF *DIE GEBORENE TUGENDREICH*

The rise in anti-Jewish sentiment and violence is reflected in the next serial fiction that appeared in the *Israelitisches Familienblatt*, Rabbi Martin Salomonski's *Die geborene Tugendreich: Ein Großstadtroman* (roughly: *The Woman Née Tugendreich* [rich in virtue]. *A Big-City Novel*). Tacit in Salomonski's novel, for all its oblique references to anti-Semitic acts, is the recognition that it had become impossible by late 1923 to publish a Jewish *Zeitroman* like *Versöhnung*. The only option remaining was a historical novel, in this case set in 1903 during the boom years of the *Kaiserreich*. Until the stabilization of the Weimar Republic in 1924, it appeared that a reconciliation between Jews and non-Jews was no longer realizable in the framework of *Zeitprosa*, or contemporary fiction.

Whereas the primary fault lines in *Versöhnung* involve consensus, the fault lines in *Die geborene Tugendreich* tend to involve plausibility. Realistic motivation and psychological causality are not always manifest, even though it was eventually published as a separate book in 1928. Aside from these compositional fissures, *Die geborene Tugendreich* seems to have been formulated as a counterpoint to *Versöhnung* and its agenda of reconciliation. Indeed, the desire for lighter, more escapist fare in a period of crisis is prefigured in the announcement of the novel a week prior to the first installment:

> In the next issue we begin with the publication of our new novel, *Die geborene Tugendreich* [in large type] by Martin Salomonski. It plays in Berlin in the prewar era, where life flowed so much more tranquilly and deliberately than today. With its empathy and friendly humor it depicts the circle of lower-middle-class [*kleinbürgerlich*] Jewish families, and tells how young people with their new ideas and designs bring commotion and agitation [*Unruhe*] to these contented confines. The main characters adopt something of the gentle and dreamy quality that so distinguished Georg Hermann's unforgettable [novel] *Jettchen Gebert*. (August 2, 1923, installment, 4)

This mode of address targeted actual (or would-be) lower-middle-class readers socially located between the working-class and upper-middle-class characters featured in the novel. It also touched a nostalgic nerve in accord with a general longing among Weimar Jews for the Wilhelmine epoch. More than ever, the retailers and white-collar workers who composed the core audience of the *Israelitisches Familienblatt* found their socioeconomic status on the decline. These subscribers and occasional advertisers likely favored arranged marriages to the "youthful commotion" of romantic coupling. *Die geborene Tugendreich* compensates them by delivering a rags-to-riches love story. Minni, the daughter of Regina Witt, who is Jewish-born but intermarried, is presumed to be a proletarian non-Jew and thus inappropriate for marriage to Dr. Max Rosenthal and—by extension—to his class- and caste-conscious parents, Jettchen and Jonas. In a series of intricate episodes, the Rosenthals' milieu of theaters, cafés, and spas (Berlin Mitte/Tiergarten) is juxtaposed to the Witts' simpler pleasures and less deluxe haunts (Berlin Friedrichshain). True reconciliation is made possible only when Minni turns out to be Max's first cousin: she is the eponymous "*geborene Tugendreich*" and not a *mamzer* (a child deemed illegitimate under Jewish law) of uncertain parentage.

As a congregational rabbi, the author of *Die geborene Tugendeich* was eminently qualified to understand Weimar Jewry's conflicts and need for consensus. Salomonski was born in Berlin in 1881, where he earned a doctorate at the Liberal Rabbinical Seminary, the *Hochschule für die Wissenschaft des Judentums*. After holding a pulpit in Frankfurt on the Oder and serving as a military chaplain in World War I, he returned to work in his hometown in 1925. A literary man of the cloth, Salomonski went on to publish other belles lettres, including a 1934 fantasy about life in Palestine, *Zwei im andern Land* (*Two in Another Country*). In *Die geborene Tugendreich,* he expressly acknowledges his debt to Theodor Fontane's satires of Berlin society.

Die geborene Tugendreich is in many respects informed by Salomonski's biography and career. Indeed, Max's characterization of himself as "the linguist who deserted 'rabbinism'" (October 11, 1923, installment, 4) could apply equally to the liberal *Doktorrabbiner* Salomonski. At times the protagonist seems to be a wish fulfillment, capable of almost anything. Having turned down the rabbinate and achieved academic prominence, he successfully modernizes the family business by upgrading office equipment and instituting other innovations. The twists and turns of *Die geborene Tugendreich* are also a type of old wine in new bottles insofar as the novel's contestations are resolved in a modern yet Jewish manner. Although love conquers all in the end, Max and Minni are technically first cousins. What might have been deemed illicit under German law is superseded by the aforementioned Judaic partiality toward matches of uncles' children. Yom Kippur once again serves as the archetypal moment in which generational, marital, and familial tensions are overcome. Jettchen ends her opposition to the young couple's matrimony when she meets Regina at services. And Jonas is sufficiently inspired by the High Holy Day sermon of Rabbi Krausnicker—who just happens to be a friend of the Witts—to reconcile with his brother for the disgrace he caused the family by getting Regina pregnant years earlier.

Here and elsewhere the realization of consensus in Salomonski's novel seems strained and artificial. The reliable depiction of women characters that had distinguished Opet-Fuß's novel is missing. One can conjecture that this omission was a response to editorial or even audience antipathy toward *Versöhnung*, although there are no documents to substantiate such a claim. By the same token, it remains unclear whether *Die geborene Tugendreich* was modified according to the sociopolitical climate of 1923 Germany.

The idea that Salomonski was composing installments of *Die geborene Tugendreich* just weeks ahead of their publication is no more speculative than was the case with *Versöhnung*. In his history of American serial authors in the same period, James L. West documents the widespread practice of contracting for serial rights on the basis of an incomplete manuscript—often less than one-quarter complete. If the editor liked the finished chapters and the synopsis of the rest, the magazine or newspaper would buy the serialization. After receiving an advance, the author would compose subsequent chapters and collect further paychecks as later chapters were delivered against specific deadlines. Frequently the early installments were running in a periodical before the final chapters had even been drafted (West 107–8). This well-established routine may explain why certain promises of the aforementioned promotional teaser for *Die geborene Tugendreich* go unfulfilled, for Salomonski's serialized fiction, no matter how buffered from events of the day, reflects the "disorder and early suffering" (to borrow a phrase from Thomas Mann) that marked the first Weimar crises. The first installment that is sober and pessimistic (October 4, 1923) comes near the midpoint of the novel as well as one week after the first reports had reached the Jewish press of the pogromlike situation in Beuthen. A mood of confusion is hinted at in the final images of this continuation: melancholic and inebriated, Max drifts through a prostitute-filled Berlin in the early morning hours, bemoaning the "misery" of the world.

In the same episode, the limits and possibilities of German-Jewish symbiosis are rendered more equivocally than ever before in *Die geborene Tugendreich*. After drinking and singing a German folk song—"Blonde Maid komme zu mir" ("Come to Me, Fair Maid")—in the Ratskeller, Max and his Jewish comrades retire to a café in the *Scheunenviertel* located suggestively at the imaginary intersection of Kaiser Wilhelm and Münz streets.[7] This establishment, dubbed Lecho daudi (Hebrew: Come my beloved), is owned by a Germanized Rumanian Jew named Berkowitz, whose "steel-blue eyes" enable him to preserve order in his chaotic saloon.

More important than this extraordinary portrait of an *Ostjude* (Eastern European Jew) is the fact that it is one of the first references to Eastern European Jews in an *Israelitisches Familienblatt* feuilleton novel since prior to *Versöhnung*. Although Regina originally hails from Poland—probably from Posen like so many other Jewish immigrants to Berlin (perhaps also Salomonski's forebears?)—she is never explicitly described as an *Ostjüdin*. Minni, for her part, believes herself to be a non-Jew although the reader learns she is actually of German-Jewish paternity, yet in the October 25, 1923, installment Minni is assisted at the spa by a young woman suggestively named Etla Fisch. While this reference can be taken as a recognition of Eastern Jewry and discrimination against them in Germany, Fisch is said to lack *Dressur und Pensionat* (proper boarding-school training) (4).

That this was a time of political disarray for Jews and non-Jews in the Reich is further alluded to in the unusual episode of November 8, 1923, in which Jettchen goes out to Friedrichshain to confront Max's girlfriend. Met by Minni's formidable (step-)grandmother, Jettchen engages in verbal violence. Grandmother Witt defends Minni's virtue against the attacks of the *Judenweib*, but Minni grows distraught and collapses, injuring herself and losing blood (6). The "violence" expands in the next-to-last chapter (November 22, 1923). Here a jealous, non-Jewish suitor—whose character has hardly been adumbrated in the novel—attempts to shoot Max and Minni. The *Scheunenviertel* pogrom of previous weeks is being cited; this notion is validated by texts in the surrounding pages of the *Israelitisches Familienblatt*. In a fantasy dénouement, the attacker is beaten down with a stick by Minni's half-brother, a non-Jew. The final installment is a tempered happy end, not unlike the breaking of glass that concludes a Jewish wedding and that recalls the destruction of the Temple. "For happiness does not always laugh at the darlings of fate and there came the time which, as old Ezekiel said, engraved itself with crying and sobbing and lamentation" (November 29, 1923, installment, 5). At the same time, the first major crisis of the Weimar Republic was being defused—if not forgotten, for the deportations of Eastern Jews inaugurated in Bavaria were soon renewed only days after the unsuccessful Hitler Beer-Hall Putsch of November 9.

The reservations toward the non-Jewish world expressed in *Versöhnung* are relatively circumscribed in *Die geborene Tugendreich*. In fact, it was the criticism of Jewish male participation in that world that made Opet-Fuß's narrative most credible on gender issues. In contrast to Adolf Thalheim, however, Max Rosenthal is strong and in control of his surroundings. Indeed, there is only one significant obstacle to his development: namely, his mother. While the antifeminism of *Die geborene Tugendreich* is somewhat assuaged by the distance of historical fiction, Jettchen epitomizes the *yidishe mame*, a caricature with an infamous history in Jewish and German-Jewish letters. It is arguable that this example was inspired by Hermann's novel, which likewise appeared originally in serialization,[8] for in Salomonski's fiction, Jettchen has the dubious honor of functioning as the primary source of conflict and misunderstanding. Max, despite recognizing that he has internalized some of her traits, is repeatedly victimized by her intrusions, nor is his father spared. This results in a sentimentalized episode of "male bonding" between Jonas and Max, described using *mame loshn,* that is, Yiddish.

The role of women and Eastern European Jewry in *Die geborene Tugendreich* points up the more convincing social dynamic of *Versöhnung.* Jettchen's foil and the model female in Salomonski's novel is Regina, the Polish-Jewish mother of Max's fiancée. While praising Minni and her mother as women of valor incapable of "betray[ing] the tribe" (September 6, 1923, installment, 9; and September 14, 1923, installment, 5), Salomonski's narrator is also issuing a disguised attack on the virtue of East European Jewish women—an attack that rehearses the discourse of the fallen Eastern Jewish woman victimized by the "white slave trade." This and other passages appear to blame East European Jewish women for their involvement in prostitution, notwithstanding the efforts of Bertha Pappenheim and others to liberate them from it. The narrator, for example, directly addresses women readers at the midpoint of the novel, issuing a proscriptive agenda for Jewish womanhood:

> Minni's evenings were not that exciting. But whoever means well by her won't lament that she usually stayed at home and hardly went out by herself. Even a very confining home is the be-all, end-all for a woman if she's able to appreciate the grandeur in little things. Comfort can be replaced by homeliness; poverty and darkness lose their gloomy aura where kindness shines radiantly through the fog.
>
> See to it in your wisdom, you mothers, that your daughters and all young women have something they can hold onto in the quiet of their own worlds. A woman can only live when she is able to dispense love in tiny ways (October 11, 1923, installment, 4).

Salomonski's favoring of domestic confinement for women, a typical discourse of mass-culture fantasy novels, stands in stark contrast to *Versöhnung.* Understanding Opet-Fuß's novel as the female *romancière's* protest against such confinement is yet another way to take serial fiction seriously as record of and response to the social realities of Weimar Jewry.

Die geborene Tugendreich not only imagines a different positioning of male readers but also elicits a variant of the putative "male gaze." For Max, it is important that he project "courage and decisiveness" when he speaks to Minni for the first time in public. After a successful encounter, he feels like a "victor" for the rest of the day (October 4, 1923, installment). This is not to say that Opet-Fuß's novel is an example of *écriture féminine.* But Salomonski's opus betrays what one can safely term a more androcentric perspective or even "style." At times its incredible plot line, where action overrides description and dialogue, results in a gendered stereotype of genre-fiction. Finally, its deemphasis of antidefamation as well as political relations are arguably implicit in the continuation of Salomonski's own life story, for like Leo Baeck and other rabbis, Salomonski remained in the Third Reich to tend to the flock. His activities on behalf of senior citizens under the auspices of the so-called *Aufbringungswerk* were designed to offer succor to the remnant. He was eventually deported and perished in Auschwitz in 1944.

DIRECTIONS FOR FURTHER RESEARCH

Compared to *Versöhnung*, Salomonski's *Familienblatt* novel is less reliable but no less helpful as a guide to the experiences and self-understanding of diaspora Jews in a troubled phase of history. Still, much work remains to be done if we are to write a truly comprehensive history of the Jewish experience in the Weimar Republic. In evaluating literary sources, comparisons are needed of other novels by the same authors, indeed of other installment fiction in the forty-year history of the *Israelitisches Familienblatt*. What is more, feuilleton novels for Jews were published in a variety of periodicals, and it is possible that the theme of reconciliation may have appealed more to readers of the *Israelitisches Familienblatt* than readers of other Jewish organs: the *Familienblatt*'s readers were more likely to be Jews in small towns than city slickers, more likely families with small businesses than the financial or cultural elite, more nonobservant than Orthodox, and more likely of middle-brow taste. Last but not least, the readers were more likely men and women than just men. The placement of serial novels next to the women's section—the *Frauenbeilage*—in the *Israelitisches Familienblatt* suggests as much.

The installment fictions discussed here also need to be placed in the larger German context in which non-Jews were publishing serialized novels for non-Jewish audiences.[9] More systematic research would be welcomed on the genres and techniques[10] of installment fiction and popular literature generally. The label *Trivialliteratur*, besides being negatively associated with women, has proved to be as durable as any other misleading prejudice. Critics of the ideology of mass culture such as Theodor W. Adorno and Max Horkheimer contend that this type of literature is informed by "bankrupt" nineteenth-century models of psychological Realism (*bürgerlicher Realismus*).

What may surprise the opponents of popular culture is the fact that the narrator of *Versöhnung* more than once makes the leap from "kitsch" to "camp." Particularly overt are the parallels between Opet-Fuß, the narrator, and the writer manqué Adolf, whose literary efforts are often specified. Even in *Die geborene Tugendreich,* the elision of author, narrator, and character subjects the mimesis to a kind of permanent parabasis (or Romantic irony) à la Schlegel. With its self-referentiality and the way it ingests previous intertexts, the feuilleton literature analyzed in this study is as suited to the satiric-grotesque as it is to Bakhtinian polyphony.

Indeed, the *Familienblatt* novels of both Opet-Fuß and Salomonski constitute an object lesson for us today about the complexities of reading and reception. Like the viewers of nighttime television soap operas, we who write about
mass culture may still respond to popular fiction and melodrama with that
strange combination of distance and intimacy signified by the term "irony."
Now, as then, irony's symbiosis of critique and appreciation may be the most
rewarding approach to the study of German Jews and their cultural productions.
It may also enable us to make educated guesses in answering important questions: How did Weimar Jewish readers interpret serialized fiction? To what extent did they identify with Jewish characters and Jewish concerns, and what
were the mechanisms involved in this identification? In the end, teasing out the
relationship between audience and text is a step en route to a reconciliation of
political history, social history, and cultural history.[11] By focusing not just on
events themselves but on their representations and recollections, an integrated
approach to the German-Jewish experience may also tell us more about the
complex relationship between narrative and history.

NOTES

1. For an overview, see Storey.
2. All translations from the German are my own and have been rendered in a contemporary American idiom so as to suggest the colloquial, contemporary quality of discourse
in *Versöhnung*.
3. For a discussion of stereotypes of Jewish male bodies, see Breines. The role of the
gymnastic movement in German/Jewish dynamics is discussed in Christopher D. Kenway's contribution to this volume. See his "Regeneration of the *Volkskörper* and the
Jew's Body: The German *Körperkultur* Movement at the Turn of the Century."
4. See also Radway.
5. For an excellent summary of the German-Jewish response to 1918, see Ruth Gay,
who writes:

> The enemies of the Jews (and of the Republic) found welcome fodder
> in the results of the wartime census of Jews in the armed forces, re-
> leased in 1919 by an unofficial, pseudonymous, anti-Semitic author,
> "Otto Armin." The statistics he offered, presumably reflecting the of-
> ficial count, supported the slander that Jews had hung back behind
> the lines. Anticipating such slander, a special consortium of Jewish
> organizations had set up a Committee for War Statistics at the be-
> ginnning of the war. It worked under the direction of two highly
> placed statisticians: Jacob Segall, head of the Berlin Bureau for Sta-
> tistics on Jews, and Heinrich Silbergleit, director of the Office of
> Statistics for the city of Berlin between 1906 and 1923. They released
> their results in 1922 and the facts were very different from the story
> in the Otto Armin report: among the 550,000 Jews of German nation-
> ality, 100,000 had served in the war, 80,000 at the front. And 12,000
> had died for Germany. What is more, 35,000 Jewish soldiers had re-
> ceived medals, and 23,000 had been promoted—2,000 of them, in

fact, to officer's rank. The Reichsbund jüdischer Frontsoldaten . . .
was founded in 1919 with the express purpose of documenting, and
thus honoring, the Jewish war dead. (Gay 243–44)

6. Right-wing anti-Semites also made an attempt on the life of Maximilian Harden, a convert to Protestantism, in 1922.

7. A *Münze* is a coin; the pun sets up the irony of the bar's name, which is the title of a hymn traditionally sung to welcome the Sabbath.

8. For a more recent example of the Jewish mother stereotype in German-language Jewish literature, see Rafael Seligmann, *Die jiddische Mamme*.

9. Most scholars have eschewed comparisons of Jewish authors and audiences with their non-Jewish counterparts; see, for example, M. Brenner 153–54.

10. It should be noted that, for all the sudden shifts and improbabilities of feuilleton fiction, there is often a high degree of close observation and milieu detail, suggesting that composition and organization were not haphazard. Some practitioners maintain that it actually requires more discipline to write on an installment basis.

11. Numerous debates in reception theory and reader-response theory since the 1960s involve the problematic notion of the "implied reader"; for a good summary, see Holub. The implied audience can be teased out from the text by drawing on social histories that use analytical categories such as class, education, gender, age, ethnicity, and religion; see Jarausch.

WORKS CITED

Adorno, Theodore W., and Max Horkheimer. *Dialektik der Aufklärung: Philosophische Fragmente*. Amsterdam: Querido, 1947.

Belgum, Kirsten. "Domesticating the Reader: Women and 'Die Gartenlaube.'" *Women in German Yearbook* 9 (1993): 91–111.

Boyarin, Daniel. Personal interview, 20 July 1996.

Breines, Paul. *Tough Jews: Political Fantasies and the Moral Dilemma of American Jewry*. New York: Basic Books, 1990.

Brenner, David. *Marketing Identities: The Invention of Jewish Ethnicity*. Detroit: Wayne State University Press, 1997.

Brenner, Michael. *The Renaissance of Jewish Culture in Weimar Germany*. New Haven: Yale University Press, 1996.

Fuss-Opet [sic], Meta. "Judentum und Pazifismus." *Jüdisch-liberale Zeitung*, 21 Jan. 1931: n.p.

Gay, Peter. *Weimar Culture: The Outsider as Insider*. New York: Harper & Row, 1968.

Gay, Ruth. *The Jews in Germany*. New Haven: Yale University Press, 1993.

Holub, Robert. *Reception Theory: A Critical Introduction*. London: Methuen, 1984.

Jarausch, Konrad. "Toward a Social History of Experience." *Central European History* 22 (Sept./Dec. 1989): 427–43.

Kaplan, Marion A. *The Making of the Jewish Middle Classes: Women, Family, and Identity in Imperial Germany*. New York: Oxford University Press, 1991.

Maurer, Trude. "Partnersuche und Lebensplanung. Heiratsannoncen als Quelle für die Sozial- und Mentalitätsgeschichte der Juden in Deutschland." *Juden in Deutschland: Emanzipation, Integration, Verfolgung und Vernichtung: 25 Jahre Institut für die Geschichte der deutschen Juden (Hamburg)*, ed. Peter Freimark, Alice Janowski, and Ina S. Lorenz, 344–74. Hamburg: Hans Christians, 1991.

Modleski, Tania. *Loving with a Vengeance: Mass-Produced Fantasies for Women.* Hamden, CT: Archon Books, 1982.

Opet-Fuß, Meta. *Johann Reuchlin:Roman. Israelitisches Familienblatt.* Installments begin Dec. 14, 1933.

———. "Jüdischer Sport in der Gegenwart." *Israelitisches Familienblatt.* 18 Jan. 1934: n.p.

———. *Versöhnung. Israelitisches Familienblatt.* Installments begin Oct. 12, 1922.

Peukert, Detlev. *The Weimar Republic: The Crisis of Classical Modernity.* Trans. Richard Deveson. New York: Hill and Wang, 1993.

Radway, Janice A. *Reading the Romance: Women, Patriarchy, and Popular Literature.* 2nd ed. Chapel Hill: University of North Carolina Press, 1991.

Salomonski, Martin. *Die geborene Tugendreich: Ein Großstadtroman. Israelitisches Familienblatt.* Installments begin Aug. 9, 1923.

Seligmann, Rafael. *Die jiddische Mamme.* Frankfurt am Main: Eichborn, 1990.

Storey, John. *An Introductory Guide to Cultural Theory and Popular Culture.* Athens: University of Georgia Press, 1993.

West, James L. W., III. *American Authors and the Literary Marketplace since 1900.* Philadelphia: University of Pennsylvania Press, 1988.

Chapter 4

Binding Together by Cutting Apart: Circumcision, Kafka, and Minority Discourse

Steven Taubeneck

"Talent for 'patchwork.'"

—Franz Kafka, *Tagebücher* 922[1]

In this chapter, Steven Taubeneck raises the question of how communities are formed and how they are broken down. Rejecting Herder's traditional criteria of exteriority and interiority in his definition of culture, Taubeneck maintains that cultural practices, and in particular, rituals of agreement, be considered paramount in understanding how cultural groups cohere or fall apart. By way of illustration, he examines tropes of binding and cutting extending from the Bible and culminating in the works of Franz Kafka, Edgar Hilsenrath, and Esther Dischereit.

Taubeneck's analysis of circumcision reveals a community-forming ritual, where the act of cutting is paradoxically tantamount to an act of binding. Yet under the onslaught of modernism, he argues, the seamlessness of such communal bondings is no longer inevitable, as evidenced in Kafka's contrastive discussions of circumcision practices among Eastern and Western European Jews. In the West, circumcision signals the internal and spiritual dissolution of the community; in the East, on the other hand, vitality and spiritual coherence. Where binding no longer results in wholeness, communities fall apart.

Taubeneck points out in his treatment of Hilsenrath, Dischereit, and Kafka that this process has implications for literature as well. Kafka observes that literature is like the circumcision that binds the child to the community by cutting his skin: where "people who hang together are lacking, literary actions that hang together fall away, too."

Two recent books on Kafka, Mark Anderson's *Kafka's Clothes: Ornament and Aestheticism in the Habsburg Fin de Siècle* and Sander Gilman's *Franz Kafka: The Jewish Patient*, have made important contributions to our understanding of him as a central representative of the modern period.[2] Both have provided many reasons for seeing Kafka as a paradigmatic cultural modernist. But with the historical, psychological, and social emphasis of these studies, at least two important features of Kafka get overlooked: the distinctive qualities of his writing, and the many links between Kafka and postmodernity.[3] My argument is that Kafka should be seen as more of a "patchwork" figure than a figure obsessed with a single concern or set of concerns.[4] He should be read as someone with many, varying concerns, at moments as light and humorous as he is dark and ponderous. If we see him this way, not only would we be acknowledging his assessment of his own talents, we would be able to see him as someone with particular relevance to our condition today.

To demonstrate the point, I want to read Kafka as an example of minority discourse. Of course, this would situate him most immediately in his own time; as Evelyn Torton Beck has emphasised: "Kafka was multiply a minority."[5] But it would also link Kafka strongly to today: "Ours is becoming the age of minorities" (Deleuze and Guattari, *Plateaus*, 469). Deleuze and Guattari have further linked the migration associated with minority discourse to patchwork: "Patchwork, in conformity with migration, whose degree of affinity with nomadism it shares, is not only named after trajectories, but 'represents' trajectories, becomes inseparable from speed or movement in an open space" (477). And, in the extent to which our world is marked by the reappearance of the archaic, Kafka can also be situated against antiquity.

To understand minority discourse, however, it would be helpful to understand in the first place how people form allegiances as communities, groups, and nations. What binds people together, and what cuts them apart? The more people there are, the more important it becomes to find ways of forming allegiances among communities. Yet that very population growth has unsettling effects, creating smaller communities, more exclusive groups, and more conflicted divisions. Consider the divisions between and within Quebec and Canada, Northern and southern Ireland, the Serbs and the Croats, or the vexed situation of the "new Eastern *Länder*" in Germany. Perhaps if we could understand how people form loyalties in the first place, how they come to feel a sense of belonging to a community, we could begin to solve the problem of human beings belonging together more generally.[6]

One place to start, I would suggest, is with culture. Of course the very word "culture" is notoriously hard to grasp. It might help to focus the discussion by considering the definition proposed by Johann Gottfried Herder, in his *Ideen zur Philosophie der Geschichte der Menschheit* (*Ideas on a Philosophy of Human History*), which appeared from 1784 to 1791.[7] Herder's concept of culture is characterized by at least three moments:

- A culture involves the practices of a specific group, or *Volk*, whose unique essence appears in the unfolding of those practices,
- The *Volk* should be ethnically and socially homogeneous,
- It should be clearly distinct from other peoples.

Herder's concept centers around a desire to unify internally and to differentiate externally. Underlying Herder's culture concept is the distinction between the inside and outside, or the insiders and outsiders, of a particular ethnic group, but today, Herder's concept seems largely inappropriate. Contemporary societies are at once so unified by, for example, computer technology, and yet so differentiated by language and values that it would be counterproductive to speak of a dialectic of inside and outside. For where would the line between inside and outside be drawn? How could the zones of interiority and externality for individuals and groups be accurately distinguished? The discussion would be made more useful if we would agree that the term "culture" refers to all forms of attitudes and behaviors practiced by any particular person or people. To study culture would mean to study any form in which attitudes or behaviors are articulated. It would mean to study all forms of expression with the aim of deriving their full significance. In regard to the problem of how people come to feel they belong together, it would involve the study of the forms of expression used to mark that sense of belonging.

Of course, such study is not really new. At least since Homer described the Greeks and the Trojans, and the Bible described the beginnings of the Jewish nation, people have tried to explain how groups are formed and loyalties arise. The problem today is that an integrated study has been broken by the very structuring of knowledge into discrete and segregated units. Instead of large, overarching arrangements, we have schools of law, faculties of arts, sciences, and medicine; departments of anthropology, geography, political science, psychology, religious studies, and sociology; and various national languages and literatures. Clearly, by their very constitution, such institutional units have a disintegrating effect. The structuring of knowledge, particularly at the university, will impede the synthesis of information needed to address larger problems. Too much specialized information will lead to an overburdening of the university's ability to respond.

What is needed in short, is an overarching unit of cultural studies.[8] Such a unit would take as its mandate the study of larger issues arising in culture. To address certain issues, such as the problem of group formation, it would assume the work of bringing together insights from all related disciplines. These might range from disciplines as widely separated as medicine, law, business, and the arts. Only when the actual work of arranging, combining, coordinating and integrating such disciplinary perspectives is accomplished will we have an appropriate basis for developing strategies to deal with many problems today.

The problem of group formation can be used as a test case for this approach.[9] Perhaps one of the first practices to consider would be the ways in which people make agreements with each other, for surely the practice of making agreements would signal the formation of a cohesive group in which people would accept certain ceremonies as binding. It turns out, of course, that there are many ways of making agreements, and they have long histories and continue even to the present day. My point is that the study of such histories can show us a great deal about the persistence of certain practices and indicate areas in which we have not changed as much as we would like to think. The persistence of these practices would suggest that, behind the rhetoric of postmodern this and that, there remains an active tribalism at work in human affairs. Perhaps we need to expose the roots of this tribalism in order to overcome many hostilities,[10] for the act of binding together is often signalled by cutting people apart, their bodies and even their body parts.

The notions of making an agreement or sealing a contract only need slight restatement to reveal the long histories embedded in each. Each could be redescribed as entering into a covenant. Once we have redescribed contractual arrangements as covenants, we need not look far afield to discover the ancient rituals marking covenantal ties. There was, for example, the ritual of circumcision from the Old Testament, which was instituted to mark the covenant between God and his chosen people.[11] The crucial passage occurs in the Book of Gen. 17.10–11, 13, when God says to Abraham: "This is my covenant, which you shall keep between me and you and your seed after you: Every manchild among you shall be circumcised. And you shall circumcise the flesh of your foreskin, and it shall be a token of the covenant between me and you . . . [My] covenant shall be in your flesh for an everlasting covenant." The covenant between God, Abraham, and his tribe was marked by cutting the flesh of the foreskin. With this cut, this loss, a bond was to be formed between the divine and the human, and among humans. The act was prescribed for the eighth day after birth, and anyone who had not undergone it should be cut off from both his people and from God. Cut flesh would seal the bond, whereas uncut flesh would break it.

This is clearly an economy of physical sacrifice. The price for establishing the covenant is the loss of the foreskin. Membership in the group was to be bought at the cost of some mutilation, pain, and suffering. Of course, the Old Testament does not dwell on the pain of the act. Instead, in a flat, matter-of-fact tone, it recalls the event itself: "And Abraham was ninety years old and nine, when he was circumcised in the flesh of his foreskin. And Ishmael his son was thirteen years old, when he was circumcised in the flesh of his foreskin" (Gen. 17.24–25). Evidently, Abraham accepted the terms of the deal without complaint. In any case, it was with that gesture that the covenant with their God and among Abraham's descendants had been sealed. The tribe was to be bound together by the cutting of skin.

My point here is that this founding gesture of tribal solidarity involves loss, mutilation, pain, and suffering. One can only belong to the tribe if one has sacrificed a part of one's skin. With this, a basic aspect of signifying group membership and sealing a contract was established. Today, this gesture continues to reinforce distinctions between who belongs to one group and who does not. The culture of belonging to one tribe or another is often organized around rituals of physical mutilation. What is further important to note is how controversial such practices have been and how many various meanings have been attached to them. From Abraham to the present, millions have died over the absence or presence of a foreskin. The loss, mutilation, pain, and suffering that marked the entrance to the group also led to embattled distinctions between the tribe and others. At the same time, physical and psychological, ethnic, religious, and social meanings have been attributed to such rituals.

To this day, the ritual of circumcision evokes many of the different features of tribal differentiation. The example suggests a model of belonging to the tribe different from the one suggested by Herder. Instead of any essential, inherent quality of the group, a very specific cultural practice or ritual is used as a tool to organize the distinctions between inside and outside, insiders and outsiders. Belonging, from this point of view, becomes a dynamic cultural process that is neither essentially reactionary nor essentially progressive. Understanding the process of belonging to a group would involve understanding the rituals used to mark that process.

The power and problematic function of circumcision appear in the transition from the Old Testament to the New. Luke wrote (Luke 2.21) that the child Christ was circumcised under the Old Law, on the eighth day following his birth. Then Paul interpreted baptism as superseding the sacrament of the Old Law. Baptism was thus to be understood as a spiritual circumcision in Christ (Col. 2.11–12). These are the scriptural records in the New Testament.

The Church Feast of the Circumcision and Naming of Christ was fixed for January 1 from the midsixth century at the latest. By this time, most of the major themes in the theological interpretation of the event had crystallized. Paul's typological parallel remained axiomatic: though circumcision and baptism differ in outward form, they agree in effect. The ritual in the New Testament, as in the Old, is a sign, the seal of the covenant between God and his chosen people.

The second major interpretation arises with Augustine. Whereas earlier commentators had interpreted Old Testament circumcisions as a token of initiation into Abraham's covenant with God, Augustine expanded its importance and declared it to have been an instrument of grace for erasing the stain of original sin. "Instituted among the people of God, circumcision availed to signify the cleansing, even in infants, of original sin . . . just as baptism . . . from the time of its institution began to be of avail for the renewal of man" (*Marriage and Concupiscence*, II, 292, cited in Steinberg, 50). This ruling prevailed in the West. Circumcision was meant to be continuous with the work of redemption.

But how relevant is all this abstruse theology to the work of twentieth-century artists? I am not suggesting, for example, that Kafka sat up nights reading Genesis, Luke, Paul, or Augustine. Yet three specific points can be made. First, the ritual of circumcision clearly extends back to the beginnings of Judeo-Christian writing and up through a long history of revisionist interpretations. Second, the ritual has been interpreted in the most various ways, as either a sign of the Old Law or a prefiguring of the New. Third, circumcision has consistently been a problem for interpreters to face. By the time this history extended to Goethe, the Circumcision of Christ, which had once been the opening act of the Redemption, had become merely bad taste. When Goethe reports on Guercino's *Circumcision of Christ*, a painting he admired in the artist's birthplace in mid-October 1786 and describes in his *Italian Journey*, he writes of it with considerable ambivalence: "I excused the unbearable object and was pleased about the execution" (cited in Steinberg 72). By this time, Christ's nakedness and circumcision had become a matter of disgust. Circumcision, for Goethe, had become the mark of a foreign, sinister tribe.

The situation in Prague, at the close of the nineteenth century, had intensified. By then, religion had lost its centrality in the lives of both Jews and Christians. Without the foundation of Judeo-Christian theological beliefs, people turned to the body as the basis for a metaphysical ground.[12] The proclamation of Nietzsche's madman that "God is dead" had led to body worship. This meant in practical terms, as Gilman writes, that

> the theological difference of the Jew from the Christian was trans-
> lated into the biological difference of the Jew from the Aryan. Jewish
> biological difference came to be understood as immutable and in-
> scribed on the Jew's imagined body. No matter what the self-
> definition of the Jew—whether religious, ethnic, cultural, or politi-
> cal—this construction of the Jew's body appeared in the Jew's self-
> perception and self-actualization. (8)

Belonging to the tribe of Abraham had become a bond of shame. Especially the act of circumcision marked the male Jew as shamefully different, and as different precisely for reasons of "hygiene," the rationale for infant male circumcisions among European and North American Jews at that time.

Kafka wrote most explicitly on circumcision and minority discourse in an important sequence of diary entries from the end of 1911. These entries have become a major site for discussion in the Kafka industry, but they contain a number of significant elements that have not received the attention they deserve. Among the first to comment on the entries were Deleuze and Guattari.[13] For them, the entry headed "Schema zur Charakteristik kleiner Literaturen" ("Schema for the Characteristics of Minor Literatures") suggests "the three characteristics of minor literature": "the deterritorialization of language, the connection of the individual to a political immediacy, and the collective assemblage of enunciation" (18). Under this description, Deleuze and Guattari see Kafka as a writer of revolutionary importance, in terms of both political significance and an intensive approach to language.

Undoubtedly, the work by Deleuze and Guattari has had a major impact on cultural theory as well as on the Kafka industry. The concept of a "minor literature" as a highly politicized form of discourse has circulated widely throughout writing on culture. As Gilman comments, "This concept is especially useful for any analysis of a literature that self-consciously positions itself outside a cultural mainstream to which it certainly belongs" (22). But as Walter H. Sokel pointed out in his review of Deleuze and Guattari, Kafka did not see his own writing as an example of "minor literature"; in fact, such a description drastically oversimplifies the complexities of Kafka's writing and the situation of a "minor literature" itself.[14] Though their analysis may be brilliantly written and compelling as far as it goes, it will have missed much of what happens in Kafka's writing in particular and minority discourse in general.

When Gilman revisits the diaries, twenty years later, he extends his analysis into other topics and other entries. For Gilman, Kafka's "minor literature" consists of "a discourse that must simultaneously be employed and transcended. It is a language and style that the 'minority' is accused of not being able to command that is captured in a special way by the writers in that minority. This is a highly psychologized political literature" (22–23). By contrast with Deleuze and Guattari, Gilman's Kafka is divided against himself, indeed, carries out a prolonged "struggle with the image of the self that is both private, psychological— and here the model of the masochist is appropriate—as well as public, political, since resistance to one's internalization of others' labeling of oneself is inherently political" (23). In a sense, Gilman supplements one book by Deleuze and Guattari with another work by Deleuze: the study entitled "Coldness and Cruelty."[15] The psychological element in Kafka's writing, which Deleuze and Guattari had displaced in favor of the political, returns in Gilman's analysis in the form of a concerted masochism.

More than Deleuze and Guattari, as well, Gilman adds a historical and specifically ethnic component to his account of the diaries. Gilman's Kafka is extremely anxious not only about himself and his father but about the relations between Jewish and Christian culture. For Gilman, these anxieties appear most vividly in the diary entries on circumcision placed around the "Schema" in Max Brod's edition. Gilman therefore analyzes in great detail the two accounts of circumcision, which for him "frame" Kafka's views on the "authentic character of Jewish identity": "[B]oth frame the notion that minor literature is a product of the ethnopsychology of a group, and is in some way as much inscribed on their unconscious by their social circumstances and historical experiences" (33). Gilman's "new psychohistorical" (9) approach to the diaries adds a significant dimension to the ethnopsychological, historico-political situation of Kafka in "high modernism" (9).

As is often the case, however, the situation becomes much more complicated when the texts themselves are considered. In the first place, it is not entirely accurate to suggest that the two texts on circumcision "frame" the entry on minor literature "for December 25, 1911" (Gilman 22). Though the earlier edition, the one edited by Max Brod, suggests this kind of "framed" structure, the more recent version in the *Kritische Ausgabe* (critical edition) tells a different story.[16] First, the passages on the circumcision and the one on the "Schema" extend from December 24, 1911, to December 27, 1911, from page 309 to page 326. The "Schema" actually appears on the last page of this sequence, in the entry from December 27, 1911, whereas one description of circumcision appears in the entry from December 24, while the other appears in the entry dated December 25. The assumption that the accounts of circumcision "frame" the description of a minor literature follows the unifying structure imposed on the material by Max Brod, whereas these are just a few of the entries scattered across the four days. It would be reductive to limit these entries to one theme or a limited set of themes. It would be preferable to conceive of Kafka's writing as a patch-work of themes, a gathering of various, often quite heterogeneous materials.

Often in these entries, Kafka is concerned about his relations with his friends and his father. He reports of a friendly visit to Baum and Weltsch, while sug-gesting that he felt "free" without Max (309). Evidently, Kafka was not entirely at ease with Max. In addition to these relations, he describes his "angst" with his father, especially when his father spoke "of the last or ultimate things" (309). In both sets of relations, Kafka appears uneasy, awkward, or unsure, while desiring a closer, friendlier connection. It is his own awkwardness with his family and friends that prefaces the discussion of the "circumcision of my nephew" (310). The general issue involves the question of where he belongs, with whom, and under what description. The concluding lines of one entry on the circumcision testify to this emphasis: "As he has now entered into the covenant, so may he enter into knowledge of the Torah, a happy marriage covenant and the perform-ance of good deeds" (311). These lines promise the group solidarity that Kafka is seeking with his father and friends.

Repeatedly, he writes about the tension between unity and fragmentation, belonging to a group and not belonging. One of the central qualities of a litera-ture like Jewish literature in Warsaw and Czech literature is the ability to hold or bind together the disparate elements of a nation: Kafka notes "the many benefits of literature—the stirring of minds, the coherence of national consciousness, often unrealized in public life and always tending to disintegrate" (312–13).[17] Kafka adds here other advantages of such literatures, including "the binding of dissatisfied elements" and "the dignification of the antithesis between fathers and sons and the possibility of discussing this."[18] For him, a better sense of unity—within a nation, between father and son, and against enemies—can be achieved by such a literature. Kafka implies that such literature is like the cir-cumcision that binds the child to the community by cutting his skin. Writing from the margins accomplishes among minds what circumcision achieves on the body.

More successful than the circumcision in Prague, the circumcision that Kafka describes in Russia resembles a festival: "The circumcision follows, often in the presence of more than a hundred relatives and friends."[19] Though the practice of the ritual may be "not very pleasant," its consequences form a narra-tive of healing: "The member is then sprinkled with sawdust and heals in about three days."[20] The implication is that despite the dirt, the scene in Russia is healthier for its unifying force. Whereas the ritual in Prague unifies the child and the community in word, the Russian version "heals" any cut between the indi-vidual and the group. As often in Kafka's writing, dirt and filth carry a healing, more powerful, significance.

Kafka thus proceeds in his writing through a gathering process of autocita-tion and textual rearrangement. In the first entry on circumcision, he describes the somewhat mechanical procedure in Prague; in the second, he returns to the ritual but casts it in an earthier, more carnivalesque, and healing light. Similarly, he returns to the descriptions of his friendships, his relations with his father, and the roles of literature. It is as if he consistently reworked certain themes, character types, and plot structures in an exploratory form of personal recycling.

This steady repetition might have carried the promise of coherence, unity, wholeness, and integration, but Kafka also recognizes the impossibility of fulfilling that promise: "Since people who hang together are lacking, literary actions that hang together fall away, too."[21] Since people are no longer coherent, literary developments will also be lacking in coherence. Though he may have wanted coherence, unity, and integration, Kafka evidently recognized that they were not available. What was available was a kind of patchwork, a makeshift series of contingent sketches out of which he would try to assemble his stories. This means that Kafka realized that no wholeness was possible, even for a "minor literature." He knew that the image was but a dream. Hence, just after he wrote the famous "Schema," which became the basis of his description of a "minor literature," Kafka commented sarcastically: "How weak this picture is. An incoherent assumption is thrust like a board between the actual feeling and the metaphor of the description."[22] It is especially the lack of coherence that bothered him about the outline.

Thus, in the writings of Franz Kafka by 1911 at the latest, the history of circumcision as a ritual of group formation had reached an important nexus point of tribal differentiation, cultural exhaustion, and, potentially, cultural renewal. For Kafka, the Prague version of the ritual was only a memory, and showed many of the symptoms of decay and falling apart. By contrast, the Russian ceremony seemed to offer the possibility of a lively community renewal. Whereas the physical, psychological, religious, and social dimensions of the ceremony had been exhausted in the West, Russian practices represented a desirable alternative for Kafka. In Kafka's world, the decayed, the dirty, and the old represent the more spiritual and sublime instances. Just before Gregor Samsa in "Die Verwandlung" ("Metamorphosis") dies and his family is saved, he is described as covered with dust and food particles from lying around on the floor. Just before Georg Bendemann's father rises up in the story of "Das Urteil" ("The Judgment"), he is described as living in a dark and dirty room. Frieda and K., in *Das Schloss* (*The Castle*), are never happier than when they are rolling around in the beer together on the floor. For Kafka, the dirty is the sign of the spiritual, and the dirtier the ceremony of circumcision, the closer the community will be bound together. Thus, it is not only the cutting apart that forms group allegiances, but also the smelly, contagious ritual of the Russian circumcision. Paradoxically, binding together is formed by cutting apart; dirt and filth carry the possibility of salvation.

Kafka's concerns with belonging, circumcision, and minority discourse persist into the present day. Examples include one text by Edgar Hilsenrath, *Der Nazi und der Friseur* (*The Nazi and the Hairdresser*), and another by Esther Dischereit, *Joëmis Tisch* (*Joëmi's Table*). The Hilsenrath text appeared first in 1977, and the Dischereit text appeared in 1988.[23] Both are pivotal examples of recent writing on the topic of minority discourse, and both show how problematic the relations between a minority and the cultural mainstream remain.

Moreover, both texts organize their narratives around the gesture of cutting apart in order to bind groups together.

The Hilsenrath text tells the story of two childhood friends, Max Schulz and Itzig Finkelstein, who eventually become identical. Max describes his birth as "purely Aryan": "I am Max Schulz, the illegitimate, but also purely Aryan son of Minna Schulz . . . at the time of my birth a servant girl in the house of the Jewish furrier Abramowitz."[24] But just two minutes and twenty-two seconds after Max was born, Itzig came into the world: "Itzig Finkelstein lived next door. He was exactly as old as I, or . . . to be more exact, and if I may express myself thus: Itzig Finkelstein glimpsed the light of the world exactly two minutes and twenty-two seconds after the midwife Gretchen Fettwanst freed me, with a forceful pull, from the dark womb of my mother."[25] The two couldn't have been closer in terms of their births, yet farther apart in terms of their ethnic background.

Max becomes a leading member of the SS during the Second World War, and presumably is involved in killing Itzig. Yet as the war comes to an end, he recognizes that his side has lost, and he begins to imagine a second life for himself. The only problem is that he will have to be circumcised: "'And you know,' Max Schulz said, 'for months I have been thinking how I can best go under . . . Only I'll have to cut off my cock,' said Max Schulz. . . . 'Not really cut off,' he said, seriously. 'Only the foreskin. Then I am circumcised . . . just like Itzig Finkelstein.'"[26]

This text can be read as a paradigmatic example of postmodernist writing. Just as the SS man Max Schulz eventually becomes the Jew Itzig Finkelstein and later opens a barber shop in Tel Aviv, so the act of circumcision has been detached from any essential practices of a group and becomes a floating, transferable signifier. When anyone, even an old SS man, can become a Jew, then the cultural, political, or religious foundations underlying circumcision have been suspended. The act becomes a fetish of commodity exchange, whereby one identity is exchanged for another. The novel explores the mutability of identity, on the one hand, and the intertwining of German and Jewish identities on the other. Andreas Graf has recently analyzed the contradictions in the novel and compared it to another postmodernist novel, Günter Grass's *The Tin Drum*.[27]

But judging from my other example, Esther Dischereit's *Joëmis Tisch*, it is not entirely likely that Germans and Jews will blend together anytime soon into a great, neo-American-style melting pot.[28] The story is told through a complicated series of brief, narrative flashbacks on the life of a Jewish woman in Germany. But the central episode involves her discovery of a swastika scratched into her school desk: "I forgot to mention one thing. One day it was there. Thick and fat, drawn with ink, scratched in with the end of the pencil. It lay there in front of me, stared at me, the whole long hour."[29] In the Dischereit text, no explicit circumcision takes place. Another kind of cutting has occurred, the cutting of the swastika into the school bench. Both the cutting of the foreskin and the cutting of the swastika mark the borderlines between groups; on the one side, the

Jews, and the Germans on the other. Both kinds of cutting bind them together into discrete groups in tension with each other.

In conclusion, I would make several points about the dynamic of binding together by cutting apart, which extends at least from Abraham to Dischereit. This kind of broad, comparative cultural analysis makes visible a number of persistent themes. It should be clear that rituals of belonging and exclusion have not changed substantially since Old Testament days. People continue to distinguish between themselves and others, their own kind and aliens, on the basis of certain markers and cultural practices. It should also be clear that tribal allegiances and sexual identity can be linked around the practice of circumcision. Groups still form around practices that involve loss, mutilation, pain, and suffering. Third, it appears that covenants still involve an economy of physical sacrifice. We are perhaps more than ever affixed to the idea of the body as the sole guarantee of certainty and reality. Finally, I would suggest that we look again at the overly triumphalist claims of those who uncritically favor the present age. To be sure, it may be that communism has waned in some of its harsher forms, and it may be that free market practices are spreading faster than ever before. But I would also like to suggest that, just under the surface of our postmodern age, there still lurks the oldest tribal instincts of human beings. More than ever, tribalism may be the way of the future.

NOTES

1. Translations are my own throughout the chapter. Versions in German are given in the notes, and cited from the following critical edition: Franz Kafka, *Franz Kafka: Tagebücher in der Fassung der Handschrift*, ed. Hans-Gerd Koch, Michael Müller, and Malcolm Pasley (Frankfurt am Main: S. Fischer; 1990). This passage appears as "Talent für 'Flickarbeit'"(922).

2. The references are to Mark M. Anderson, *Kafka's Clothes: Ornament and Aestheticism in the Habsburg Fin de Siècle* (Oxford: Clarendon Press, 1992), and Sander L. Gilman, *Franz Kafka: The Jewish Patient* (New York: Routledge, 1995). With their emphasis on Kafka as a literary modernist, Anderson and Gilman agree with the recent article by Walter H. Sokel, "Kafka and Modernism," in *Approaches to Teaching Kafka's Short Fiction*, ed. Richard T. Gray (New York: Modern Language Association, 1995), 21–34.

3. The point is also to see how close Kafka is to contemporary perspectives. The literature on postmodernity is enormous, but one could begin with the essay by Fredric Jameson, "Postmodernism and Consumer Society," in *The Anti-Aesthetic: Essays on Postmodern Culture*, ed. Hal Foster (Seattle: Bay Press, 1983), 111–25. On Kafka and postmodernity, see my "Irony, Contingency, and Postmodernity: 'In the Penal Colony,'" in *Approaches*, 114–22.

4. By the term "patchwork" I have in mind the definition by Deleuze and Guattari: "An amorphous collection of juxtaposed pieces that can be joined together in an infinite number of ways." See Gilles Deleuze and Félix Guattari, *A Thousand Plateaus: Capitalism and Schizophrenia*, trans. Brian Massumi (Minneapolis: University of Minnesota Press, 1987), 476.

5. From "Gender, Judaism, and Power: A Jewish Feminist Approach to Kafka," in *Approaches*, 35.

6. Compare, for example, the journalistic account of the problem by Michael Ignatieff, *Blood and Belonging: Journeys into the New Nationalism* (Toronto: Penguin Canada, 1993).

7. Compare my account with the analysis by Wolfgang Welsch. See, for example, his articles "Transkulturalität—Lebensformen nach der Auflösung der Kulturen," *Information Philosophie* 2 (1993): 5–20, and "Transkulturalität—die veränderte Fassung heutiger Kulturen," *Sichtweisen: Die Vielheit in der Einheit* (Weimar: Edition Weimarer Klassik, 1994), 83–122.

8. Of course the development of cultural studies has gone on for some time, and by now there is a large bibliography on the concept and its applications, but it has consistently met resistance from more entrenched interests in the university. See, for example, the anthology edited by Lawrence Grossberg, Cary Nelson, and Paula Treichler, *Cultural Studies* (New York: Routledge, 1992).

9. One of the most suggestive books on this clearly very large topic is by Benedict Anderson, *Imagined Communities: Reflections on the Origin and Spread of Nationalism* (London: Verso, 1983). A more recent collection, which follows Anderson's study but extends it into the areas of gender and sexuality, is edited by Andrew Parker, Mary Russo, Doris Sommer, and Patricia Yaeger, *Nationalisms and Sexualities* (New York: Routledge, 1992).

10. My suggestion could be brought together with, for example, Freud's analysis of neurosis and tribalism in *Totem and Taboo: Resemblances between the Psychic Lives of Savages and Neurotics*, trans. A. A. Brill (New York: Random House, 1918).

11. The discussion about the advantages, the disadvantages, and the significance of circumcision is long and acrimonious. For the history of the concept, I would like to draw on the work of the art historian Leo Steinberg, *The Sexuality of Christ in Renaissance Art and in Modern Oblivion* (New York: Pantheon, 1983).

12. Gilman makes a similar point in his *Kafka*, 6–12.

13. See *Kafka: Pour une littérature mineure* from 1975 (Paris: Les éditions de minuit), translated by Dana Polan as *Kafka: Toward a Minor Literature* (Minneapolis: University of Minnesota Press, 1986).

14. See Sokel's "Two Views of 'Minority' Literature: Deleuze, Kafka, and the German-Jewish Enclave of Prague," *Quarterly World Report* 6 (1983): 5–8.

15. In Gilles Deleuze and Félix Guattari, *Masochism*, trans. Jean McNeil (New York: Zone Books, 1991).

16. The comparison is between *Franz Kafka: Tagebücher 1910–1923*, ed. Max Brod (Frankfurt am Main: S. Fischer, 1951), and Franz Kafka, *Franz Kafka: Tagebücher in der Fassung der Handschrift*, ed. Hans-Gerd Koch, Michael Müller, and Malcolm Pasley (Frankfurt am Main: S. Fischer, 1990).

17. See "viele Vorteile der litterarischen Arbeit, die Bewegung der Geister, das einheitliche Zusammenhalten des im äußern Leben oft untätigen und immer sich zersplitternden nationalen Bewußtseins" (312–13).

18. See "die Bindung unzufriedener Elemente" and "die Veredlung und Besprechungsmöglichkeit des Gegensatzes zwischen Vätern und Söhnen" (313).

19. "Die Beschneidung erfolgt meist in Gegenwart von oft über 100 Verwandten und Freunden" (317).

20. "Das Glied wird dann mit Holzmehl bedeckt und ist in 3 Tagen beiläufig heil" (317).

21. "Weil die zusammenhängenden Menschen fehlen, entfallen zusammenhängende litterarische Aktionen" (321).

22. "Wie wenig kräftig ist das obere Bild. Zwischen tatsächliches Gefühl und vergleichende Beschreibung ist wie ein Brett eine zusammenhanglose Voraussetzung eingelegt" (326).

23. Edgar Hilsenrath, *Der Nazi und der Friseur* (1977; reprint, München [Munich]: R. Piper, 1990). Esther Dischereit, *Joëmis Tisch: Eine jüdische Geschichte* (Frankfurt am Main: Suhrkamp, 1988).

24. "Ich bin Max Schulz, unehelicher, wenn auch rein arischer Sohn der Minna Schulz . . . zur Zeit meiner Geburt Dienstmädchen im Hause des jüdischen Pelzhändlers Abramowitz" (Hilsenrath 7).

25. Itzig Finkelstein wohnte im Nachbarhaus. Er war genauso alt wie ich oder . . . um genauer zu sein, und wenn ich mich so ausdrücken darf: Itzig Finkelstein erblickte das Licht der Welt genau zwei Minuten und zweiundzwanzig Sekunden nachdem mich die Hebamme Gretchen Fettwanst mit einem kräftigen Ruck aus dem dunklen Schoß meiner Mutter befreite.

26. "'Und wissen Sie,' sagte Max Schulz, 'Seit Monaten denk' ich darüber nach, wie ich am besten untertauchen soll. . . . Nur den Schwanz muß ich mir abschneiden,' sagte Max Schulz. 'Und das gefällt mir gar nicht. Nicht wirklich abschneiden,' sagte er ernst. 'Bloß das Vorhäutchen. Dann bin ich beschnitten . . . so wie Itzig Finkelstein'" (Hilsenrath 125–26).

27. Andreas Graf, "Mörderisches Ich: Zur *Pathologie der Erzählperspektive in Edgar Hilsenraths Roman Der Nazi und der Friseur,*" in *Edgar Hilsenrath: Das Unerzählbare erzählen*, ed. Thomas Kraft (München [Munich]: R. Piper, 1996), 135–49.

28. The point is further strengthened by the recent controversy over Daniel Goldhagen's interpretation of the roles of "ordinary Germans" in the Holocaust. See his *Hitler's Willing Executioners: Ordinary Germans and the Holocaust* (New York: Knopf, 1996).

29. "Eine Sache habe ich noch vergessen. Eines Tages war es da. Dick und fett, mit Tinte nachgezeichnet, mit der Bleistiftspitze eingeritzt. Es hat geklingelt. Ich setze mich auf meine Bank. Da liegt es vor mir, stottert mich an, die ganze lange Stunde" (Dischereit 64–65).

WORKS CITED

Anderson, Benedict. *Imagined Communities: Reflections on the Origin and Spread of Nationalism*. London: Verso, 1983.

Anderson, Mark M. *Kafka's Clothes: Ornament and Aestheticism in the Habsburg Fin de Siècle*. Oxford: Clarendon Press, 1992.

Beck, Evelyn Torton. "Gender, Judaism, and Power: A Jewish Feminist Approach to Kafka." In *Approaches to Teaching Kafka's Short Fiction*, ed. Richard T. Gray; 35–42. New York: Modern Language Association, 1995.

Deleuze, Gilles. *Masochism*. Trans. Jean McNeil. New York: Zone Books, 1991.

Deleuze, Gilles, and Félix Guattari. *Kafka: Toward a Minor Literature*. Trans. Dana Polan. Minneapolis: University of Minnesota Press, 1986.

———. *A Thousand Plateaus: Capitalism and Schizophrenia*. Trans. Brian Massumi. Minneapolis: University of Minnesota Press, 1987.

Dischereit, Esther. *Joëmis Tisch: Eine jüdische Geschichte*. Frankfurt am Main: Suhrkamp, 1988.

Foster, Hal, ed. *The Anti-Aesthetic: Essays on Postmodern Culture.* Seattle: Bay Press, 1983.

Freud, Sigmund. *Totem and Taboo: Resemblances between the Psychic Lives of Savages and Neurotics.* Trans. A. A. Brill. New York: Random House, 1918.

Gilman, Sander. *Franz Kafka: The Jewish Patient.* New York: Routledge, 1995.

Goldhagen, Daniel. *Hitler's Willing Executioners: Ordinary Germans and the Holocaust.* New York: Knopf, 1996.

Graf, Andreas. "Mörderisches Ich: Zur Pathologie der Erzählperspektive in Edgar Hilsenraths Roman *Der Nazi und der Friseur.*" In *Edgar Hilsenrath: Das Unerzählbare erzählen,* ed. Thomas Kraft, 135–49. München [Munich]: R. Piper, 1996.

Gray, Richard T., ed. *Approaches to Teaching Kafka's Short Fiction.* New York: Modern Language Association, 1995.

Grossberg, Lawrence, Cary Nelson, and Paula Treichler, eds. *Cultural Studies.* New York: Routledge, 1992.

Herder, Johann Gottfried. *Reflections on the Philosophy of the History of Mankind.* Chicago: University of Chicago Press, 1968.

Hilsenrath, Edgar. *Der Nazi und der Friseur.* 1977. Reprint, München [Munich]: R. Piper, 1990.

Ignatieff, Michael. *Blood and Belonging: Journeys into the New Nationalism.* Toronto: Penguin Canada, 1993.

Jameson, Fredric. "Postmodernism and Consumer Society." In *The Anti-Aesthetic: Essays on Postmodern Culture,* ed. Hal Foster, 111–25. Seattle: Bay Press, 1983.

Kafka, Franz. *Tagebücher in der Fassung der Handschrift.* Ed. Hans-Gerd Koch, Michael Müller, and Malcolm Pasley. Frankfurt am Main: S. Fischer, 1990.

———. *Tagebücher 1910–1923.* Ed. Max Brod. Frankfurt am Main: S. Fischer, 1951.

Kraft, Thomas, ed. *Edgar Hilsenrath: Das Unerzählbare erzählen.* München [Munich]: R. Piper, 1996.

Parker, Andrew, Mary Russo, Doris Sommer, and Patricia Yaeger, eds. *Nationalisms and Sexualities.* New York: Routledge, 1992.

Sokel, Walter H. "Kafka and Modernism." In *Approaches to Teaching Kafka's Short Fiction,* ed. Richard T. Gray, 21–34. New York: Modern Language Association, 1995.

———. "Two Views of 'Minority' Literature." *Quarterly World Report* 6 (1983): 5–8.

Steinberg, Leo. *The Sexuality of Christ in Renaissance Art and in Modern Oblivion.* New York: Pantheon, 1983.

Taubeneck, Steven. "Irony, Contingency, and Postmodernity: 'In the Penal Colony.'" In *Approaches to Teaching Kafka's Short Fiction,* ed. Richard T. Gray, 114–22. New York: Modern Language Association, 1995.

Welsch, Wolfgang. "Transkulturalität—Lebensformen nach der Auflösung der Kulturen." *Information Philosophie* 2 (1993): 5–20.

———. "Transkulturalität—die veränderte Fassung heutiger Kulturen." In *Sichtweisen: Die Vielheit in der Einheit,* ed. Freimut Duve et al., 83–122. Weimar: Edition Weimarer Klassik, 1994.

Part 2

Bridges and Gulfs: Intergenerational Ruptures and Connections

Chapter 5

From Big Daddy to Small Literature: On Taking Kafka at His Word

Scott Spector

Since the end of the Second World War, Kafka's difficult and complex relationship with his father has been at the center of Kafka research. In this contribution, Scott Spector puts into question conventional interpretations of filial inferiority and defeat in the face of ponderous paternal oppression both in Kafka's life and in his texts. Adapting criteria developed by Deleuze and Guattari in their understanding and elaboration of the concept of "minor" literature, Spector reads the father-son relationship as one of intergenerational conflict in which the major discourse is literally embodied by the acculturating father, the minor discourse by the skeptical son. Spector's analysis reveals Kafka's use of tropes of "big" and "little" as metaphors of the two discursive planes. He also argues that traps in Kafka's texts deliberately invite misinterpretations by those who adopt a "major" perspective. By examining Kafka's use of "weakness" and "smallness," Spector shows how the author evolves textual forms and strategies that allow an escape from "major" discourse, enabling the artist—both historical and fictional—to take flight and attain spiritual height. Read from this perspective, Kafka's texts assume the subversive and political functions ascribed to minor literature by the French theorists.

Franz Kafka's life and work are of special significance not only to discussions of modern German-Jewish identity and culture, but also to the study of the broader field of minority discourse and "minor literature." Furthermore, they are critical to debates on the potential of minority voices to have political effects on their dominant cultures. It is easy to trace this centrality to a decade ago, to the publication in English of the late Gilles Deleuze and Félix Guattari's seminal book, *Kafka: Toward a Minor Literature.*[1] Paradoxically, though, while these ten years have seen a veritable explosion of scholarly interest in minority literatures, this popularity has been accompanied by a certain skepticism toward the little book by Deleuze and Guattari. Briefly put, this text sought to identify the complex political function of "deterritorialization," the subversive deployment of a major language within a majority culture, which the authors saw so manifestly represented in Kafka's writing.[2] It seems, then, that the critical line initiated by these thinkers is not being reworked or furthered in much current discussion of minority literatures. There seems instead to be some sort of multiculturalist agenda at work, a claim to a place in the canon rather than a threat to dis-place it. In its most liberal form, the agenda amounts to the absorption of the exotic element into a more tolerant cultural system, when in fact it is the resistance to this absorption, the indigestibility of minor literature from the position of the majority culture, which in earlier discussions of minor literature gave it its power.[3] Thus, in the last decade and a half we can map the move from a critical consciousness of the function of "small" literatures to the revision of their status as enrichments of canonical national literatures. More sophisticated work today focuses on the concept of "hybridity" in a way that, intriguing as it can be, ultimately reinforces the structures it is meant to dissolve—but that is the subject of another essay.[4] What I want to do here is rehearse some easily misread moves in a few familiar Kafka texts and reread these moves within the ideological contexts that surrounded Prague German-Jewish cultural products in the early twentieth century.

Any discussion of the ideological contexts contemporary with Kafka's texts will gravitate toward two major issues, which are actually closely related to one another. The first is the nationality conflict in Prague, Bohemia, and the Habsburg monarchy as a whole until its dissolution in 1918. The clash in Prague and Bohemia between German and Czech nationalism put Prague's German-speaking Jews, Kafka's cohort, in an uneasy position as the ideological options available to their parents' generation fast disappeared. This brings us to the second important context, that of the famed "father-son" conflict of Kafka's generation. This conflict, revolving around an ethical distinction of liberal and postliberal generations, belongs not only to Prague in this period, and has been described by historian Mary Gluck as a struggle between a Victorian moralism, utilitarian ambition, and rationality on the one hand, and spontaneity, instinct, and spirituality on the other.[5] These contexts are linked to one another because in Prague, where more than half of the 10 percent hegemonic minority of German speakers were of Jewish origin, bourgeois German liberalism was clung to long after its obsolescence was apparent.[6] Yet the strange persistence of faith in that decaying order is apparent in the memoir of Stefan Zweig, the Viennese Jew who describes the prewar period in Austria as "The Golden Age of Security," in which everyone knew her place and every duty was exactly proscribed, where a benevolent state guaranteed the predictability of steady progress, conservative profit, carefully measured justice, reason.[7] Could Zweig really have been describing the experience of Central European Jews at the turn of the century, where, for the first time anywhere, the power of anti-Semitism was being successfully tested in national as well as regional and local politics, where the liberal nineteenth century had given way to anti-Semitic rioting among local populaces, where the ancient and antirational accusations of Jewish ritual murder had suddenly and forcefully resurfaced? [8]

The readings I want to offer of Kafka's "Brief an den Vater" ("Letter to His Father") and certain passages from *Der Proceß* (*The Trial*) will not focus on moments of reference to the "actual world" of German-Jewish Central Europe in this period. To the contrary, I would like to call attention to the potential for a misreading of such referents in these texts. There is a structural similarity between the "multicultural" appropriation of marginal elements into great literatures and the reading of inferiority complexes, persecution, and paranoia in Kafka's work, even as readers are in a sense seduced into these positions. The quite different encounters of the young Kafka in the household of his father and the character K. in the setting of the court are sites where such trap-readings are available in different ways, and so it will be useful to examine them side by side. In each case, the question of power is radically opened through textual devices, in utter opposition to what seem to be literal readings of the texts as victimization narratives. In fact, such readings are not literal at all in that they are only made possible by pulling away from the letter of the text, by taking Kafka's words out of his mouth, as it were, and taking them as vocalizations of a marginalized subject within an oppressive context. "Taking Kafka at his word" means in this context not taking binary oppositions like big/small, strong/weak, and prosecutor/persecuted at face value and as unproblematic references to power relations in Kafka's life, but rather tracing the way these binaries operate within his text. Read this way, this literature will not come forth as a minority or marginal creature, knocking meekly at the door of great literature, like the man from the country bidding entry to the law; minor literature, instead, makes doors of its own through walls that seemed impenetrable.

Kafka's well-known, undelivered letter to his father was written at the height of a generational conflict, then, which not only took place within Kafka's family, but also came to characterize this sociohistorical period. To get a grasp on this unwieldy text, I will focus on the trope of size and, in particular, of size anxiety, a theme that is explicit in the letter and that relates directly to Deleuze and Guattari's reading of the political function of Kafka's minor—or, in Kafka's parlance, "small"—literature. There are three discrete and yet intimately bound levels on which we can speak about the father-son conflict in this context. The first, and most obvious, is the personal level, which would lead almost inevitably, and misleadingly, to the diagnosis of an Oedipal conflict in the Kafka home. This is misleading first and foremost because it forgets that Franz Kafka was perfectly familiar with Freud, and quotes him therefore sometimes as parody, sometimes as a trap. [9] The second level is historico-political: that is, the ideological valence of the generational conflict in Prague at this time, the revolt by young writers against a worldview that was powerfully identified with the generation before them, Hermann Kafka's generation.

Belonging to this level is the issue of the relations of the personal to the political in "minor literatures" pointed out by Deleuze and Guattari. In their following remarks on this relation there is a striking inversion of valuations relating to images of size—these inversions, I will argue, come straight out of Kafka and are directly applicable to a reading of the "Letter:"

> [E]verything in small literatures [minor literatures—*kleinen Litera-turen*] is political. In major [large—*großen*] literatures, by contrast, the individual concern (familial, marital, and so on) joins with other no less individual concerns, the social milieu serving as a mere environment or a background; this is so much the case that none of these Oedipal intrigues are specifically indispensable or absolutely necessary but all become as one in a large space. Minor literature is completely different; its cramped space forces each individual intrigue to connect immediately to politics. The individual concern thus becomes all the more necessary, indispensable, magnified because a whole other story is vibrating within it. In this way the family triangle connects to other triangles—commercial, economic, bureaucratic, juridical—that determine its values. When Kafka indicates that one of the goals of a minor literature is the "purification of the conflict that opposes father and son and the possibility of discussing that conflict," it isn't a question of an Oedipal phantasm but of a political program. "What Is a Minor Literature?" 17

This theoretical statement raises the final level on which the father-son drama was played out, and that is the historiographical or methodological. For now, I will just warn against looking at the social milieu, as Deleuze and Guattari say here, as "a mere environment or background," as the "big picture" in which to understand the littler picture of Kafka's life and his own representations. Thus, there is a mode of interpretation that benefits the position of the father, a liberal interpretation for a liberal generation, a mode of analysis that preserves the size advantage of Hermann, and a reading that rescues the son from these forces larger than he or, more precisely, that records Kafka's own self-rescue.

The letter was inspired as an answer to Hermann's question of why his son feared him. At the moment of this question, Franz was unable to answer, "in part just because of the fear I have of you, and in part because so many details [*Einzelnheiten*, little individual parts] belong to the grounding of this fear that I cannot hold them at all together in speech" (Schillemeit 143).[10] Even in writing, he knows his explanation will be partial or incomplete (*unvollständig*, not in possession of all its parts) because it is crippled by the fear and "simply because the mass of the material [*Größe des Stoffs;* emphasis mine] goes far beyond my memory and my understanding" (Schillemeit 143). Already in the contrast between Hermann's booming question and the writer's ability to respond, between critical faculties and "material," there is the suggestion of size anxiety.

Very early in the long letter, Franz describes himself, already shrinking in anticipation of the comparison with Hermann, as "weak," "frightened," "restless" (*unruhig*) (Schillemeit 146)—the figure of mobile restlessness is opposed to the stable groundedness of what Zweig called "The Age of Security," the obsession with stability of the father's generation. But the figurative comparison is made stark, or presented nakedly, a few pages later with the memory of the two Kafka men in the changing room. This plain comparison of the two men's bodies serves as the emblem of the size anxiety trope we are exploring: "I was already oppressed by your plain corporeality. I can still remember for instance how we used to undress together in a changing room. Me skinny, weak, delicate, you strong, big, broad" (Schillemeit 151).

This comparison was the source for Franz's early recognition of his diminutive "wretchedness," not merely in relation to the father, but "to the whole world, for you were for me the measure of all things" (Schillemeit 151). The trap Franz lays throughout for the reader (whether the father and addressee, the mother who holds the letter and could never deliver it, or the literary public for which it has been salvaged) is to read this comparison as an inferiority complex, to forget that "world" and "things" might not represent the neutral ground of a stable reality, but values that only seem self-evident and uncontestable to the generation of the father. Further reading will make this point clearer.

Franz is willing to concede everything if he is understood within the value system of the father: Hermann worked hard his whole life, has done everything for his children, whereas Franz had the "freedom to study what I wanted" (Schillemeit 143). This, too, belongs to the letter's taxonomy of size, as the heavy substance of the bourgeois life, responsibility, and worries is opposed to the light, fleeting, fairly insubstantial figure of Franz's writing. Faced with the father's enormous, massive and weighty generosity, the son's ungrateful and unsympathetic reaction is: "Instead I have drawn away [*verkrochen*] from you" (Schillemeit 144). He shrinks from the father, *verkriechen*, as a tortoise into a shell. The German word is also used in this way: "*Neben ihm kannst du dich verkriechen*," which means "You can never measure up to him."[11] Franz associates books and ideas with an escape from the world of Hermann and with this word *verkriechen*.

Thus, the notion of shrinking is identified with escape, and explicitly tied to the realm of thinking and reading. It is a very incautious reading—a "confident" reading, one that someone like Hermann might engage in—that sees this shrinking as submission. The trap Kafka lays for a certain reader, perhaps for the intended reader, lies in the assumption of the valence of these terms of self-deprecation. The adjective "weak" (*schwach*), for instance, must have seemed to Hermann to be a simple enough term to judge. The (to Hermann) very negative quality of weakness evoked disgust in the father, Kafka strongly implies in the letter. In contrast, in the short text "Elf Söhne" ("Eleven Sons"), where the position of the narrator is occupied by the father, weakness has a more complex function:

> My eleventh son is delicate, probably the weakest of my sons; but deceptive in his weakness; he can be at times powerful and determined, although even then is weakness somehow fundamental. However it is not a shameful weakness but rather something that only on our earth [*Erdboden*] appears as weakness. Is not for instance readi-

> ness to flight weakness, since it is after all wavering and indetermi-
> nation? My son displays something like that. Such qualities are natu-
> rally not pleasing to a father; they obviously take off from the de-
> struction of the family. Sometimes he looks at me as if he wanted to
> tell me: "I will take you with me, father." Then I think: "You are the
> last one I would trust myself to." And his gaze seems again to say:
> "Let me then at least be the last one." (Schillemeit, *Franz Kafka Buch*
> 244)[12]

The grounded earth, *Erdboden*, is this sphere from which the deterritorializing gesture escapes. In its flight from that earth, the distressed father notes, the
weakness becomes strength, the fear becomes threat. Gustav Janouch has reported Kafka's equation of the term literature with "flight from reality"(47).[13]
While the veracity (or at least the literal accuracy) of Janouch's reports have
been more than questioned by now, this figure of flight associated with writing
is one that resonates with the "Eleven Sons" and other texts as well. We recall
"The Bucket Rider," whose last grasp on the material world slips away from him
as he is refused a few bits of coal, and the flight of the weightless bucket away
from the *Erdboden*; or the asceticism of the hunger artist in the dying Kafka's
last piece, where this opposition could be read as well. Obviously, I do not mean
to offer this dichotomy as a key to these complex texts. Rather, the recurrence of
figures of earth and the pulling away from earth in these and many other moments in Kafka's writings begin to point to the way that a univocal reading of
submission, weakness, persecution, in these texts is wrongheaded. This flight of
language is Kafka's new definition of strength, the coefficient of deterritorialization. The central figures in the stories "The Bucket Rider" and "A Hunger
Artist" pull away from the world in their insubstantiality, denied or denying
themselves the particle of matter that would allow them to walk upon the earth.

By now we are at the point where we can clearly generalize the principles of
the letter writer *Ich* and recipient *Du* in terms of generations. The boundary between these generations, as in Mary Gluck's previously cited definition, is a
clash of class values, or a "postliberal" revolt against a bourgeois order of life.
But this conflict is also mapped onto the opposition of mass and flight: the big-
ness of Hermann's will to life, business, conquest (*Lebenswillen, Geschäftswil-
len, Eroberungswillen*) seems to threaten to crush the son's wings. Franz is
fighting for his life against this monstrous will, and it is a struggle to the death:
"In any case we were so different from one another, and in this differentness so
dangerous to one another . . . one could have assumed that you will simply
stamp me out until nothing is left of me" (Schillemeit 147).

And yet the bigger they come, the harder they fall. Franz's sly reference to a
Hermann once "younger, therefore fresher, wilder" (Schillemeit 148) is implicitly contrasted to a more decrepit Hermann posed to receive the deadly letter.
The illusions of Hermann's generation—"big" Prague German liberalism, the
German-Jewish ruling class that fancied itself the cultural center of Bohemia, a
cultural power closely associated with sociopolitical hegemony—these illusions
had been utterly shattered by World War I.

"I did not have your strength, nor your appetite," writes Franz, "Your self-confidence was so great [*groß*]" (Schillemeit 152), while Franz trades this self-confidence for "a boundless sense of guilt" (*ein grenzenloses Schuldbewußtsein* —a guilt without borders) (Schillemeit 184). Guilt and shame are the products of the father's "education" of the son, and when Franz compliments Hermann as a good father for having educated or "raised" the children well, he calls him *"ein guter Erzieher"* (Schillemeit 155). Earlier in 1919, the year in which the letter was written, Kafka explored this notion of *Erziehung* through the sadistic military figure at the center of the story *"Die Strafkolonie"* ("The Penal Colony"). The letter's confident father and shameful son are complementary; in "The Penal Colony," the torturer leads the object of his sadism to understanding, and shame pares away at the mass of the body to reach toward the core of existence. The profit of the industrious father is paid for with the guilt of the son (the letter puns with the words guilt [*Schuld*] and debt [*Schulden*]). Thus, the hardy gourmand gives way to the Hunger Artist, the "greatness" of the former's confidence collapses before a shame that breaks down borders (*grenzenloses Schuldbewußtsein*) (Schillemeit 184).

This play of terms plunders optimistic misreadings of the frequent and exalting references to family that litter Kafka's notes and letters. "Marriage is the greatest of all," and if Franz could only marry, he could become Hermann's son. This is precisely because marriage belongs to the substantive, material, territorial world that the father represents for the son. The territorial is explicitly invoked in the letter: "Sometimes I imagine the map laid out before me with you stretched out over it. And then it seems to me as if the only regions which would come into question for my life would be those that you either do not cover or which do not lie within your reach. And in light of the image I have of your size, those are not many and not very satisfying regions" (Schillemeit 210).

Of course, there is nothing left—nothing earthly. Hence the escape, the deterritorializing gesture, the mercurial flight which, destroying territoriality along the way, opens new horizons. The possibility that this flight is superior to mass is really only barely concealed. The rhetorical strategy to invite misreadings that identify in Kafka the assimilation of the discourses marginalizing him is directed against the territorialized reader (that is, Hermann). The generational conflict represented the struggle against those really very "big" discourses of territory that went beyond the value system of the individual bourgeois life to cover essential assumptions about nation and race, borders and political power, identity and the body. The creative moment is not that in which K. is defeated in the face of dangerous, colossal, insurmountable discourse, but rather the construction of a text that is a very cautiously and deliberately engineered instrument, a technology developed to provide a way out of the confines of the body.

. This reference to K. brings us to *Der Proceß* (*The Trial*), one episode of which I would like to examine in the context of these questions of big and minor discourses. Before discussing that episode, the "First Interrogation," it is significant to point out how the text as a whole is opened: the first chapter heading, "Verhaftung" ("Arrest"), is followed by the famous first line, "Someone must have been telling lies [*verleumdet*] about Joseph K., for without having done anything wrong he was arrested [*verhaftet*] one morning."[14]

This opening sets the tone for a reading of the "First Interrogation" in several ways. First of all, I am interested in the triple iteration of the prefix "*ver*," which in German implies a veering from the standard course of the root of the word, a departure or a corruption. The arrest itself is in this case an unexpected departure from the routine of the bourgeois K.'s otherwise perfectly normal morning (not "one fine morning," as in the Muirs' translation, but simply "*eines morgens*"). The active verb in the first clause (*verleumden*, to distort the truth in speech) points already to the suggestion that this departure or corruption is taking place in the realm of language. The subject of the sentence is significantly ambiguous —"someone"—and its ambiguity is called attention to by means of the circumlocutious construction "*Jemand mußte Josef K. verleumdet haben.*" It is well known that the question raised in this first clause remains unanswered in the novel, and in fact falls to the background so quickly and with so little trace that the whole of *The Trial* is thought of as a persecution without a persecutor, but with one torturously persecuted victim, K., so often identified with the author Kafka.

The caricature of Kafka's work as a relentless victimization narrative may be present in more subtle form in critical literary treatments than in the popular imagination, but it is by no means absent. It plays an important part in the movement against seeing these works as active, even as it allows them to stand as testaments of a cry against the oppression of The Powers That Be, even a premonition of totalitarianism. Yet, inconsistent with the structure of oppression of totalitarianism, power in a text like *The Trial* is monumental precisely because it is dispersed and uncentered, fragmented and without a definable locus. Just as critical attempts in the 1950s and 1960s to see Kafka's pieces as allegories with direct referents in the world were doomed to fail, the tendency to see the apparatus of the trial as a representation of univocal and monolithic power, say state power, runs exactly counter to the movement of the text itself. In fact, the trial has no revealed apparatus; *The Trial*, though—that is, the text—exposes a complex apparatus in glimpses throughout. Again, it is a machine made of writing, and that puts power in quite different kinds of hands.

One more opening clue to how to read the novel is left to be discussed: the title *Der Proceß*. We do not know whether Kafka would have kept this title had he completed the work, but he did refer to the manuscript in progress with this term. Certainly the first translation to come to mind is "trial," although no trial actually takes place in the novel, nor is the sentence that is carried out ever actually pronounced. Yet, there are other meanings of the word *Proceß* (or in today's German, *Prozeß*). The German word may operate as its English cognate, a generic process without the specificity of the juridical procedure. This suggests the possibility of another sort of shadow referent of the title, such as the writing process for instance, or the particular process of writing this novel. I will come back to this important double meaning later. Finally, the word is also a synonym for "progress," for the process of civilization, the element of forward propulsion implied by the prefix "*pro*."[15] *Proceß* is thus ironically paired with words that stand in for it, such as *Verfahren* (K.'s term for what he is undergoing, this "procedure"), and those that stand near it in this opening that share the prefix *ver-*, indicating a diverted rather than a forward movement. But who has led this confident forward march astray?

Ernst Pawel struck a compelling chord with the suggestive title of his Kafka biography, *The Nightmare of Reason*.[16] Indeed, it is easy to sense that the diversion in *The Trial* from the security and justice that the rule of law is supposed to guarantee is more "rationalist" than "irrationalist." If K.'s persecution represents a distortion of the ideals of rational justice proceeding from the Enlightenment, this distortion is effected through the very intensity of concentration on the mechanisms of rationalism—it is a rationalist orthodoxy. Rather than having been attacked by external irrationalist elements, the system that promised emancipation of the bourgeois subject, in particular, the Jewish assimilationist, is itself the instrument of his/her subjection. This focus on the continuity of rationalism and the failure of emancipation puts in a different light the major public trials of Kafka's lifetime, which have often been identified as backdrops for Kafka's *Trial*: the Dreyfus affair (which one commentator called "[t]he archetypal court case in the background of *The Trial*") and the sensational Hilsner case, a revival of the blood libel in rural Bohemia, when Kafka was a teenager.[17] We know that these cases occupied Kafka, that he collected newspaper clippings and made numerous notes and references to the cases throughout the years. All of this preoccupation only makes more striking how Kafka's *The Trial* departs from the pattern that would seem to be set by these cases: the normally accepted assumption that they ran counter to the progressive line of rationalism, with rationalist defenders of the persecuted in Émile Zola and the Dreyfusards in France, and the heroic positivist Tomáš Masaryk in Bohemia. There are no Dreyfusards in *The Trial*. The persecution of K. belongs to the same world as the bourgeois liberal stability from which K. is torn. Further, the dichotomy between antirationalism and rationalism, or myth and mechanism, is completely broken down in this representation of law, so that the notion of "sides" available in the Hilsner and Dreyfus cases is not even left as a question.

The persistent ambiguity of the opening word "someone" is the site of the breakdown of clear power relations in the text, as opposed to the reinforcement of a violent dichotomy between a persecuting context and persecuted narrative subject that is so often perceived as the stable structure of *The Trial*. The first part of this dichotomy to be destabilized is the subject of the incrimination. If the "someone" responsible for K.'s persecution is any figure appearing in the text, it is K. himself, who seems to be producing a discourse over which he has no control; if, on the other hand, there is any suggestion that the power of incrimination is held by an omnipotent subject not appearing in the text but in control of it, that can only be the author. Either of these possibilities, if taken seriously, would work against a simple kind of reading of the novel as a reflection of individual powerlessness in the face of monolithic power. Let us look at

K.'s first visit to the court in the third chapter of the novel, the "First Interrogation," to trace these dual and apparently contradictory possibilities.

Telephoned at his office, K. is told he must appear before the court but not
given a time. He arbitrarily decides to appear at 9:00 A.M., and yet this designation immediately becomes realized at the appointed hour—he worries he has
slept in and skips breakfast, he rushes when it seems he will be late, and when
he finds the court at 10:05 A.M., he is told, "You were supposed to appear an
hour and five minutes ago." Similarly, in the labyrinthine and nonofficial apartment complex where the court is supposed to be, there is no signage, and K.
must invent the way to the court himself. He is confident about his decision of
which stairway to take not because of any external indication, but because he
had been told "that an attraction existed between the Law and guilt, from which
it should really follow that the Court of Inquiry must abut on the particular flight
of stairs K. happened to choose."[18] Similarly, in searching for the inquiry room,
he decides to invent a carpenter named Lanz, whom he pretends to be seeking,
and this becomes the code that provides access to the court—he asks for Lanz
and is told to enter. When he feels stifled in the room and asks for Lanz again,
the woman compels him to enter, saying, "I must shut this door after you, nobody else must come in." This is obviously a quotation, in reverse, of the famous fragment "Before the Law," which appears in the crucial penultimate
chapter "In the Cathedral"—"No one but you could gain admittance [to the
Law] through this door, since this door was intended for you. I am now going to
shut it."[19]

If the terms of the court are in fact being set by K., then he damns himself
several times in his dramatic monologue before it. "You may object that [this] is
not a trial at all; you are quite right, for it is only a trial if I recognize it as such.
But for the moment I do recognize it, on grounds of compassion, as it were."
What seems to K. to be a fantastically controlled and rhetorically brilliant indictment of the system, a turning of the tables of accused and accusers, goes
astray and is turned back upon himself in a single stroke. His complaint that he
has been robbed, for instance, is transformed into the judgment of the court that
K. has robbed himself of the advantages due any accused person in an interrogation ["*daß Sie sich . . . des Vorteils beraubt haben*"].[20] His indictment,
which becomes increasingly generalized as he improvises his own defense, finally attacks all officials and officialdom as definitionally corrupt. Thus, his
starting point for declaring his own innocence—namely, that he is not a house-
painter at all, as the court has declared, but an official, the chief clerk at a
bank—becomes proof of his own complicity. And in an even more ominous
moment of self-infliction, announcing the approach of the end of his discourse
indicting the corrupt system, he actually sentences himself: "*Ich bin gleich
zuende*" ("I am nearly finished").[21]

The key moment where this double movement of K.'s discourse is revealed
is the examining magistrate's curt reply to his tirade: "[T]oday—you may not
yet have become aware of the fact—today you have flung away with your own
hand all the advantages [*des Vorteils*] which an interrogation [*Verhör*] invariably

confers on an arrested man [*den Verhafteten*]." Thus, the course from presumed advantage to assumed guilt has been charted by K.

Of course, there is a built-in resistance to the ascription of agency to Joseph K. in a text that repeatedly sets his controlled discourse in a narrative defined by his lack of control. That is, the uncanny mark of the novel is precisely this pairing of compulsive precision and control, with effects that jettison K. out of the realm of stability and justice to which he feels entitled. This pattern is laid out in the first interrogation scene, where, as I have indicated, K. is given the appearance of producing a triumphantly controlled discourse that turns out to have a life of its own, indicting rather than vindicating the speaker. As I have also tried to show, K. is arrested and tried in the field of language. This language is, it seems, never the instrument of intentioned users, but rather itself serves as the subject of action. This is a brief, perhaps abbreviated, route to what has increasingly been recognized as the paradigmatic modernity of Kafka's writing: that it is about writing. This brings us to a potential answer to the question opened by the novel's initial word "someone": we are made conscious of the authorship of this labyrinth by Franz Kafka—although here, as in the case of Joseph K.'s controlled/out-of-control discourse, there is also the question of which figure, the author or the text, is manipulating the other.

I am describing a nesting of a figure of writing, dramatized by a painful struggle between author and text, within a text where a similarly dramatic struggle is enacted on the body of a persecuted subject who seems to be the author of his own persecution. But this complex of crossings between texts and authors needs to be nested within another figure, that of context, the world outside of the text, which the text tempts the reader to recognize within it. *The Trial* invites the reader to fall into an interpretive trap where the role of writer and writing in the text is oversimplified to the point of misreading. Instead of the constant trespass across the boundaries of writer (the author Kafka), writing (the figure of the writing process), and written (fictive characters and actions within the story), merely one example of which I have just discussed, the reader is seduced into reinforcing those boundaries first by assuming the discrete nature of these fields, and then by seeking referents in the outside world that K.'s persecution seems to reflect. The assumption that "K." stands for "Kafka" is the founding wrong move of such a reading, if not a surprising one, since it is a wrong move baited by the author.

One illustration of the complexity of context is the previously mentioned father-son or generational conflict. Max Brod reports an illuminating incident from the period leading up to Kafka's composition of *The Trial*. In Brod's biography of his friend Kafka, he expounds at some length on the element of "soul-destroying 'work'" as an anti-creative force, contrasting the father's side of the generational split (respectability, responsibility) to what Brod defines as "Franz's idea of art" (Brod 78). This dichotomy, in Brod's report, seems to have been taken so seriously as to cause a crisis in 1911, when Kafka contemplated suicide after having been asked to look after a factory for a short time on his father's behalf: "I saw perfectly that I had only the alternatives of either waiting until everyone had gone to bed and then jumping out of the window, or of going every day to the factory . . . for the next two weeks" (Brod 92). Brod, "gripped by cold horror," begged Kafka's mother to intervene for the sake of her son's life, and all conspired to deceive Kafka's father. This anecdote, even though its mediation by Brod clearly served Brod's own critical agenda, is nonetheless useful in two ways. First of all, it demonstrates the very literal way in which the respectable, bourgeois daily life of the father was viewed as an artistic and spiritual death for the generation of the sons, whether Kafka or Brod. Franz's reactions and those of his friend and mother work comically in the re-telling of this story precisely because of the slip from the metaphorical lifeless-ness of bourgeois drudgery to the physical death represented by the "alternative" of jumping out of the window. In the second place, it highlights the place of what Brod calls "soul-destroying 'work'" in the image of the life of the father. In *The Trial*, after all, K. is caught between the "alternatives" of life as chief bank clerk and death by execution. Or, put differently, what encourages readers to identify the bourgeois protagonist K. with Kafka the son and not the father? Or even with the Habsburg regime itself, which, both imperial and royal (*kaiserlich und königlich*), called the monarchy and its administrative institutions "k. and k."?

In the parable within a parable, in the famous fragment "Before the Law" recited to K. in the cathedral scene, the reader is given a lesson on how to read the word of the law. K.'s initial interpretation of the parable parallels the reading of *The Trial* against which I have been arguing: K. focuses on the deception and persecution of the man from the country, who, wishing entry to the law, seems to be impeded by the doorkeeper. In fact, as K. is told, his focus on the predica-ment of the country man impedes his reading of the text: "Don't be too hasty . . . don't take over someone else's opinion without testing it. . . . You have not enough respect for the written word and you are altering the story."[22] Indeed, the priest demonstrates how a close reading of the words of the doorkeeper can reveal the doorkeeper's generosity, humor, and helpfulness. Rather than hinder-ing the countryman, the priest shows, the doorkeeper himself can be seen as the victim of deception. In just this way, Kafka offers the reader of *The Trial* alter-natives to the trap of a victimization narrative. But that is not to say that one of these is a route to the text's actual meaning, for the hermeneutic lesson offered by the priest is that none of these exegeses can achieve the status of the text it-self: "I am only showing you the various opinions concerning that point. You must not pay too much attention to them. The scriptures are unalterable and the comments often enough merely express the commentators' despair."[23]

By now it is clear that I do not mean to argue that the impossibility of pin-ning down the figures within Kafka's texts, whether novels or letters, frees them from history and demands a reading confined within a decontextualized aes-thetics. The self-representation of the texts as scripture, as systems of writing to which the multiple available allegorical interpretations are secondary, can itself be read within the historical contexts in which they were created. It is a particu-lar brilliance of both the letter and the novel that the most defiant answer to the world of the father does not come through any representation of it, but instead through this bearing down on the word of the text, the creation of a world of writing that takes precedence over its assumed referentiality. This is how, by taking Kafka at his word, his readers can find respite from the world of paranoia and persecution they might have imagined him to be portraying—and how the minor literary function of a major literary figure can be recovered.

NOTES

1. Gilles Deleuze and Félix Guattari, *Kafka: Toward a Minor Literature*, trans. Dana Polan (Minneapolis: University of Minnesota Press, 1986).

2. The trend referred to here is indicated less importantly in this sense by the formal scholarly challenges to Deleuze and Guattari than by the more generalized resistance to "minor literature" I subsequently describe below. The early response of Walter Sokel is an understandable plea for close readings of contexts; see "Two Views of 'Minority' Literature: Deleuze, Kafka, and the German-Jewish Enclave of Prague," *Quarterly World Report* 6 (1983): 5–8. The more recent piece by Stanley Corngold, "Kafka and the Dialect of Minor Literature," *College Literature* 21, 1 (1994): 89–101, is more symptomatic of the resistance on grounds both aesthetic and ideological to a view of minor literature that identifies its subversive, always-already political character.

3. For a broad view of this position, see the special issues on minor literature of *Cultural Critique* 7 and 8 (1987) and *New German Critique* 46 (Winter 1989).

4. The proliferation of the term follows Homi Bhabha's seminal essays collected in *Nation and Narration* (London: Routledge, 1990). It is chiefly in the broad use of the term of hybridity following Bhabha's more self-conscious deployment of it that categories of purity and hybridity seem to have been reified, reiterating the essentialist foundation of racisms even as the relative valuations of pure (hegemonic) and mongrel (subversive, or representative of a newly centralized marginality) types are reversed.

5. Mary Gluck, "Liberal Fathers, Postliberal Children," in *Georg Lukács and His Generation 1900–1918* (Cambridge, MA: Harvard University Press, 1985) 107.

6. National/linguistic demographics in Prague in this period are considerably more complex than this rough figure suggests. The best analysis remains Gary Cohen, *The Politics of Ethnic Survival: Germans in Prague 1861–1914* (Princeton: Princeton University Press, 1981) 86–111.

7. Stefan Zweig, *The World of Yesterday* (New York: Viking, 1943) 1–2.

8. In lieu of a long bibliography that could be listed here, I refer to one work which concisely and yet rather thoroughly covers the terrain in question: Christoph Stölzl, *Kafkas böses Böhmen: Zur Sozialgeschichte eines Prager Juden* (München [Munich]: Text + Kritik, 1975), especially the chapter "Aus dem jüdischen Mittelstand der antisemitischen Epoche 1883–1924," 44–107.

9. See Sander L. Gilman, *Franz Kafka: The Jewish Patient* (New York: Routledge, 1995) 32, 159, 162, and 182.

10. All quotations from the text are my translations and taken from the Critical Edition edited by Jost Schillemeit, *Nachgelassene Schriften und Fragmente II* (Frankfurt am Main: S. Fischer, 1992).

11. See "verkriechen," *Wahrig Deutsches Wörterbuch*, 1986.

12. "Elf Söhne," *Das Franz Kafka Buch* (Frankfurt am Main: S. Fischer, 1983) 243.

13. Gustav Janouch, *Conversations with Kafka*, trans. Goronwy Rees (London: Quartet, 1985), 47.

14. Franz Kafka, *Der Proceß*, ed. Malcolm Pasley (Frankfurt am Main: S. Fischer, 1990), 7. My English citations are adapted from the standard English translation of Willa and Edwin Muir, *The Trial by Franz Kafka* (New York: Knopf, 1965).

15. See *Wahrig*, 1020: The German word is derived from the Latin *processus*: *Fortschreiten, Fortgang*, progression or progress, and *processus* from *procedere, vorwärts schreiten*, to step forward.

16. Ernst Pawel, *The Nightmare of Reason: A Life of Franz Kafka* (London: Collins Harvill, 1988).

17. See Gilman, 112–19. The commentator was Frederick Karl in *Franz Kafka, Representative of Man* (New York: Ticknor & Fields, 1991) 501, cited in Gilman, 70.

18. *Der Proceß*, 55.

19. *Der Proceß*, 294–95.

20. *Der Proceß*, 72.

21. *Der Proceß*, 68.

22. *The Trial*, 269–70.

23. *TheTrial* 272–73.

WORKS CITED

Primary Literature

Kafka, Franz. *Das Franz Kafka Buch*. Frankfurt am Main: S. Fischer, 1983.

———. "Der 'Brief an den Vater.'" *Nachgelassene Schriften und Fragmente*. Ed. Jost Schillemeit. Vol. 2. Frankfurt am Main: S. Fischer, 1992.

———. *Der Proceß*. Ed. Malcolm Pasley. Frankfurt am Main: S. Fischer, 1990.

———. *The Trial by Franz Kafka*. Trans. and ed. Willa and Edwin Muir, trans. New York: Knopf, 1965.

Secondary Literature

Bhabha, Homi. *Nation and Narration*. London: Routledge, 1990.

Brod, Max. *Franz Kafka: A Biography*. Trans. G. Humphreys Roberts and R. Winston. NewYork: Schocken, 1947.

Cohen, Gary. *The Politics of Ethnic Survival: Germans in Prague 1861–1914*. Princeton: Princeton University Press, 1981.

Corngold, Stanley. "Kafka and the Dialect of Minor Literature." *College Literature* 21, 1 (1994): 89–101.

Deleuze, Gilles, and Félix Guattari. *Kafka: Toward a Minor Literature*. Trans. Dana Polan. Minneapolis: University of Minnesota Press, 1986.

Gilman, Sander L. *Franz Kafka: The Jewish Patient*. New York: Routledge, 1995.

Gluck, Mary. "Liberal Fathers, Postliberal Children." *Georg Lukács and His Generation 1900–1918*. 76—105. Cambridge,MA: Harvard University Press, 1985.

Janouch, Gustav. *Conversations with Kafka*. Trans. Goronwy Rees. London: Quartet, 1985.

Pawel, Ernst. *The Nightmare of Reason: A Life of Franz Kafka.* London: Collins Harvill, 1988.

Sokel, Walter. "Two Views of 'Minority' Literature: Deleuze, Kafka, and the German-Jewish Enclave of Prague." *Quarterly World Report* 6 (1983): 5–8.

Stölzl, Christoph. *Kafkas böses Böhmen: Zur Sozialgeschichte eines Prager Juden.* München [Munich]: Text + Kritik, 1975.

Wahrig Deutsches Wörterbuch. Ed. Gerhard Wahrig et al. Wiesbaden: Brockhaus, 1986.

Zweig, Stefan. *The World of Yesterday.* 1943. Reprint, New York: Viking, 1947.

Chapter 6

"A Frosty Hall of Mirrors":
Father Knows Best in Franz Kafka and Nadine Gordimer

Iris M. Bruce

> People live on the street as if in a frosty hall of mirrors, and every decision, every stop becomes incredibly difficult.
> —Walter Benjamin, *Moscow Diary* (1926/27): 35

In Nadine Gordimer's "Letter from his Father" (1984),[1] the ghost of Kafka's father is conjured up from the dead and allowed to present his perspective of the family situation in the Kafka household. This chapter examines the nature of self-representation assigned to the father, showing it to be highly ironic, even a caricature. Bruce sees Gordimer reveal that "the frosty hall of mirrors" (Benjamin 35), which Kafka encounters through his father's objections and rejections, is made up of socially and culturally determined values and acceptable norms of behavior. By shifting the focus from Kafka's self to that of his father and the historically determined class within which he speaks, Gordimer's letter acts as a much-needed corrective to the all too frequent psychobiographical readings of Kafka's *Brief an den Vater* (1919). Gordimer's letter exposes the father as a typical representative of his generation, whose values are defined by prejudice, racism, and a petty middle-class morality. Terming the son's rebellion *Selbstwehr* (self-defense), ironically, the name of the Zionist Prague newspaper, Gordimer ridicules the younger generation's complex values: its rejection of assimilation, preoccupation with Jewish self-hatred, and flight from historical reality into literature and the arts. Bruce explores how Gordimer deconstructs the father's monological discourse of domination, of middle-class patriarchy, which arbitrarily defines "Otherness." The thematics of alterity must ultimately be seen within a larger political framework of relationships of power and self-awareness—specifically, within the postcolonial situation of Gordimer's South Africa.

In Nadine Gordimer's "Letter from His Father," the ghost of Franz Kafka's father, Hermann Kafka, is conjured up from the dead and allowed to respond to his son's version of the family situation in the Kafka household, as recounted in *Brief an den Vater* (*Letter to His Father* [1919]). Gordimer's "Letter" appears in a collection of short stories entitled *Something Out There* (1984), a collection that depicts various forms of betrayal (Marchant 257) and many unsuccessful attempts to "picture" someone or something else. One of the dangers "out there" is the ghost of Kafka's father, an outraged father who challenges Kafka's representation of his paternal self and counters it with his own narrative. A question one might well ask is why Gordimer would bring the father back to life and thus give him the last word. Is it to allow Hermann Kafka to defend himself and to crush his son once and for all? This is rather unlikely, given Gordimer's preoccupation with the political nature of Otherness in a variety of power relations based on class, gender, or race, and we should not ignore the presence of irony in this text. In fact, one scholar who considers irony an "essential element" of Gordimer's narrative technique (Riis 102) also points out that it is sometimes hard "for a 'new' reader, with no frame of reference to Gordimer's writing as a whole, to grasp the meaning, for there are hardly any fixed points" (Riis 103). In the following we will see that what looks like the father's hoary hand stretching out beyond the grave to administer the final blow to the son's identity is really a highly ironic representation of the father's projected self-image.

Both Hermann and Franz Kafka feel betrayed because their self-image does not accord with the picture the other party has created of them. Their charge is one of "false" representation, which already indicates the larger problematics inherent in anyone's attempt at representation—be it an interpretation of someone else's "lived experience" or one's own self-representation by recording one's life in an autobiographical discourse. Kafka, in his letter, recognizes the limits of such representations and ends on a note of resignation; however, it is also apparent that his father is not so self-aware, and Gordimer uses this to her advantage. Not only does she reverse Kafka's rhetorical structure by giving Hermann Kafka a voice, her letter indeed continues where Kafka left off by creating a space for the father in which he can present his position without the son's mediating interference. The result is the opposite of what one might expect: ironically, the strongly opposed perspectives in Kafka's and Gordimer's letters complement each other. Gordimer's "surgical analysis" (Smith 6) traps the father in a mirror that magnifies the values and presuppositions underlying his discourse and thereby restores truth-value to Kafka's original representation.

Franz Kafka's *Brief an den Vater* is an autobiographical narrative, which is defined by Philippe Lejeune as a "retrospective prose narrative written by a real person concerning his own existence, where the focus is his individual life, in particular the story of his personality"(4). In this letter, Kafka narrates the story of his life by leading the reader through a "frosty hall of mirrors," to use Walter Benjamin's phrase (35), and recreating the pictures his father has formed of him in his mind. They are bent and distorted and certainly do not correspond to the image the son has of himself. Kafka recounts how his father always stressed their irreconcilable differences:

> To you the matter always seemed very simple . . . : you have worked hard all your life, have sacrificed everything for your children, above all for me, consequently I have lived "like a fighting-cock," have been completely at liberty to learn whatever I wanted, and have had no cause for material worries, which means worries of any kind at all. You have not expected any gratitude for this, knowing what "children's gratitude" is like, but have expected at least some sort of obligingness, some sign of sympathy. (K 157)

Father knows best: Hermann Kafka's discourse is monological and leaves no room for dialogue. Thus, "worries" to him mean only material worries, and from this it follows that his son cannot have any worries at all, given his social position. His judgment is arbitrary and even contradictory, yet it is always absolute.

According to Sander Gilman, arbitrary judgments raised to the level of absolutes are characteristic of the discourse of stereotyping where "[t]he line between the projections of the self and the Other does not exist and therefore must be internalized as absolute" (Gilman, *Other*, 13). It follows that Hermann Kafka creates not truthful representations of the Other but rather "stereotypical mental representations" (Gilman, *Other*, 12–13). The values and presuppositions that enter into the creation of this stereotyped Other are apparent in his discourse. Here he largely relies—in an unreflective manner—on preconceived ideas: we can see this in the clichés and common expressions that he employs, as when he resorts to dismissive phrases such as "lived like a fighting cock" (*"in 'Saus und Braus' gelebt"*) (Kafka, *Brief* [1953], 5–6) or draws on commonplaces, as in his complaint about the lack of gratitude shown by children. Such preconceived notions about children living too well, having it much too easy, and his resentment thereof stem from the father's vivid memory of his own difficult childhood and his struggle to make his way in society. It is clear that Hermann Kafka was torn between contradictory impulses: on the one hand, he strove for material well-being, yet on the other hand, when he saw his success manifested in his children, he resented this and punished them for it. Such contradictory impulses are responsible for the ever-shifting lines between self and Other, between good and bad, which Hermann Kafka created for himself and turned into absolute barriers. It is important to note that the "line between 'good' and 'bad'" responds to the stresses that occur within the psyche" (Gilman, *Other*, 13). Kafka's father was either unable or felt there was no need to control his frequent mood changes, which meant that his verbal abuse could not be foreseen, indeed could be caused by anything at any moment: "But you struck out with your words without more ado, you weren't sorry for anyone, either during or afterwards, one was utterly defenseless against you" (K 166).

Nevertheless, despite the arbitrary nature of the father's punishments, there was a recognizable method in the way they were inflicted: Kafka recalls the father's many "means of drilling me and humiliating me" (K 174) (*"Erziehungs-*

und Demütigungsmittel") [*Brief* (1953), 25]). One such example may be taken as representative:

> It was only necessary to be happy about something or other, to be filled with the thought of it, to come home and speak of it, and the answer was an ironical sigh, a shaking of the head, a tapping of the table with one finger: "Is that all you're so worked up about?" or "I wish I had your worries!" or "The things some people have time to think about!" or "What can you buy yourself with that?" or "What a song-and-dance about nothing!" (K 165)

Hermann Kafka's method was to use both verbal irony and body language in order to undermine the self-confidence of his son when the latter was most vulnerable: the fact that he is taking particular pleasure in destroying any feelings of happiness verges on the sadistic. His distorted representation of Franz Kafka is easily unmasked, though, for his ironic remarks consist of clichés that again say more about the father than about the son. They reveal, for instance, what Hermann Kafka considered important in life, that is, the values he regarded as absolute, values that formed the barrier between himself and his son. His sarcastic rejoinder "Is that all you're so worked up about?" not only ridicules the feelings of the child but diminishes them by implying that they are trivial compared to the serious matters of the world, of which the father thinks he is a part (or would like to think he is!). Moreover, the cliché "What can you buy yourself with that?" reflects the materialist, consumer values of the father's society, his belief that one's importance in the world is measured largely by the amount of one's income and by one's possessions. Naturally, one cannot buy anything with happiness; thus, the child is made to feel worthless. Kafka lists many more examples of clichés and commonplaces, such as, "Not a word of contradiction!" (K 170) or, "Of course, that's too much to expect of our worthy son" (K 173). Such recreations of the father's discourse are time and again juxtaposed with the son's refutations and his feelings of hurt and frustration.

For the reader it may be obvious that the father's "special trust in bringing children up by means of irony" (K 172) (*"Erziehung durch Ironie"* [*Brief* (1953), 23]) is more an indication of his own psychological instability than an accurate description of his son. It is not difficult to see that the father is mostly concerned with his own self-esteem, which he boosts by using his son as a receptacle for his own frustrations. Moreover, Hermann Kafka's envy of his son and his frustrated desire for recognition are all too evident in his dramatic exaggeration of his own hard work, his sacrifice.[2] However, what predominates thematically in Kafka's letter is the son's victimization, and his feelings of resignation and despair: Stanley Corngold therefore rightly remarks that "Kafka explicitly portrays himself . . . as the wretched product of his father's design." (*Fate* 227). And Walter Benjamin's description of a painfully slow progression, "as if in a frosty hall of mirrors" (35), aptly describes the difficulty involved in Kafka's attempt at self-representation. The "frosty hall of mirrors" can be understood as the son's mind-forged prison, well established already in his childhood, in which father and son now confront each other with refracted and distorted representations of each self. Kafka's letter is an attempt to break out of the prison hall and represents a journey *toward* the father: in the words of Jacques Derrida, he can be said to *"write himself to the other* who is infinitely far away and who is supposed to send his signature back to him [emphasis added]" (88). However, the father was also the gatekeeper, and the message could never reach the addressee, which is why Kafka's mother never delivered the letter to the father in real life (Brod, *Biography*, 16).

At the same time, though, another and very different reason for Kafka's feelings of resignation and despair is his realization that the father's "frosty mirror" cannot help but refract and distort their relationship. This is because Hermann Kafka's inability to render a "truthful" picture is true of *any* representation, including Kafka's own. Any textualization of real-life events is not so much an accurate reflection but rather a refraction, a mediation, an interpretation of these events. Kafka realized this himself since he highlighted this problem at the end of his letter, when he allowed his father to respond to and refute him (K 215–17). It is interesting, though, that Kafka scholars, in their response to this text, have generally ignored the boundaries between lived experience and textual worlds, between real people and texts, and have focused predominantly on the personal, confessional nature of the letter.

Wilhelm Emrich, for instance, sees it as a document "in which all the anguish of his childhood is still not overcome and weighs upon him as strongly as ever, indeed we feel an intensification of this excruciating pain."[3] What speaks against Emrich's limiting personal approach is Kafka's telling his friend Milena Jesenská not to forget that his letter is a "lawyer's letter": "And as you read it understand all the lawyer's tricks: it is a lawyer's letter. And at the same time never forget your great Nevertheless" (*Letters to Milena* 63) ("*Dein Großes Trotzdem*" [*Briefe an Milena* 85], that is, literally, "your great Despite-it-all"). This quotation is actually reprinted on the cover of the most recent German edition of Kafka's letter, the 1994 Fischer facsimile edition of *Brief an den Vater*, which immediately suggests to the reader quite a different angle for understanding this text. It certainly emphasizes Kafka's awareness of rhetoric and textuality, even in a personal letter of this kind, and cautions the reader not to establish facile relationships between real-life events and their fictional representation.

Perhaps it would be useful to consider the whole structure of the letter as an advocate's discourse that employs the rhetorical tricks of a lawyer. The juxtapositions of father and son are clearly significant for what they can reveal about the psychological realism of the father-son relationship. At the same time, though, this is also the major structural principle of Kafka's letter, which is composed in terms of ironic juxtapositions of recreated situations that reveal each party's respective lack of understanding for the position of the Other. Here, it is not Joseph K. or Gregor Samsa but the father who is put on trial, while the son is playing the roles of both accuser and advocate. Charges are laid by the son, refuted by the father, and refuted again by the son. Ironically, this very structure, which continually juxtaposes the positions of father and son in order to present both sides as objectively as possible, is really an attempt to undermine the father by not only *re*-constructing his discourse but by *de*-constructing it at the same time. Indeed, one could ask, how does the *Brief an den Vater* differ from Kafka's other writings where, in the words of one critic, "deconstruction" is "built right into the text itself" (Sandbank 8)? During the course of the trial, the father's authority is increasingly diminished as we listen to Kafka's voice until, at the very end, Kafka suddenly reverses the narrative structure. Instead of ending with a condemnation of the father, Kafka now gives Hermann Kafka a chance to defend himself and to refute his son, and this, in turn, leads to Kafka's final deconstruction of his whole initial representation of the father-son relationship from the son's point of view. Just as deconstruction questions "the idea of an immediate, intuitive access to meaning" (Norris 30) and resists "any kind of settled or definite meaning" (Norris 31), Kafka's deconstructive technique in this letter (and elsewhere) consists of increasingly deferring or demolishing narrative authority: first, by eliminating one "center of meaning" (which here lies in the arbitrary authority and judgment of the father) and second, by exposing his own authority as a writer as equally flawed and arbitrary, even if, ironically, this means throwing the truth-value of the entire previous narration into doubt.

Stanley Corngold, too, focuses on the letter's confessional intent and regards it as Kafka's "most deluded work" (*Necessity* 88). Even though Corngold acknowledges that it is "full of lawyer's tricks," he still sees it as "arising from an inferior order of 'motivation,' which Kafka defines as flight from the knowledge that self-knowledge, as the knowledge of good and evil, is already given along with the Fall—as flight into the belief that self-knowledge is something still to be achieved by a struggle resembling litigation" (*Necessity* 107). But is Kafka's letter really his "most deluded work"? Naturally, it arises from the "hope" (rather than "belief") that self-knowledge and communication might be "achieved by a struggle resembling litigation," but this hope is quickly shattered in the very process of writing the letter.

On the one hand, the representation of both father and son is clearly one-sided, with Hermann Kafka emerging as the victimizer and the son as the victim. In this sense, Kafka's text certainly illustrates, as Derrida puts it, that any "auto-explanation . . . can very quickly turn into an auto-justification, even auto-celebration" (77). But Kafka himself was quite aware of this, and later (again in a letter to Milena Jesenská) he criticized the all too obvious rhetorical construction of his letter: "the letter is much too focused on its purpose" (*Letters to Milena* 56); literally, "much too *constructed* toward its goal" ("*der Brief ist doch zu sehr auf sein Ziel hin* konstruiert" [*Briefe an Milena* 75; my emphasis]). One critic suggests that any attempt to textualize real-life experiences is invariably a fictional creation, for it is "precisely an author's *readerly* knowledge of the effect of autobiographical narrative that would lead him or her to exploit its potential for reference to endow that principal referent, the self, with a reality it might not otherwise enjoy" (Eakin xxiii). Kafka, too, realized that he had created not a truthful reconstruction of real life but rather a self-serving fictional account of his suffering at the hands of his father. This was not mere hindsight, for otherwise he would not have exposed his arbitrary fabrication of the two opposed selves at the end of the letter. When he gives his father a voice and a chance to defend himself, Kafka reveals his awareness of the inherent arbitrariness of fictional creation, which enables him not only to play out one side against the other, but also allows him to make his opponent construct an equally arbitrary portrait of the son, which is diametrically opposed to Kafka's earlier self-representation. In this "correction" (K 217) the father not only asserts his self, but he now calls his son's representation lies and charges him with "insincerity, obsequiousness, and parasitism" (K 215).

By subjecting his whole narrative to this devastating critique, Kafka also questions his earlier representation of himself as victim. His initial "desire" for self-articulation has given way to fundamental "doubt" that the representation of himself vis-à-vis his father was successful: "Naturally things cannot in reality fit together in the way the evidence does in my letter" (K 217). It is equally clear, though, that the father's "correction" alone will not amount to a truer representation, either: according to Kafka, it is only *together* that the two opposed representations approach something "so closely approximate to the truth that it may be able to reassure us both a little and make our living and dying easier" (K 217). Kafka's self-critical discourse therefore implies not only that "true" representation of the self or the Other is ultimately impossible, a belief that is shared by poststructuralists, who stress the "apparently limitless possibilities for the production of meaning that come about when the language of the critic enters the language of the text" (Murfin 205). This "language of the critic" can be the father's reading of the son, Kafka's reading of father and son, Nadine Gordimer's reading of father and son, or, for that matter, the present reader's reading of all of them. Each individual reading may complement the other reading or even contradict it, but does this state of affairs necessarily imply an affirmation and celebration of a general arbitrariness of meaning? Quite the contrary, for Kafka's juxtaposition of the two parties' different perspectives ends on a note of resignation but not in *aporia*, as is so characteristic of many poststructuralists (Norris 49). In the final analysis, Kafka is clearly aiming for a reconciliation of opposite views rather than celebrating their irreconciliability: for him, both representations of father and son *together* come as close to truthful representation as one can get. Nor does Nadine Gordimer's recreation of the father's monological discourse end in *aporia*. We will see that her ironic depiction of Kafka's father, like Kafka's own, "holds itself provisionally open to further deconstruction of its own operative concepts" (Norris 48) and that by doing so, Gordimer decidedly takes a stance.

Nadine Gordimer's "Letter from His Father" shows that an awareness of the inherently untruthful and arbitrary nature of any self-representation does not necessarily mean a dead end. Kafka's letter ended with the recognition that his self-representation was a fictional labyrinth of mirrors, which refracted and distorted, but never reflected, an accurate picture of father and son. Nadine Gordimer's letter continues where Kafka left off. Here, Paul Eakin's words on an

author's relation to her/his constructed autobiographical discourse are particularly revealing, for he remarks, "[I]f the premise of autobiographical referentiality that we can move from knowledge of the text to knowledge of the self proves
to be a fiction, the text becomes paradoxically not less but more: in making the
text the autobiographer constructs a self that would not otherwise exist" (xxiii).
Kafka saw this state of affairs as flawed, as a limitation; however, Gordimer
takes this insight as her starting point and creates a clearly fictional father with
no explicit claims to accuracy and referentiality.

Moreover, the main operative mechanism behind Gordimer's reading of
Kafka's letter—of the father's projections of his own and of Kafka's supposed
self—is irony. It is significant that elsewhere, Gordimer connects her use of
irony specifically with her immediate cultural-political environment, South Africa under the rule of apartheid, where political oppression and ideological cen-
sorship made it impossible for a writer to write the truth, and where the reader
knew not to trust the surface but to read between the lines: "In a society like that
of South Africa, where a decent *legal* life is impossible, a society whose very
essence is false values and mutual distrust, irony lends itself to you." (Riis 102).
The connection between South African society and Prague society lies in the
fact that Kafka's father can also be seen as representative of a "society whose
very essence is false values and mutual distrust," as someone who has internalized these values and regards them as absolute. In view of this, Eakin's comment that "the reader, perhaps especially the critic, is potentially an autobiographer himself or herself" (xxiii) suggests that Gordimer's reading of Kafka's father does not need any special, historically verifiable, autobiographical legitimation. Even though such parallels between the father's doctrinaire views and
those of South African society are never openly addressed in her letter, they do
not need to be stated directly; this parallel is intimated beneath the surface, and
constitutes an important affinity on Gordimer's part with Kafka's autobiographical narrative. Moreover, according to Philippe Lejeune, autobiography is,
in any event, not restricted to direct personal relationships and experiences with
the subject matter at hand, because it is "a *mode of reading* as much as it is a
mode of writing" (30; my emphasis). In the same way, then, Gordimer's ironic
mode of reading Hermann Kafka can be said to complement and even magnify
Kafka's own reading.

By bringing the father back to life and allowing him to condemn the son,
Gordimer depicts what seems to be the frostiest mirror of all. However, there is
much to be said for this reversal of roles. Stanley Corngold's insightful comment that Kafka portrayed himself *"more thoroughly than could his father*, his
adversary, as the wretched product of his father's design" (*Fate* 227; my emphasis) identifies the main psychological reason for Kafka's inability to portray a
truthful picture of the father-son relationship: in his self-representation, Kafka
was certainly his own worst enemy because he kept searching for guilt in himself.[4] By reversing the dialogical technique in Kafka's letter, that is, by removing the son, the commentator, entirely, Gordimer lets us hear Hermann Kafka's
monological discourse alone. She thus creates an inversion of the dialogical

structure in Kafka's *Brief an den Vater*, where the son played himself off against the father. This, in particular, enables her to make *explicit* the values of Kafka's father that Kafka himself left largely *implicit*. What even in Gordimer's text, though, remains implicit is her own political subtext—her indirect critique of societies like South Africa, of power structures (and here, the Kafka family situation represents a microcosm of the macrocosm) that work through domination and humiliation, and that are run and maintained by individuals who share views similar to those of Kafka's father.

In order to demonstrate Hermann Kafka's values and presuppositions, I will follow Gordimer's own method. Just as her letter continues where Kafka left off, my analysis in turn will fill in where Gordimer left off and deconstruct and recontextualize "her" father's self-representation. A hall of mirrors will become alive that will refract various pictures of father and son in their respective social environments. In addition, Gordimer's representation of the father will be complemented by biographical and extra-biographical evidence such as Kafka's fictional/autobiographical commentary (including dream narration), personal memoirs of friends, other literary, journalistic, and historical narratives, and literary criticism. This will allow us to situate Franz Kafka vis-à-vis his father within a larger sociohistorical discursive framework in order to create a more multifaceted picture of the father-son relationship than is generally provided by psychobiographical readings.

To begin with, before we hear the father speak, a few words are necessary on his social background and career. Hermann Kafka (1852–1931) was born in the village of Wossek (near Pisek in Southern Bohemia), which had a predominantly Czech population. His father, Jakob Kafka (1814–1889), was a kosher butcher who barely managed to make a living to support his six children (Wagenbach, *Biographie*, 16; Binder, *Handbuch*, 111). Hermann was the fourth child. He did not have much schooling, and at the age of fourteen was forced to earn his living as a peddler. From 1872–1875, he was drafted into the Austrian army. As Kafka's friend Max Brod recounts, "Hermann did three years' military service, and liked to talk about his soldiering even when he was an old man—used to sing soldiers' songs when he was in a good mood—which was not very often, admittedly" (*Biography* 6). The father's love of the army also surfaces in a dream Franz Kafka had in 1916, and then recorded, in which he saw a regiment marching down the street. In this dream he sees Hermann Kafka watching the soldiers and exclaiming, "That's something to look at as long as one can" (*Diaries 1914–1923*, 146). After military service the father resumed his earlier life as a peddler until 1881, when he decided to move to Prague. Only a year later, in 1882, he married and opened his own store; in 1883 Franz Kafka was born. In the Prague Jewish ghetto, Hermann Kafka moved from synagogue to synagogue, a trajectory that paralleled his upward social mobility. By 1911, we hear that Kafka attended a service in the oldest and most prestigious synagogue, the Old-New Synagogue (*Altneusynagoge*) (*Diaries 1910–1913*, 72), where the famous rabbi Loew, who today is best known for the legend of the golem, had taught. Despite Hermann Kafka's very modest beginning, it did not take him long to raise his family's social status, and by 1911, the Kafkas were moving in the circles of the rich and prestigious, who had seats in the Old-New Synagogue, who identified with the dominant German culture, and who sent their children to German schools.

Hermann Kafka's personal circumstances are representative of many who moved to the city and assimilated quickly into German culture. Kafka himself considered his father representative of a whole social group: "The whole thing is of course not an isolated phenomenon. It was much the same with a large section of this transitional generation of Jews, which had migrated from the still comparatively devout countryside to the towns" (K 195). And regarding his father's views on the choice of a profession, Kafka also states: "[H]ere too you were conforming with the general method of treating sons in the Jewish middle class, which was the measure of things for you, or at least with the values of that class" (K 198). The father's values, then, are those of the assimilated Jewish middle class of his time.

Hermann Kafka's self-representation in Gordimer's "Letter from His Father" makes explicit some of these norms and presuppositions. For one, he is adamant about distancing himself from his lower-class origins, and does not share Kafka's enthusiasm for the Yiddish actors who performed in Prague in 1911–1912, and with whom Kafka became acquainted.[5] Kafka himself attended many performances and even saw some of their plays several times: "I love the Yiddish theater; last year I may have gone to 20 of their performances, and possibly not once to the German theater" [November 3, 1912] (*Letters to Felice* 26). But for his father, an interest in Yiddish—the language of the ghetto—, the Yiddish theater, and Yiddish actors is totally unacceptable: "Those dirty-living traveling players you took up with at the Savoy Café. Your friend the actor Jizchak Löwy . . . . You had the disrespect to bring him into your parents' home, and I saw it was my duty to speak to him in such a way that he wouldn't ever dare to come back again" (G 46).

By rejecting the actors, Hermann Kafka rejects anyone or anything that reminds him of his own lower-class origins. His new "German" values, on the other hand, show in the term "disrespect," and in the concept of "duty," which he invokes to justify his insult of the actor Jizchak Löwy (G 46). The rhetoric he uses reveals that he has internalized Prussian values about law and order. "Respect" and "duty" are also essential in the army. *Father knows best:* like a dutiful army officer he enforces his private set of rules at home with an abrasive military tone. It is telling that Kafka, who was quite critical of the frequently poor quality of the performance in the Yiddish plays, told Felice in a letter that he did not mean his criticism to come across as ironic and judgmental: "What I said about the Yiddish theater was certainly not meant to be ironical; I may have laughed at it, but that is part of loving" (November 6, 1912, *Letters to Felice* 29). Hermann Kafka was not so generous, as we can see in the following remark, where he expresses indignation at the thought of his son falling in love with a married woman, a Yiddish actress at that: "[Y]ou thought you were in love with her, a married woman (if you can call the way those people live a marriage)" (G 46). Again, *Father knows best*: here, German middle-class morality is mixed in with his disdain for the lower-class Eastern European Jews. He knows what the "norm" is, what it means to be "normal," to be "human"—the Yiddish actors certainly were not, they were "those people," the lowest of the low. Gordimer is more vocal than Kafka by naming the proverbial expression he used for them, "I say it again as I did then: if you lie down with dogs, you get up with fleas" (G 46), whereas Kafka left this implicit.[6] It was their rootless lifestyle in particular that did not meet with the father's approval, and another element of the *doxa* becomes clear—that a "normal" young man is supposed to be "rooted," to have "a decent marriage" (G 52) with a devoted wife and children in "a home of his own" (G 52). Hermann Kafka could not understand that his son felt he was incapable of marrying. "How is any ordinary human being to understand that?" (G 52), he says.

As for the choice of a woman, she must be a good connection. Felice Bauer, the first fiancée, was acceptable: "At least the Bauer girl came from a nice family" (G 52). Felice's family belonged to the upper middle class: she was the daughter of a Berlin insurance agent and worked in Berlin as a chief clerk (Binder, *Handbuch*, 418). The second fiancée, Julie Wohryzek, had the same type of profession, but she was the daughter of a shoemaker and local *shammes* (sexton) in a synagogue on the outskirts of Prague (Wagenbach, "Julie," 40; Northey 6). For Kafka's father, this was too low, even though in reality the family was not poor: they had been involved in trade; Julie's father's family had owned a butcher shop as well as an inn, and her father had had his own grocery store before he came to Prague (Northey 6). But their social background was very close to Hermann Kafka's own, and he ridiculed his son for choosing to marry into this class: "I can't make you out, after all you are a grown man, here you are in town, and you can't think of any way of managing but going straight off and marrying the next best girl" (K 208). Here, in Kafka's letter, the emphasis is still on Kafka himself, on his inability to choose the right partner, but in Gordimer's letter it shifts increasingly toward Hermann Kafka: "A man doesn't have to marry a nothing who will go with anybody" (G 53), he remarks. This statement is highly revealing—not so much in regard to Julie, who, incidentally, was not very eager to get married at all,[7] but for what it tells us about the father's presuppositions concerning women. What is implicit is that any woman just wants a man, and if she is from a lower class, she will go with anyone. The father also sees nothing wrong with directing sexual insults against Julie—to him she was "some Prague Jewish tart who shook her tits in a thin blouse" [G 51]). Again, unlike Kafka, who attempts to render the father's insults in somewhat more polite terms, Gordimer is explicit and blunt.[8] From the father's point of view, as Gordimer portrays him, his treatment of women is quite normal. This is how men treat women: "I'm human, after all. But I was frank with you, man to man" (G 53). His attitude to women is sexist, patriarchal, and he considers this the norm, "I was normal man enough, eh!" (G 53).

Kafka's last companion, Dora Diamant, was an embarrassment to the family; she was "that woman" (G 55); meeting her would have meant to "swallow our pride" (G 55): "Living with that Eastern Jewess, and in sin. . . . We knew she was giving you the wrong food, cooking like a gypsy on a spirit stove. She kept you in an unheated hovel in Berlin . . . may God forgive me (Brod has told the world), I had to turn my back on her at your funeral" (G 55). Prejudice, racism, and a petty, middle-class morality characterize the father's values. When he likens Dora to a gypsy with whom his son is living "in sin," Hermann Kafka reveals not only that he rejects lower-class Eastern European Jews because they remind him of his own origins, but that he has also internalized the common racist stereotypes about the rootlessness of Jews and gypsies, their loose morality, improper living conditions, and so forth—stereotypes that are embodied in the dominant German culture.

Another element of the *doxa* is that one has to fulfill one's social duties and act and behave in socially acceptable ways. According to Kafka's father, his son's writing habits interfered with this. Kafka did much of his writing at night, and in the father's eyes, "normal" people sleep at night: "Always crawling off to bed, sleeping in the day (oh yes, you couldn't sleep at night, not like anybody else), sleeping your life away" (G 49). The parents went as far as removing Kafka's ink. This was "for your own good, your health" (G 48), the father says, because "[s]cribbling away half the night, you'd have been too tired to work properly in the mornings, you'd have lost your position " (G 48).

As for the content of Kafka's writing, it does not conform to the "norm" because it is not "decent" and shows "[n]o respect" (G 45). The father is convinced that Kafka's stories are not made up "by a normal young man" (G 45):

> [Y]our animal obsession. *Dafke!* Insect, ape, dog, mouse, stag, what
> didn't you imagine yourself. They say the beetle story is a great
> masterpiece, thanks to me—I'm the one who treated you like an infe-
> rior species, gave you the inspiration. . . . You wake up as a bug,
> you give a lecture as an ape. Do any of these wonderful scholars
> think what this meant to me, having a son who didn't have enough
> self-respect to feel himself a man? (G 45)

Decency, respect, to be "a man," a "normal" young man, to "work properly," to do one's "duty"—all of these are bourgeois clichés. It must be stressed that they derive from the class, but they have, of course, become part of Hermann Kafka's discourse through a process of internalization. He represents them; indeed, he embodies them. As Kafka puts it, "At bottom the faith that ruled your life consisted in your believing in the unconditional rightness of the opinions prevailing in a particular class of Jewish society, and hence actually, since these opinions were part and parcel of your own nature, in believing yourself" (K 194).

Franz Kafka rejected the values his father stood for, and it cannot be an accident that in *Brief an den Vater* the son's rebellion against the father is called "self-defense" (K 215), or *Selbstwehr* in the original German (*Brief* [1953], 72). The term *Selbstwehr* had a particular meaning for Kafka: this was the name of the Zionist newspaper in Prague, with which Kafka and many of his friends were involved. *Selbstwehr* was founded in 1907 in response to increasing anti-

Semitism in Prague. The paper regarded it as one of its main duties to report on anti-Semitism, because there was really no other paper that did. It therefore filled a need as "[t]he only Jewish weekly in Bohemia, Moravia, and Silesia," and by advertising *Selbstwehr* as "the cheapest Jewish newspaper," the editors tried to ensure that they would reach everyone, even the lower social classes.[9] The following chronological overview briefly establishes the extent of Kafka's involvement with this paper.

Kafka's name is mentioned in *Selbstwehr* for the first time on May 13, 1910, in honor of his promotion in the *Arbeiter-Unfall-Versicherung* (Workers' Accident Insurance Company) where he was working. On January 26, 1912, he published a circular entitled "Jüdisches Theater" ("Jewish Theater") in *Selbstwehr* in which he tried to find further guest performances for the Yiddish actors (See also *Diaries 1910–1913*, 223). He then appeared in a review by Hans Kohn on the Prague writers Kafka, Max Brod, Oskar Baum, and Franz Werfel (20 December 1912, 2–3). Moreover, in 1914 Kafka attended editorial meetings for *Selbstwehr* on a regular basis, together with Max Brod (Binder, *"Selbstwehr,"* 284). In September 1915, Kafka's parable "Vor dem Gesetz" ("Before the Law") was published in *Selbstwehr* (7 September 1915, 2–3), and in December 1915 *Selbstwehr* announced that Kafka had received the Fontane prize: "Our colleague and sympathizer Dr. Franz Kafka, Prague, received the *Fontanepreis* from Carl Sternheim, who had been awarded the prize originally."[10] In addition, Kafka's name appeared "in *Selbstwehr*'s advertisement in Martin Buber's monthly *Der Jude* (*The Jew*), which lists Kafka among the contributors to the 1916 volume."[11] From 1917 on Kafka's contact with *Selbstwehr* was even closer because several of his friends became actively involved in the board of directors. Nelly Thieberger, sister of Kafka's Hebrew teacher and herself a good friend of Kafka's, edited *Selbstwehr* in 1918 (Binder, *"Selbstwehr,"* 285); and a year later, in 1919, when Kafka wrote *Brief an den Vater*, his close friend Felix Weltsch became editor and began to publish extensively in *Selbstwehr* as a commentator on social and political events.

In view of these developments, Kafka's use of the term *Selbstwehr* and his request of Milena Jesenská—"And at the same time never forget your great Nevertheless" (*Letters to Milena* 63), that is, "your great Despite-it-all"—should be seen in relation to Kafka's involvement in Zionist affairs. Many years later, Max Brod characterized their whole generation after World War I as "a generation of courage, a generation of the Despite-it-all."[12] If we place Kafka's letter within the Zionist climate of his time, we recognize that there is a further dimension to the father complex, which goes beyond the clash between a particularly strong and overbearing father and his oversensitive son. Instead, the letter becomes representative for a whole generation of young people who rebelled against their assimilated fathers because they had internalized the bourgeois values of German middle-class culture.

In Gordimer's letter, the father recognizes that his very existence, everything he stands for, is rejected: "If it's what I am that's to blame, then I'm to blame . . . for what *I am*, for being alive and begetting a son! You! Is that it? Because of you *I* should never have lived at all!" (G 44). For the Prague Zionists, the father's major "crime" would have been called "assimilation." According to Hartmut Binder, the main concern of the Zionist Bar Kochba organization was a reaction against the assimilated Jew and "within Prague society above all the fight against the assimilated fathers who were not yet able to see the error of their ways."[13]

Kafka shared many of the Zionists' concerns. Regarding his relationship to his father, he acknowledged that "it would have been thinkable that we might both have found each other in Judaism" (K 191), particularly since Hermann Kafka "had really brought some traces of Judaism with [him] from that ghetto-like little village community" (K 194). However, for Kafka it was "too little to be handed on to the child" (K 194). Most of the time Kafka considered his father's religious practices no more than "a mere scrap, a joke, not even a joke" (K 192). It did not take long for him to realize that going to the synagogue was primarily a social occasion for the father. One would go mainly to see people and be seen in return: the presence of "'the sons of the millionaire Fuchs,' who were in the synagogue with their father at great festivals" (K 193), seemed to be of greater importance than the religious occasion. These remarks were made in hindsight, in 1919, but even by 1911 Kafka's criticism of his assimilated environment revealed his closeness to the Zionist position. For instance, at his nephew Felix's circumcision (December 24, 1911), he was greatly struck by the gap between modern reality and traditional religious practice:

> Today when I heard the *moule*'s assistant say the grace after meals and those present, aside from the two grandfathers, spent the time in dreams or boredom with a complete lack of understanding of the prayer, I saw Western European Judaism before me in a transition whose end is clearly unpredictable and about which those most closely affected are not concerned, but, like all people truly in transition, bear what is imposed upon them. It is so indisputable that these religious forms which have reached their final end have merely a historical character. (*Diaries 1910–13*, 190–91)

And in February 1912, when Kafka organized a performance for the Yiddish actors with the Zionist Bar Kochba association (at which he himself made the introductory speech),[14] the generational gap is noticeable again, when he comments, "(My parents were not there)" (*Diaries 1910–1913*, 235), for his parents typically did not attend. Because of his assimilated upbringing, or rather "despite it all," Kafka, like many of his contemporaries, became involved in Jewish activities, and his interest increased over the years, particularly in the last ten years of his life: he attended at least one of Martin Buber's three lectures in Prague in 1909–1910—his *Drei Reden über das Judentum* (*Three Lectures on Judaism*)—, met Buber personally in 1913, corresponded with him, and contributed to his journal *Der Jude* in 1917; he went to the Eleventh Zionist Congress in Vienna in 1913, and attended many Zionist meetings and lectures over the years; from 1914 on, he was very concerned about furthering the notion of Jewish education, participated in parent-teacher meetings, and strongly supported the foundation of the first Jewish elementary school in Prague (1920); he also began learning Hebrew in 1917, and seriously thought about emigrating to Palestine. Kafka's increasing involvement in Zionist affairs had much to do with growing anti-Semitism in Prague: living in an atmosphere of constant racial tensions profoundly influenced his skepticism about the value of assimilation. For him, as for many of his friends, it was not really a question of rejecting the assimilation that had been the goal of their fathers; rather, their skepticism grew out of the conviction that assimilation was a very idealistic concept that could not be realized since acceptance by the dominant culture was a near impossibility.

In Gordimer's letter, all the Jewish activities that were important for the Zionists are belittled by the father. Kafka's many years of studying Hebrew are dismissed in a derogatory fashion, and the plan to go to Palestine is sneered at as "some wild dream" (G 47). The most ironic accusation, though, is the father's charge of anti-Semitism: "The fact is that you were anti-Semitic, Franz" (G 46). The most damaging "proof" he cites is the following:

> When your great friend Brod wrote a book called "The Jewesses" you wrote there were too many [Jews] in it. You saw them like lizards. (Animals again, low animals.) "However happy we are to watch a single lizard on a footpath in Italy, we would be horrified to see hundreds of them crawling over each other in a pickle jar." From where did you get such ideas? Not from your home, that I know. (G 47)

The charges of "self-hatred" and "anti-Semitism," the accusation that the assimilated Jews were not "Jewish" enough and unable to pass on Jewish culture, all these were generally leveled against the father's generation by the Zionists. However, by turning this around and calling his son an anti-Semite, Hermann Kafka is able to escape these charges; significantly, his violent reaction indicates how much he actually did feel threatened by his son's involvement in Jewish affairs.

Moreover, the father's misrepresentation of Kafka's argument is obvious when one relates Kafka's "offensive" remarks to the sociohistorical situation in which these statements originated. Kafka's comments are made in response to a review of Brod's *Die Jüdinnen (The Jewesses* [1911]) in *Selbstwehr*. One of the main characters in Brod's novel is a young Jew who rejects Judaism and identifies only with German culture, and Brod was attacked for this by the Zionist Hugo Herrmann, whose argument ran as follows: this is not a "Jewish" novel, even though all the characters in it are Jewish; in fact it is not even a "novel" but a "depiction" of the most typical, the most common and ordinary Jews around us. The main character in particular, Hugo Rosenthal, seems a very self-satisfied person, not someone who is a fighter for a cause (that is, a Zionist). There are not many conflicts, there is no tragic end; instead, the author simply wishes his character good luck at the end of the book. This is very poor construction. The greatest flaw, though, is that Brod never takes a stance vis-à-vis his characters. This is why his work is "definitely not the Jewish novel."[15]

For the reviewer, the Jewish element is not obvious because the gentile characters are missing, and without this contrast, Otherness is not clearly visible. Kafka's commentary seems laconic for the most part, but he also parodies Hugo Herrmann's dogmatic stance (*Diaries 1910–13,* 54–55, 59–60).[16] One can see this in the type of vocabulary he employs in order to criticize the reviewer's hasty judgment.[17] In both diary entries, Kafka uses the phrase *kurz entschlossen* (*Tagebücher* 36, 160), which is rendered as "offhand" (*Diaries 1910–13* 55, 60) in English but really implies jumping to conclusions and thus ridicules the reviewer's impatient response and his lack of thought. These stylistic formulations, which give away the irony, suggest that Kafka is not only recreating the Zionist argument but parodying it at the same time. Unaware or unwilling to see the irony, Hermann Kafka distorts Kafka's statement, "The *Jüdinnen* lacks non-Jewish observers" (*Diaries 1910–13,* 55) into "you said there were too many Jews in Brod's novel" (G 47).

As for Kafka's "offensive" anecdote, which likens the Jews to lizards, it must be seen as a response to the reviewer's criticism that there was no ethnic specificity, not even one Jewish hero with whom the reader could identify; for this reason, the Jews in Brod's novel were all equally nondescript. Again, Kafka is parodying here the objection that we really do not know with whom we are dealing by creating the following ironic anecdote: "In the same way, too, the convulsive starting up of a lizard under our feet on a footpath in Italy delights us greatly, again and again we are moved to bow down, but if we see them at a dealer's by hundreds crawling over one another in confusion in the large bottles in which otherwise pickles are usually packed, then we don't know what to do" (*Diaries 1910–1913,* 55).

Moreover, the Jew as reptile or lizard was a common anti-Semitic stereotype (Gilman, *Patient,* 17). By employing anti-Semitic rhetoric here, Kafka is associating Zionist discourse with racial stereotyping and thus giving a scathing critique of the reviewer's dogmatic position. Brod himself countered the reviewer's attack on the front page of *Selbstwehr* (26 May 1911, 1–2) by referring to Homer, Shakespeare, and Flaubert, none of whom created unambiguous one-dimensional characters, monological in the extreme. Within this context, Kafka's judgment, "This is just what we demand, no other principle for the organization of this Jewish material seems justified to us" (*Diaries 1910–1913,* 55), must be seen as ironic. The use of "we" alone indicates that Kafka is mimicking the dogmatic Zionist viewpoint. Kafka always kept a critical distance from dogmatic positions in the Zionist movement and the Zionist press.

Furthermore, it seems strange and even contradictory that Hermann Kafka first charges Kafka with anti-Semitism and then continues: "And look how Jewish you are, in spite of the way you despised us—Jews, your Jewish family! You answer questions with questions. I've discovered that's your style, your famous literary style: your Jewishness" (G 47). Why would the father attempt to portray Kafka first as anti-Semitic and then immediately throw back in his face just how Jewish he is? The most plausible explanation is that here again we have a projection of the father's confused psyche onto the son: since it is not the son who did not want to be Jewish, this is the father speaking—the assimilated Jew voicing his frustrations at a fundamental dilemma. Even though he rejects his origins, he knows full well he will never be accepted as an equal by the dominant German culture or by the Czechs, whom he called, after all, "paid enemies" (K 181). Kafka and his Zionist friends never tired of analyzing the effects and consequences of assimilation. Hermann Kafka incorporates them all: Jewish anti-Semitism, self-hatred, resentment toward the gentiles: "(you should have had to deal with those lazy *goyim*)" (G 55), he says. The father's frustration finds an outlet in his poor treatment of his gentile employees in the shop (K 181) and in his humiliation of his son, particularly when the latter becomes ever more interested in Jewish affairs. Within this context, the father's charge—"and look how Jewish you are"—reveals that he is still indebted to essentialist thinking and that he has quite internalized Jewish stereotypes, which he here employs himself in order to humiliate his own son. This is what the Zionists called "sickness," the sickness of the assimilated Jew, for which they sought a cure.

Kafka's seemingly arbitrary black-and-white portrayal of father and son, which manifests itself in their inability to find a common ground, does not seem so implausible any more. In Gordimer's letter, we have seen Hermann Kafka present his view of the world in equally black-and-white terms: what he believes is "[c]lear as daylight" (G 41), "isn't that a law of life" (G 44). But Gordimer has gone beyond reproducing the father's commonplaces and clichés in terms of their psychological effect on the son. The political nature of the father's arbitrary imposition of "difference" has become increasingly obvious. Thus, seemingly personal statements that arbitrarily attribute Otherness—as when the father says, "Because you were never like any other child" (G 42)—are located not only on the level of individual psyches. The charge of "Otherness" or "difference" as a negative category must be seen within a larger sociopolitical framework, such as the postcolonial situation of Gordimer's South Africa during apartheid, or the clash in Prague between assimilated Jews and Zionists, German Jews and Czech Jews, Jews and gentiles. Just as "race" in South Africa has been constructed through the discourse of the dominant white power structure, Kafka's father has arbitrarily constructed an image of his son as Other. The very language employed by father and son can be related to constellations of political power, for when Kafka allows his father to have the last word, the latter's monological speech proceeds to crush all dialogue.

Kafka himself points out the dogmatic and inflexible manner of his father, who will not be contradicted: "From your armchair you ruled the world. Your opinion was correct, every other was mad, wild, *meshugge*, not normal" (K 164). And the political dimension is also addressed by Kafka when he compares his father to "all tyrants . . . whose rights are based on their person and not on reason" (K 164). In Gordimer's letter the father's rhetoric is exposed as politically dangerous. He is vehemently anti-intellectual and inflexible. Since he does not understand his son's writing—"What did you *want*? . . . What did you mean . . . ? What's the sense . . . ?" (G 48)—he can deal with it only in a dismissive fashion. Thus, he ridicules "the great writer's beautiful words" (G 44), and aggressively asserts, "I'm not a deep thinker like you" (G 44). It is in keeping with his middle-class mentality that he feels both awe and resentment for higher education and learning: "[Y]ou see, sometimes I'm not so *grob*, uneducated, knowing nothing but fancy goods, maybe I got from you some 'insights'" (G 50), "Hah! I know I'm no intellectual, but I knew how to live" (G 55). We can see that his aggressive assertion of the value of his mediocrity compensates for his feelings of insufficiency. But psychological explanations aside, Hermann Kafka's monological discourse in Gordimer's text contrasts sharply with Kafka's dialogical discourse, which at least invites the father to a dialogue.

The reason for this becomes obvious in Gordimer's letter: Hermann Kafka is completely unable to go beyond HIMSELF—not to mention his inability to see the presuppositions underlying his own arguments, or their political implications. At the end of Gordimer's letter he becomes sentimental, contradicts himself, and thus undermines his whole argument: "[Y]ou should never have moved out of your own home, the care of your parents. . . . We had some good times, didn't we? Franz? When we had beer and sausages after the swimming lessons? At least you remembered the beer and sausages, when you were dying" (G 55–56). Sentimentality. Beer and sausages. . . . Indeed, no self-representation, even the most self-assured one, can escape its own "frosty mirror." By placing Hermann Kafka within this parodic framework, Gordimer makes him expose himself—her recreation of the father's rhetoric does not lead to *aporia*. In fact, Hermann Kafka's "failure to think through the problems engendered by his own mode of discourse" (Norris 27) and to see the limits of self-representation leads him to fall into his own trap.

Both Gordimer and Kafka distort and/or refract images of the Other and present critiques of self-representations that are based on self-justifications and lies. Kafka's letter ends in resignation because he becomes increasingly aware that he is deceived by his own discourse. In Gordimer's letter, on the other hand, the father is deceived by his own discourse, but without ever knowing this. Nadine Gordimer's highly ironic "Letter from His Father" is a caricature of Kafka's father that exposes his middle-class values and presuppositions. More importantly, Gordimer foregrounds relationships between discourse, social history, class, and power structures, and highlights the political nature of Otherness. By allowing Hermann Kafka to speak and represent himself, she allows us to deconstruct his values and presuppositions; through his blindness, his inability to transcend his monological discourse, and his arbitrary imposition of Otherness as a negative quality, she reveals the locus for totalitarian thought in middle-class ideology and underscores Kafka's need for "*Selbstwehr*."

NOTES

1. The following abbreviations are used throughout this text: Kafka's "Letter to His Father" (K); Gordimer's "Letter from His Father" (G).

2. The father's inferiority complex is also apparent in Kafka's following comment: "For instance, there was the way you so easily let yourself be dazzled by people who were for the most part only seemingly your social superiors; you would keep on talking about them, as of some Imperial Councillor or other and the like (on the other hand such things pained me too, to see you, my father, believing you had any need of such trifling confirmations of your own value, and boasting about them)" (K 175–76).

3. "in dem alle Qualen seiner Kindheit noch ebenso unbewältigt und beklemmend anwesend sind wie ehedem, ja in dem sogar eine Steigerung dieser Qualen spürbar wird" (Emrich, "Nachwort," *Brief* [1953], 75; my translation).

4. Kafka knew this full well: "Not even your mistrust of yourself [*sic*], after all, is as great as my self-mistrust which you inculcated in me" (K 217). Note that the original German does not say "mistrust of yourself" but rather "mistrust of others" ["Dein Mißtrauen gegen andere" (*Brief* [1953], 74)]. The 1954 edition of *Dearest Father*, which also includes "Letter to His Father" by the same translators and which was published the same year as *Wedding Preparations*, translates "Not even your mistrust of yours," which is also inaccurate (*Dearest Father* [New York: Schocken, 1954], 196).

5. See Evelyn Torton Beck's study *Kafka and the Yiddish Theater*; Baioni, *Kafka,* 34–58 and "Zionism," as well as Robertson 14–28.

6. "Without knowing him you compared him, in a dreadful way that I have now forgotten, to vermin and as was so often the case with people I was fond of you were automatically ready with the proverb of the dog and its fleas" (K 166). See also *Diaries 1910–1913,* where Kafka is explicit: "Löwy. My father about him: 'Whoever lies down with dogs gets up with fleas'" (131).

7. See Kafka's letter to Julie's sister in Wagenbach, "Julie Wohryzek, die zweite Verlobte Kafkas," *Kafka-Symposion* 47. For a discussion of Kafka's chauvinism in his relationship with Julie see Northey.

8. What he did say about Julie, according to Kafka, was something like the following: "She probably put on some specially chosen blouse, the thing these Prague Jewesses are good at and straightaway, of course, you made up your mind to marry her" (K 207–8).

9. "Billigste jüdische Zeitung. Einziges jüdisches Wochenblatt in Böhmen, Mähren und Schlesien" (*Selbstwehr,* 7 Feb. 1908, 8; my translation).

10. "Unser Mitarbeiter und Gesinnungsgenosse Dr. Franz Kafka, Prag, erhielt von Carl Sternheim den diesem verliehenen Fontanepreis" (*Selbstwehr,* 10 Dec. 1915, 7; my translation).

11. "in einer Anzeige der 'Selbstwehr' als Mitarbeiter des Jahrgangs 1916" (Binder, "*Selbstwehr,*" 288–89; my translation).

12. "eine Generation des Mutes . . . ; eine 'Generation des Trotzdem'" (Brod, *Leben* 218; my translation).

13. "innerhalb der Prager Verhältnisse vor allem Kampf gegen die Assimilation der Väter, die ihren Irrweg noch nicht einzusehen vermochten" (Binder, *Handbuch,* 371; my translation).

14. Hartmut Binder points out that "the recitation evening, which was organized by Kafka himself, was a regular event of the Zionist 'Bar Kochba' association" ("der von [Kafka] organisierte Rezitationsabend war eine reguläre Veranstaltung des Vereins 'Bar Kochba'") ("Selbstwehr" 289–90; my translation). See also *Letters to Felice,* where

Kafka mentions, "I even made a short introductory speech in front of what now seems like a countless number of people; then Löwy came on, acted, sang, and recited" (29).

15. "nie der jüdische Roman" (Hugo Herrmann, "Jüdinnen: Ein Roman von Max Brod," *Selbstwehr* 19 May 1911, 2–3; my translation).

16. There has been much controversy regarding these passages. Hartmut Binder argues that Kafka's critique is so similar to the tendentious Zionist critique in *Selbstwehr* that Kafka seriously intended it as a critique in a Zionist spirit (*Handbuch* 376). See also "Franz Kafka und die Wochenschrift *Selbstwehr*," where Binder finds it remarkable "that Kafka's commentary on Brod's novels 'Jüdinnen' and 'Arnold Beer' corresponds in its tendentiousness with the reviews in 'Selbstwehr'" ("bemerkenswert . . . , daß Kafkas eigene Stellungnahme zu Brods Romanen 'Jüdinnen' und 'Arnold Beer' in der Tendenz genau den Rezensionen in der 'Selbstwehr' entspricht") (288; my translation). But Binder ignores the ironic tone of Kafka's review. To my mind Giuliano Baioni rightly stresses that Kafka's review reveals his "disagreement with the Zionist position" ("Zionism" 95).

17. It is interesting to note that the courtroom metaphor in Hermann's review is all-pervasive and that the word *Urteil* (judgment) comes up sixteen times. Kafka wrote his own "The Judgment" in September 1912.

WORKS CITED

Baioni, Giuliano. *Kafka—Literatur und Judentum*. Trans. G. and J. Billen. Stuttgart/Weimar: Metzler, 1994. [*Kafka: letteratura ed ebraismo*. Torino[Turin]: Einaudi, 1984].

———. "Zionism, Literature, and the Yiddish Theater." In *Reading Kafka: Prague, Politics, and the Fin-de-Siècle*, ed. Mark Anderson. 95–115. New York: Schocken, 1989.

Beck, Evelyn Torton. *Kafka and the Yiddish Theater: Its Impact on His Work*. Madison: University of Wisconsin Press, 1971.

Benjamin, Walter. *Moscow Diary*. Ed. Gary Smith, trans. Richard Sieburth. Cambridge, MA: Harvard University Press, 1986.

Binder, Hartmut, ed. *Der Mensch und seine Zeit*. Vol.1 of the *Kafka Handbuch*. Stuttgart: Alfred Kröner, 1979.

———. "Franz Kafka und die Wochenschrift *Selbstwehr*." *Deutsche Vierteljahrsschrift für Literaturwissenschaft und Geistesgeschichte* 41 (1967): 283–304. English version in *Yearbook XII of the Leo Baeck Institute*, ed. Robert Weltsch. (London: East and West Library, 1967), 135–48.

Brod, Max. *Die Jüdinnen*. 1911. Reprint, Leipzig: Kurt Wolff, 1915.

———. *Franz Kafka: A Biography*. Trans. G. H. Roberts and R. Winston. New York: Schocken, 1960.

———. *Streitbares Leben 1884–1968*. München [Munich]: F. A. Herbig, 1969.

Corngold, Stanley. *The Fate of the Self: German Writers and French Theory*. New York: Columbia University Press, 1986.

———. *Franz Kafka: The Necessity of Form*. Ithaca, NY: Cornell University Press, 1988.

Derrida, Jacques. *The Ear of the Other: Otobiography, Transference, Translation* [texts and discussions with J. Derrida]. Ed. Christie McDonald and Claude Levesque. 1982. Reprint, Lincoln: University of Nebraska Press, 1988.

Eakin, Paul John, ed. Foreword to *On Autobiography,* by Philippe Lejeune, vii–xxvii. Trans. K. Leary. Minneapolis: University of Minnesota Press, 1989.

Emrich, Wilhelm. Nachwort to *Brief an den Vater,* by Franz Kafka, 75–85. Frankfurt am Main: Fischer Taschenbuch, 1953.

Gilman, Sander L. *Franz Kafka: The Jewish Patient.* New York: Routledge, 1995.

———. *Inscribing the Other.* Lincoln: University of Nebraska Press, 1991.

Gordimer, Nadine. "Letter from His Father." *Something Out There.* 1984. Reprint, Harmondsworth: Penguin, 1985.

Kafka, Franz. *Brief an den Vater.* Frankfurt: Fischer Taschenbuch, 1953.

———. *Brief an den Vater: Faksimile.* Ed. Joachim Unseld. Frankfurt: Fischer Taschenbuch, 1994.

———. *Briefe an Milena.* Ed. Jürgen Born and Michael Müller. Frankfurt: Fischer Taschenbuch, 1986.

———. *The Diaries of Franz Kafka 1910–1913.* Ed. Max Brod, trans. J. Kresh. New York: Schocken, 1948.

———. *The Diaries of Franz Kafka 1914–1923.* Ed. Max Brod, trans. Martin Greenberg, with the cooperation of Hannah Arendt. New York: Schocken, 1949.

———. "Letter to His Father." In *Wedding Preparations in the Country and Other Posthumous Prose Writings,* trans. E. Kaiser and E. Wilkins. London: Secker and Warburg, 1954.

———. *Letters to Felice.* Ed. E. Heller and J. Born, trans. J. Stern and E. Duckworth. 1967. Reprint, New York: Schocken, 1973.

———. *Letters to Milena.* Trans. Philip Boehm. New York: Schocken, 1990.

———. *Tagebücher in der Fassung der Handschrift. Kommentarband.* Ed. Hans-Gerd Koch, Michael Müller, and Malcolm Pasley, Critical Edition. Frankfurt am Main: S. Fischer, 1990.

Lejeune, Philippe. "The Autobiographical Pact." In *On Autobiography,* edited and with a foreword by Paul John Eakin, trans. K. Leary, 3–30. Minneapolis: University of Minnesota Press, 1989.

Marchant, P., J. Kitchen, and S. Rubin, "A Voice from a Troubled Land: Conversation with Nadine Gordimer." In *Conversations with Nadine Gordimer,* ed. N. Topping Bazin and M. Dallman Seymour, 253–63. Jackson: University of Mississippi Press, 1990.

Murfin, Ross C. "What Is Deconstruction?" In *Joseph Conrad, Heart of Darkness: Case Study in Contemporary Criticism,* ed. R. C. Murfin, 199–209. New York: St. Martin's Press, 1989.

Norris, Christopher. *Deconstruction: Theory and Practice.* London : Methuen, 1982.

Northey, Anthony. "Julie Wohryzek, Franz Kafkas zweite Verlobte." *Freibeuter* 59 (Apr. 1994): 2–16.

Riis, Johannes. "Nadine Gordimer: Interview" (1979). In *Conversations with Nadine Gordimer,* ed. N. Topping Bazin and M. Dallman Seymour, 101–7. Jackson: University of Mississippi Press, 1990.

Robertson, Ritchie. *Kafka: Judaism, Politics, and Literature.* Oxford: Clarendon Press, 1985.

Sandbank, Shimon. *After Kafka: The Influence of Kafka's Fiction.* Athens: University of Georgia Press, 1989.

Selbstwehr—Unabhängige jüdische Wochenschrift (1907–1921); *Selbstwehr—Jüdisches Volksblatt (1922–39).* Ed. R. Brandeis and F. Steiner. Prague, Czechoslovakia.

Smith, Rowland. Introduction to *Critical Essays on Nadine Gordimer.* Ed. R. Smith, 1–21. Boston: Hall, 1990.

Wagenbach, Klaus. *Franz Kafka: Eine Biographie seiner Jugend 1883–1912*. Bern: Francke, 1958.

———. "Julie Wohryzek, die zweite Verlobte Kafkas." In *Kafka-Symposion*, ed. J. Born, L. Dietz, M. Pasley, P. Raabe, and K. Wagenbach, 39–53. Berlin: Klaus Wagenbach, 1965.

Chapter 7

Narrative Strategies to Disclose Pious Lies in the Works of Irene Dische

Diana Orendi

This chapter is intended as an introduction to a writer who is a virtual unknown in her native country, the United States, while enjoying cult figure status in the country of her choice, Germany. The product of Catholic schooling, Irene Dische has reluctantly affirmed her half-Jewishness and positioned her search for self-definition as central theme of her oeuvre. The blame for her uncertainty about identity questions has been placed squarely on the shoulders of the parents' generation. This apportioning of responsibility finds expression in narrative strategies that invariably encourage acts of violence and re-crimination against parental figures in Dische's prose. The "pious lies" fed to the "Children of the Holocaust" are decried as patronizing and paralyzing attempts to keep the offspring at a safe emotional distance. By interpreting the older generation's gesture as harmful rather than protective, Dische has joined forces with a group of younger German-Jewish writers who reject the stance of the official German-Jewish community as too meek and conciliatory and lobby for a stronger, more self-confidently assertive presence of this minority in German majority culture.

In a recent volume entitled *Jewish Voices, German Words*, an anthology containing selections by fifteen young writers of German-Jewish origin, editor Elena Lappin states that "fifty years after the virtual elimination of their communities by the Nazi regime, Jewish writers are, once again, a distinctive and important voice on the German . . . cultural scene" (9). As the predominant theme in the short stories and poems presented in this collection, the authors confront the question of their often tormented, never unquestioned identity as Jews living in Germany. Their work reflects the problematics that this generation has had to contend with: not personally touched by the Holocaust, they still have to grapple in various ways with its legacy. Unlike German writers, who can choose to ignore this sociohistorical thematic complex, for young Jewish writers "the Holocaust is not an abstract notion, but a tangible issue affecting their lives and their writings" (11). The task to memorialize dominates in complex and emotionally charged ways their personal lives as well as their artistic strategies.

The past, and the ways in which it reaches into the present to haunt its inhabitants, also governs the work of a writer not listed by Lappin. Irene Dische is a Jewish-German-American writer whose life could stand as a paradigm for the cycle of enforced "displacements,"[1] begun in the thirties, that has now created several generations of exiles. For the past five years, the ashes of Zacharias Dische, winner of a Nobel Prize in biochemistry, have been standing in a box in a New York apartment. "It is a sign of true homelessness when you have no place on earth to be buried in,"[2] says his daughter, the writer Irene Dische, who, however, not only continues her father's peregrinations in her own life but cultivates the existence of an expatriate with singular determination.

On the one hand, her father seems to have had an extraordinary influence on her life, and this is evidenced by the fact that the figure of the aged, slightly mad, and maddening scientist crops up in her work frequently, but there are also indications of strongly ambivalent attitudes toward father and other parental figures in Dische's narratives. As a consequence, there is a discrepancy between the author's claims of an idyllic childhood whose guardians, her parents, allegedly have served as revered models and the role the writer assigns to parental figures in her fictional works. No Dische reader can long remain blind to the fact that in her short stories, novels, and dramatic monologues she has created a universe where elders are prone to meet violent deaths, suicides, and assorted acts of recrimination.

The sheer preponderance of parent figures in Dische's work is remarkable. A Zacharias-like character is one of the major players in the autobiographical story "Pious Lies" in Dische's first collection of short stories, which made the bilingual author an immediate celebrity and veritable cult figure upon its publication in Germany in 1989. Her father's life also figured in a prize-winning 1986 documentary Dische filmed for German television about Washington Heights, New York, the "Fourth Reich," as it was called due to its German exile inhabitants. And in 1990, Zacharias's final battle with Alzheimer's disease was chronicled with the particular Dischean mixture of compassion and cynicism in the author's second book, *Der Doktor braucht ein Heim* (*The Doctor Needs a Home*).

In this short volume, the author traces the stations of her father's life to reconstruct a biography typical for that of so many Jews of his generation: born in the provincial town of Lemberg, Poland, Zacharias Dische moved to the metropolis Vienna to pursue a medical degree. He escaped the German occupation just in time by emigrating to the United States in 1938. While the rest of his family perished in concentration camps, Zacharias Dische settled in New York, found university employment, and in his forties married the daughter of Catholic Austrian immigrants, a medical student who would later become a pathologist in the New York morgue. Though her parents' marriage faltered when Irene Dische was only ten, the author's memories of childhood and adolescence are consistently those of a household where only German was spoken and a strict Catholicism was practiced. For many years the religion of at least one of her parents was kept as something she later scathingly referred to as a "pious lie."

In a 1990 German television program about foreign writers living in Germany, Washington Heights in uptown Manhattan, where Dische was born in 1952, was again featured. On this occasion, Dische reminisced with both amazement and uneasiness about growing up in the "Fourth Reich," where German-Jewish refugee residents would wear long-sleeved sweaters in summer to hide camp numbers tattooed on their forearms. In the somewhat melancholic and nostalgic tones reserved for narrating her early years, the usually flippant Dische talked about women who sold dark bread and Black Forest torte in their Alpine Bakery. These, she claims, were just some of the attempts to recreate a German culture on foreign soil and thus squash feelings of alienation and homesickness, absurd and pathetic though such tactics may appear.

It is hard to believe that Dische was raised, as she sneeringly describes it, "like a trained dog, strictly Aryan, strictly Catholic," in this environment by parents who sent her to parochial school and consciously kept her in ignorance about her father's past and racial origin. American culture—and the English language—were held at bay and contemplated with a mixture of contempt and grudgingly admitted gratitude. "We children of the forties and fifties who grew up with German clothes, food, and language," Dische mused in a 1982 interview, "were forced to accept as reality what was actually a merely spiritual realm and discovered only later that this world actually existed in another world to which contacts had been severed."[3]

Not surprisingly, the adventurous and gifted adolescent soon decided to free herself from parental supervision. Originally sent to Austria to attend only a summer camp in music training, Dische resolved forthwith to make her permanent home in Europe. The precocious teenager cashed in her train ticket to Salzburg and instead embarked on a hitchhiking tour through Africa. Having barely escaped the erupting revolution in Lybia, Dische met up with anthropologist Louis Leakey, for whom she worked for a while as observer and transcriber of notes on ape behavior. Though she was soon bored with the employment, she impressed Leakey enough to win him as the first of a series of mentors: he procured a scholarship to study anthropology at Harvard for the girl without a high school diploma. Three weeks after Leakey's death later that year, Dische switched her major to literature, a field for which she had meanwhile developed a greater affinity. Commissioned to write a journalistic piece on "Wealthy Jews in Today's Germany" for the upscale German journal *Transatlantik* in 1981, Dische discovered Germany as the true place of departure for her quest of self-definition. She has lived there ever since.

The fractured experience of Dische's early upbringing has resulted in a life-long inner struggle and an ongoing search that have clearly left their marks not only on the writer's life but on her literary strategies. Her conflicted attitude about who she really is and where she belongs is played out in her personal life with an insistence on remaining in the posture of the Other; though she has made

Germany her home for fifteen years now, has raised a family there, and even seems to feel relatively at home in Berlin, Dische chooses to remain the migrant, the temporary guest who writes in English and still lives in Germany on a mere visitor's visa.

Just as father Zacharias remained forever the stranger in New York, so too does his daughter defiantly remain an outsider in the Berlin of the nineties. Her defense mechanisms are acutely developed, her antennae always up to detect danger signals: she senses these, for example, in the unremitting desire for order and cleanliness in contemporary German culture. She observes—and writes about—the hostility and indifference to the foreign element in a country that vainly resists the change from a homogeneous to a multiethnic society. For someone who thus embraces fully the role of the Other, it is both a fitting and revealing gesture when the author, at the end of a television program devoted to an outsider's look at Germany, leads the film crew to her favorite spot in Berlin—Zoo train station. For Dische, this vibrant and colorful locale, way station and exchange for wanderers of many nationalities, approximates as closely as any in Europe the Jewish shtetl's marketplace. Seated boldly on the steps, which have been freshly painted with the injunction "Do not sit here," Dische reflects on the dangers of becoming too emotionally drawn into the sphere she now inhabits. Yet her scruples about feeling completely at home in her adopted culture have little to do with the clichéd notion that as a foreigner and a Jew she might be sitting on the proverbial suitcase, paralyzed by the fear of xenophobia or anti-Semitism. It is a more deep-seated personal trauma that proscribes the coping mechanisms she employs in the private realm as well as in her narrative techniques.

In her first short story, the one she entitled "Pious Lies," a family of devout Catholics turns out to be of Jewish descent; this novella is clearly part autobiography, part childhood fantasy, revolving around the writer-as-child's idée fixe that her immigrant grandfather is in reality the now aged Hitler living out his last years in a New York suburb of the late fifties. After the dramatic conclusion, which climaxes in this father figure's violent death, the female protagonist, mother of the writer's adolescent persona, apologizes: "We wanted to spare the next generation the shame of knowing the truth. Not all knowledge is desirable" (Dische 282).

What fundamentally seems to have propelled Dische's early work is a revolt against what she considered a criminal collusion of the older generation against the younger: in keeping the truth about their real identity from them, the elders, in her view, robbed their progeny of something very basic but irretrievable. Prose in the short stories written during the eighties often explodes with the fury and vehemence one would expect from someone harboring a terrible emotional hurt. If it appears that the experience of her upbringing has turned her into an avenging angel, this is an image Dische would approve of wholeheartedly, considering that its origins lie within the realm of the faith that first laid hold on her. Today she claims that "[t]he mumbo-jumbo of the Catholic liturgy, the Gregorian chants I heard in church, the sacraments of confession, the prayer rituals, that's where I really feel at home" (*Zeitmagazin*). Nonetheless, the sense of outrage about the betrayal of trust has left her with a clearly ambivalent attitude toward Catholicism as well. It is this sense of distrust that has fitted her with a laserlike look at reality, a look that spares nothing as sacrosanct. As a consequence, her characters and plot scenarios often turn wildly upon "the beloved," tearing down what they seemed to cherish most highly. In this autobiographical story, in which Dische appears as an eight-year-old, trusting and innocent, the author mercilessly calls into question the Catholic rituals that dominated her childhood, exposing them as breeding pools of hypocrisy and as emotional crippling.

In the deftly constructed narratives of her two collections *Pious Lies* and *The Intimate Confessions of Oliver Weinstock*, Dische dismantles the legitimacy of the elder's apology and lays it bare as dishonesty and cowardice. In the title story of the first volume, the deception is wrapped in the parents' naive desire to save the offspring the anguish of the Holocaust generation. However, in the course of the narrative, which essentially takes place in the New York morgue, the lie is exposed as a cancer, a malignant growth that metastasizes in the host body and ultimately kills it. A physician, tellingly both a loyal Catholic and a forensic pathologist, establishes the parallels between the physiological and the metaphysical dimensions of lived lies: "Again and again I see how lies can spread like a disease; they lie in wait and work like toxins which disturb the vital functions. The uglier the lie, the more total the devastation caused in the human body. There are lies which turn against the mind and cause madness; there are lies which breed other lies spreading all through the body, slowly obliterating all truth" (*Fromme Lügen* 240).

In the story's cataclysmic dénouement, the secret of a baptized Jew, having painstakingly been maintained for a lifetime and having slowly festered for all these many years, does indeed kill him. This resolution must be read as nothing less than Dische's indictment of an act considered benign by the elders. In her narrative, the deceit turns out to be both suicidal and murderous: the heart attack that follows upon the discovery of the *Lebenslüge* (lived lie) is for one the only logical consequence of an existence lived clandestinely. Conversely, Dische is at least as interested, if not more so, in the effect this duplicity had on the adolescents. In her view, the solicitous desire of the older generation to spare the younger ones knowledge of the full truth is not appreciated, painful though this may be. She sees her own conflicted identity as the archetypal stigma with which the young Jewish, post-Holocaust generation was branded. Uprooted and unsure of their own identity, young diaspora Jews have had, in Dische's words, "to live through a trauma worse than our parents" (*Zeitmagazin*). At least, she proclaims, they knew who they were and could take this knowledge along on their diaspora wanderings.

An American living abroad, a European who grew up in the United States, a Jew who was raised with incantations of the rosary—call this fate an oddity or a fluke, a curse, or simply a confluence of many factors. As the recent volume *Displacements: Cultural Identities in Question* makes clear, Dische's life is less unique than one might expect; Marianne Hirsch's and Angelika Bammer's contributions to this volume prove that Dische can instead be considered representative of an ever-growing minority group whose members' lives are characterized by crossing and inhabiting "borderlands." Having learned to negotiate multiple cultures rather than resting rooted in one, a new generation of truly multicultural, multilingual artists, springing from this minority, is evolving. Their utilization of language shows them constantly traversing boundaries, merging identities out of complexly assorted cultural particularities, and thus constantly inventing and reinventing themselves in no one else's image but their own. Seen in this light, Dische's use of her racial/ethnic and linguistic heritage assumes paradigmatic significance, a phenomenon that is of particular interest within the framework of this volume.

Growing up in New York, Dische spoke only German at home and remembers her bafflement at hearing the strange sounds other children were making on her first day in kindergarten. Her subsequent education, however, especially her training in creative writing at Harvard, was conducted exclusively in English. Today, after fifteen years in Germany, Dische's spoken German is perfectly fluent, but she insists on writing in English. As a publishing oddity, her works are immediately translated into German and published in that country before appearing in their original in the United States. Just as odd is the fact that even in translation, Dische's fiction has been termed brilliant and masterful, and that the author has been fashioned into a German media star. Her first collection of short stories, *Fromme Lügen* (*Pious Lies*), was championed by Hans Magnus Enzensberger, another one of her mentors, who placed her book in a series he edits entitled *Die andere Reihe* (The Alternative Series), which is normally reserved for the often quaint oeuvres of posthumously discovered, but highly deserving, authors.

For those of my readers who have never read anything by Irene Dische, it may come as a surprise after the elaborations given that most of her stories are exceedingly funny, albeit in a wickedly morbid and mocking way. This is perhaps the only appropriate mode for a writer whose agenda focuses on the business of debunking long-held secrets, deflating overblown egos, and disclosing her characters' petty and calculating schemes—and yet achieving this without letting rancor and cynicism win out. If my appraisal of Dische's approach makes her sound mischievous and not altogether likeable, I may just have it right. Not surprisingly, her work has aroused its share of negative criticism; her prose has sometimes been called cold, even heartless, her plot constructions far-fetched and fabricated, and her writing informed by an overarchingly dark view of the world. She evades easy classification, and moreover, makes a sport of provoking public misgivings. When it comes to snubbing her reading public and especially the critics of literary magazines, Dische has developed a mastery in the utilization of derisive and black humor.

Surely no one in our business wants to hear yet another writer quoted as saying that there are no taboos that he/she is willing to leave untouched. Yet it happens in Dische's short story "A Jewess for Charles Allen," her best known and most controversial piece of writing: one of the few unspoken taboos in postwar, post-Holocaust Germany is indeed ignored here. The stereotype of the sainted Jewish literary character is disrupted and displaced by a female figure, whom writer colleague Maxim Biller maliciously characterized as "an ugly, horny, greedy, stingy, wealthy, lazy, criminal antique dealer" (cited in Seligmann). In reality, Esther Becker is only a typical Dische heroine: a painstakingly self-constructed control freak, and, as such, a walking time bomb ready to detonate. She is temporarily managing an antique store in preunification West Berlin, the owner of which has recently disposed of himself in a hideous fashion. Johannes Allerhand, after his escape from the Nazis to the United States, after a baptism and a name change, after a bungalow in Oregon, a decent, menial job, and the birth of a son, had returned to Germany in 1957 to the *Schöne Heimat* (Beautiful Homeland), appropriately enough, the name of his antique store. In the following twenty-five years, he had been making a living with shady deals, selling *Nazibeute* (Nazi loot) to foreigners, stolen madonnas to rabbis, and similarly acquired menorahs to priests. In the sixties, he had had a flourishing trade with stolen and faked West German passports, with which he helped Easterners escape from the GDR through underground tunnels. One such escapee, a young Jewish woman named Esther, had been his protégée, his lover, and increasingly his business partner. He never showed signs of the strain created by the tension of his schizophrenic existence: only the priest of St. Alban's knew of the nights Allerhand spent praying in church, asking forgiveness for the mortal sins he had committed under his Jekyll mask during the day. Then, one day, Allerhand senior's inner spring broke and the cancer erupted, and before Esther's horrified eyes, he slowly sank his mouth into a kitchen knife.

Summoned from his native Oregon to solve the question of an inheritance—or should this read heritage?—Allerhand's son Charles Allen presents the picture-perfect image of a young American of the western region. Clad in a white overcoat and polyester pants, reading only the sports pages of U.S. dailies, and subsisting almost exclusively on candy, Charles is, of course, too much of a perfect stereotype to be real. He may be the son of baptized Jewish immigrants, and he may surprisingly have spent many of his thirty-six years within the confines of the Order of the Immaculate Conception as the convent's accountant. Now, however, he is confronted with the tasks of assessing his genuine past and with assuming his role in an oedipal scenario that may force a complete redefinition of his self. Charles has come to Germany to make a decision about accepting or rejecting his father's bequest, and included in this legacy is the showdown with Esther, the image of a *yidishe mame*: if he is to assume ownership of the store and possibly replace his father as her lover, nothing less than a total conversion back to his origins will do for Esther. Very soon, Charles is knee-deep in her criminal schemes and thus implicated. "You're up to your neck—in money" (*The Jewess* 67), says Esther, offering as bait both herself and material wealth.

But the unlikely idyll unravels with the appearance of the furies coming back from the past: Esther's mother arrives on the scene to clear up the mystery of Esther's birth, and with it, the myth of her Jewish origins. Becker senior replaces the fiction of a birth in the barn of an Alsatian farm house and a childhood of misery with a tale no less full of pain, but of a different sort. Mrs. Becker brings proof—the photo of a blond little girl sitting on her SS-man father's knee clearly shows Esther as a child. To her parents' amazement, the teenager rejected her given identity as daughter of a Nazi lawyer who was forbidden to practice after the war; Esther dyed her blond hair black, hung a star of David around her neck, left the East, and disavowed any connection with her family. None of this can, of course, be ascertained with absolute clarity, but as this act of dismantling unfurls before the eyes of the perplexed Charles, the women's contradictory claims demand a decision, his decision. Timid Charles looks at the evidence and sees a soul mate. All he knows is that Esther has also been abused as a child and has been forced into living a lie: the horrible scar on little Esther's mouth that still disfigures the adult Esther combines in his memory with the set of false teeth he recently saw on her night stand. Here finally is someone who has lived his own lifelong dilemma and has solved it in a way he never dared and never will. He sees a woman who had the courage and independence of spirit even as an adolescent to turn in disgust against her parents, who repudiated their claim on her, and who painstakingly constructed herself into her own notion of an ideal self.

Yet what he sees arouses his envy as much as a sense of his own failure: while he is the product of his parents' fantasies, a willing or oblivious victim of their manipulation to construct the perfect new man on a new continent, Esther has liberated herself from her parents' grip. She is all he will never be. In this moment of recognition, all of Charles's characteristic serenity gives way to sensations of violent resentment. Feelings of his own inadequacy and envy combine to create the final element of eroticization needed to break down his reservations. A scene perhaps meant to be scurrilously funny but in reality starkly schematic and stilted follows: Charles throws himself upon the unresisting Esther, a violence both committed and received in absolute silence and with an almost stunning indifference on both parts.

The next day, Charles makes the decision to reject his father's material inheritance and to return to the United States; what he cannot escape is the freight with which he is burdened by the paternal "pious lies," the baggage of his questionable identity. He is too deeply steeped in the paternal tradition of inner conflict to ever be totally at peace. After a night spent praying in St. Alban's, Charles leaves for Oregon the next morning. As he hurriedly enters the taxi to the airport, a yarmulke falls to the ground and is left behind in the hasty retreat. Charles's last minute escape, however much it looks like a rescue from the abyss, does not fool the Dische reader. The question how long it will take the inner conflict to get the better of him is left unanswered; unquestioned is that a catastrophe of as yet unknown dimensions awaits him somewhere in the future.

After the publication of *Fromme Lügen* and *Der Doktor braucht ein Heim*, Dische was swiftly labeled a specialist in the "Jewish theme," a classification the writer strenuously tried to denounce. "It is true that the diaspora of the Jews has circumscribed my own life, but it in no way should be considered a restricting factor in my choice of topics," she has admonished interviewers. In works published during the last three years, she has tried to demonstrate that she can shed the ticket that ties her to the exclusive treatment of Jewish-German problematics: her protagonists have been, among others, a gay physicist,[4] a New York–born cook,[5] and an Italian composer of the Baroque era.[6] To be sure, several of these figures have also been of Jewish origin, but their Jewishness has been moved into the background, into a realm of secondary significance. As has become apparent, identities are prone to slippage in this author's universe; they are unstable and certain to be deconstructed. Thus, individual personality, as provided by ethnic or racial origin, is of less concern than the stability supplied by other more fixed elements: lifelong grudges, revenge fantasies, and other "cancers" eating away at the tissue of her protagonists' store of conscious and unconscious drives.

A case in point is the short story "A Prior Engagement," published in German as "Die intimen Geständnisse des Oliver Weinstock" ("The Intimate Confessions of Oliver Weinstock"), where Dische explores the long-term effects of early sexual traumatization. The reader is informed that the adolescent Oliver Weinstock, scion of a wealthy New York Jewish family, became infatuated with a handsome waiter while vacationing in Switzerland. The short-lived affair ended with the rape by the older and sexually more practiced man, an experience that apparently crippled young Oliver's emotional and spiritual growth. Proving the efficacy of the Freudian truism evoked here as a motto, namely that "early disappointments cause deformations," Oliver's fetish is a never-delivered love letter to his paramour; he has never been without this billet doux, carrying it along with matches, which he has occasionally been known to use in pyromaniac episodes. Now owner of a gourmet restaurant in Berlin, where he has sought refuge, Oliver is yet another nutty character in the Dische gallery of weirdos, jovial and generous to his friends and guests, but internally a cauldron of unresolved conflicts. As the letter contains the never-conveyed message of love, it is an emblem of the lack of connectedness in which Dische protagonists characteristically live out their lives: they may intersect with others, but most never link. Their isolation would be heartrending were it not for the fact that the reader senses the approach of a violent but cathartic turn of events. Some fateful twist will produce an eventually harmonizing and stabilizing effect, resulting in the restitution of justice, the kind of restoration Dische delights in, scenarios where an eye is exacted for an eye and pardons are not easily given.

Fixated on his harrowing encounter as a teen, Weinstock has never had a normal sex life: due to his "prior engagement"—used here to convey the word's multiple denotations of appointment and betrothal—he remains perversely faithful to a lover who first abused and then completely forgot him. Then, the lives of the lovers manqué finally converge one more time when Mr. Tonne, now an aged and invalid businessman, shows up in Weinstock's restaurant. After an evening of regaling his bemused but clueless guest, Weinstock carefully prepares his revenge. Having shredded the no longer needed love missive, he readies himself to deliver its now perverted message personally: he drags the invalid on crutches across icy streets to his hotel, and there Weinstock's matches finally are permitted to do their intended work. The arsonist's act of vengeance consumes the long-lost and never-to-be-won object of desire. Tonne burns for a deed long forgotten, committed thoughtlessly and in the heat of youthful sexual attraction; he dies unaware that he has caused the other a life of stunted growth and loveless homosexual encounters, none of which could simulate or replace the authentic object of his passion. "The present time protects us from the horrors of the future but not from those of the past" ("Engagement" 264), one of Weinstock's admonitions to his friends, has thus been carried to its logical conclusion in yet another Dische scenario that pits patient waiting for a long-delayed revenge against the ravages of the past.

In "Prior Engagement," Dische's protagonists were engaged in settling scores of a personal nature. The author next aimed her sharp pen at personages moving about the public sphere; more specifically, she takes on the world of the media and with deft ridicule mounts an assault on the foibles of the entertainment critics' guild. An accomplished pianist herself, Irene Dische has long been fascinated by the creative processes leading to great music; as a result, she has "composed" a novel based on Diabelli's Beethoven variations.[7] In her most recent work, the 1995 drama *The Second Life of Domenico Scarlatti*, however, she uses the events of the Baroque Italian composer's life as a point of departure, only to arrive eventually at a conclusion of starkly Dischean dimensions. In the process, the author alters the original paradigm to achieve a resolution that both confirms and subverts the basic law of the Dische universe: the desire for parricide.

The real-life Domenico Scarlatti was an eighteenth-century cembalo player whose genius lay dormant for most of his life and erupted into wild fits of creativity only after the composer's father had died. Even then, the Italian, who had long lived as minor composer and tutor at the Spanish court, would have remained in obscurity had he not been sought out by his Scottish childhood friend, Thomas Roseingrave, who consequently became his publisher, his public relations man, and the architect of his fame and immortality. Destitute himself and paralyzed in his own musical endeavors by a mixture of envy and admiration of his friend's unquestionable genius, Roseingrave attached himself to Scarlatti. In this age predating rapid publication and circulation of musical scores, the composer was still carving out a meager existence in Spain and would have continued to do so without Roseingrave's business acumen, which soon made Scarlatti the most widely performed artist of his day.

The conflicted and ambiguity-laden connection of art with the media and with the public sphere in general thus serves as subtext in the "second coming" of the Baroque composer, whose biography provides Dische with material she can construct into a postmodern plot. In Dische's rendition, life's vagaries and casual perambulations are rejected as just that and replaced by a deft construct where eliminating the father figure is seen as required for opening the gateway to success. In the modern scenario, Scarlatti senior's death no longer results from old age and infirmity, but is brought about by the ambition-driven schemes of a media figure, a pseudoson, an adoptee, a traitor, no less.

The Scarlatti clan, now reincarnated as the Polish-Jewish Scarlinskys who have settled in Berlin, find their nemesis in the person of Thomas Roseingrave, a busboy aspiring to prominence at any cost. Like the author a New York Jewish expatriate, the youth's only detectable talent lies in attaching himself to visiting dignitaries and providing unspecified "special services." Roseingrave quickly manages to insinuate himself into the famous composer's family and to negotiate this connection into a budding career as music critic. Upon being made aware of his eighteenth-century predecessor's fate, Roseingrave realizes that his grand ambitions will not ripen until the son's sun can rise after the father's demise. So he instrumentalizes the older Scarlinsky's suicide by writing a devastating critique of the aged composer's long-awaited musical *Scarlatti*.

Expectations are, of course, thwarted, the too-obvious parallels derailed: instead of fame and wealth, rejection by his friend and beloved and his own death by heart attack become Roseingrave's honoraria. Dische's "Melodrama for one Actor and one Extra who needs no Acting or other Skills, only Patience" consists entirely of Roseingrave's monologue. Stretched out on a couch in a littered basement apartment, with his composer friend playing cembalo in the adjoining room, the theater and music critic reflects on his entanglement with the composer family and outlines the stratagems he devised to bring about Scarlinsky/Scarlatti senior's recent suicide. Baring himself to the son of the deceased, the brother figure, the alter ego with whom he is connected in a web of strangely incestuous sexual relationships, Roseingrave gives expression to his naked ambitions, his greed, his ruthless drive for prominence and wealth. His exhortations are designed to soothe and seduce Scarlinsky junior: "I will take care that my name and your ouevre will remain prominent for many hundreds of years," Roseingrave wails while his alter ego next door continues to be unmoved, and while the sweet sounds of his cembalo playing waft in.

In the final moments, with Roseingrave clutching his heart and expiring a grotesque and agonizingly slow death on stage, the schemer finally is forced to realize the immensity of this total and oh, so unexpected rejection. His offering has been dismissed as unsuitable and unwanted by the person he thought was his to manipulate and to exploit. Scarlinsky junior has decided to elude the seduction of public approval and material comfort. Moreover, he is supremely indifferent to the demise of his former ally, the brother figure who entered on a path of crime on his, the rising new star composer's, behalf. In a final gesture of disdain, just before the curtain closes, the young musician, a magnificently clad figure in richly ornamented Baroque costume, struts across the stage, scarcely dignifying the dead Roseingrave on the couch with a careless glance.

Thus, in this her latest piece, Dische's plot scenario has evolved as a variation of her usual constellations and as such requires a modification of her traditional narrative strategies. This development could well be a signal of the eccentric writer's new maturity and greater self-confidence. In bifurcating the son figure into the artist on the one hand, the media personage on the other, the author apportioned herself a twofold opportunity to play out solutions to the parent-progeny relationship. The ambition-driven Roseingrave is willing to murder the father to reach his objectives. The composer, however, is content to stand idly by while the door to his success closes with the death of his critic friend. His apathy could even be interpreted as a passive act of homicide, committed to guarantee his obscurity and peace of mind.

In the paradigm, as it was presented by the Baroque composer's biography, the father's stifling presence paralyzed the son's creative powers. The elder man's death unleashed a splendid flow of creativity, marking on the one hand the son's artistic liberation and maturation. But this moment also inaugurated the modern artist's shackling to the forces of commercialization: without the original Roseingrave's skill of promotion, posterity would have remained ignorant of the young composer's works. In having her modern-day Scarlinsky reject out of hand the Faustian pact between art and the media, Dische makes a rather unexpected yet refreshing statement.

Where acts of savagery were almost de rigueur in Dische's earlier stories, her latest piece shows a more conciliatory and compassionate auctorial stance. Rather than self-realization, her artist persona opts for self-denial, an unselfish gesture in a world where most would be supremely gratified to enjoy just fifteen minutes of fame, and where few are granted a more extended measure of this all-important aspect of the artistic endeavor. Is this to signal the intent of the author, who has for the past seven years been a highly visible media personality, to withdraw more from the public glare? Or is it merely the blasé star's expression of disdain for a currency she has seemed to enjoy wholeheartedly until now? Time—and the certain-to-appear next publications from Dische's desk—will tell. What Dische's next works will also have to explore is a universe in which parental—especially father—figures no longer meet with havoc and violence but may be permitted to live to a ripe old age.

Furthermore, the latest scenario indicates an evolving acceptance by a member of the "second generation" of this group's difficult relationship with their elders, the Holocaust survivors. As she herself is entering middle age, Dische seems to be hard at work on resolving her generation's struggle for identity. In her earlier prose, she had instrumentalized the intergenerational conflict as one where the progeny felt strangely impoverished, as though they felt robbed by their parents of the mantle of victimhood. Second-generation exiles and children of survivors figure prominently in Dische's fiction. Yet as varied a lot as they are, there is one characteristic they share: their inability to get comfortable within the identity that fate has assigned them. This must be attributed to the fact that their understanding of themselves lacks precisely the element that in the children's eyes has been their parents' most horrible and yet most precious possession: their status as victims, which has equipped them with an unmistakable role, a uniqueness of fate, a stability of self. Judging from Dische's treatment in her earlier prose, such as "Pious Lies" and "A Jewess for Charles Allen," she blamed the older generation for withdrawing into this realm, into a space shrouded in secrecy and silence, inaccessible to their offspring. As a result, she had her characters play out oedipal fantasies of father-murder and violation of the mother. In the light of these beginnings, the rejection of parricide by young

Dominic Scarlinsky in her recent drama has to be welcomed as a major shift toward a more acquiescent posture by one of the angrier members of the "second generation." Since Dische is also one of this circle's most vocal and most prominent fellows, her shift may signal a softening of the belligerence vis-à-vis the parent generation that could well rub off on fellow German-Jewish writers such as Rafael Seligmann and Maxim Biller.

NOTES

1. This is the title of a recent publication proffering the thesis that "physical dislocation from one's native culture or the colonizing imposition of a foreign culture—is one of the most formative experiences of our century," a paradigm suitable to my discussion of Dische's circumstances. See Angelica Bammer, ed., *Displacements: Cultural Identities in Question* (Bloomington: Indiana University Press, 1994).

2. *Zeitmagazin* 4 (19 Jan. 1990).

3. "Das Vierte Reich verkrümelt sich: Deutsche Emigranten in Washington Heights," *Transatlantik* 1982, trans. Bernd Samland in Dische, *Die intimen Geständnisse des Oliver Weinstock* (Berlin: Rowohlt, 1994).

4. Irene Dische, *Ein fremdes Gefühl*, trans. Reinhard Kaiser (Berlin: Rowohlt, 1993).

5. Irene Dische, "Die intimen Geständnisse des Oliver Weinstock," *Die intimen Geständnisse des Oliver Weinstock: Wahre und Erfundene Geschichten*, trans. Robin Cackett, Reinhard Kaiser, and Bernd Samland (Berlin: Rowohlt, 1994).

6. Irene Dische, *Das zweite Leben des Domenico Scarlatti: Eine Nachstellung*, trans. Michael Walter (Berlin: Rowohlt, 1995).

7. *Ein fremdes Gefühl*. See note 4.

WORKS CITED

Bammer, Angelika, ed. *Displacements: Cultural Identities in Question*. Bloomington: Indiana University Press, 1994.

Biller, Maxim. *Wenn ich einmal reich und tot bin* [*One day, when I'm rich and dead*]. Köln [Cologne]: Kiepenheuer & Witsch, 1990.

Dische, Irene. *Der Doktor braucht ein Heim* [*The Doctor Needs a Home*]. Trans. Reinhard Kaiser. Frankfurt am Main: Suhrkamp, 1990.

———. *Ein Fremdes Gefühl* [*A Strange Feeling*]. Trans. Reinhard Kaiser. Berlin: Rowohlt, 1993.

———. *Fromme Lügen* [*Pious Lies*]. Trans. Otto Bayer and Monika Elwenspoek. Frankfurt am Main: Eichborn, 1989.

———. *Die intimen Geständnisse des Oliver Weinstock* [*The Intimate Confessions of Oliver Weinstock*]. Trans. Robin Cackett, Reinhard Kaiser, and Bernd Samland. Berlin: Rowohlt, 1994.

———. *The Jewess: Stories from Berlin and New York*. London: Bloomsbury, 1992.

———. *Das zweite Leben des Domenico Scarlatti* [*The Second Life of Domenico Scarlatti*]. Trans. Michael Walter. Berlin: Rowohlt, 1995.

Gilman, Sander and Karen Remmler, eds. *Reemerging Jewish Culture in Germany*. New York: New York University Press, 1995.

Lappin, Elena, ed. *Jewish Voices, German Words*. Trans. Krishna Winston. North Haven,

CT: Catbird Press, 1994.
Seligmann, Rafael. *Mit beschränkter Hoffnung: Juden, Deutsche, Israelis.* Hamburg:
Hoffmann und Campe, 1991.

Chapter 8

Through a Distant Lens:
Cultural Displacement, Connection, and Disconnection in the Writing of Maxim Biller

Linda E. Feldman

As a post-Shoah writer, Maxim Biller faces the task of overcoming the multiple cultural, social, and genealogical ruptures characterizing the lives of children of survivors. Linda E. Feldman shows that paradoxically, this task entails extending existing fissures in the social and literary spheres.

Biller's realization that Germany, as the site of oblivion, can sustain neither Jewish life nor Jewish death results in aesthetic and cultural displacement becoming the writerly precondition for exploring these possibilities. Fiction supplants journalism, the Jewish/Slavic worlds the Germanic, in the search to bridge ruptures left by the past.

Feldman traces the author's use of two topoi of social intercourse—language and sexuality—to show how their connective capacities are used to reestablish ties to the generation of the survivors, to the cultures that shaped them, to the traditions and practices that bind together what Biller terms *amchu* (common people). What serves to connect can also be seen to disconnect, however: the consolidating notion of *amchu* has, as its corollary, a growing sense of disconnectedness to the non-Jewish world, also reflected narratively in the deployment of language and sexuality. At the same time, however, the model of diversity represented to the German readership by the author critiques and erodes monolithic notions of German identity.

A famous Chassidic legend relates how, during the Holocaust, two concentration camp prisoners at the Jankowska road camp—a rabbi and his freethinking friend—survive a midnight selection by miraculously jumping over an impossibly wide pit.[1] Enabling the leap, we learn, are the prisoners' direct or indirect links to the merits of past generations. While this connection to tradition saves the survivors, their offspring are, metaphorically speaking, still in the breach. For the children, the impulse to write represents the will to emerge from the void and reach the vantage point on the other side. In a recent seminal monograph, Thomas Nolden enumerates the particular difficulties and challenges besetting prospective young Jewish writers in Germany: bereft of the usual familial, cultural, intellectual, linguistic, and narrative traditions, these authors lack the wellsprings of continuity from which most young writers draw their initial inspiration and first authority. If a state of rupture can thus be said to constitute the precondition of much literary production in this cohort, then the task of these "third-generation" writers is to overcome the break in continuity, and to find or invent some tradition into which they can place their work.

In this chapter, I shall focus on the writing of one increasingly prominent representative of this group, Maxim Biller, born in 1960. Unlike well-known contemporaries such as Rafael Seligmann, Irene Dische, or historian Michael Wolffsohn, whose progenitors stem from the German-speaking world, Biller, like the majority of Jews living in Germany today, has Eastern European roots. We shall see that this circumstance is critical to his strategies of cultural reconnection, which necessitate initially extending, rather than closing, fissures left by the Holocaust between the writer and his German milieu. Only with the resultant establishment of a creative free space in fictional terrain, can the possibilities of reconnection to the past, and potential rearticulation of Jewish identity in the German present, be explored. In the process, we shall see that in Biller's recent fiction, two forms of social intercourse—language and sexuality—arguably assume a pivotal dual function, mediating connection to and consciousness of *amchu* (common people), while at the same time underscoring the often unbridgeable cleft between the narrator and those on the far side of the void.

THE CASE FOR DISPLACEMENT

Elsewhere in this volume, contributor Sabine Gölz defines the difficulty of publicly assuming Jewish identity in Germany today: to come out Jewishly—that is, to allow readings that associate the individual with the official representative community—is, at its supraindividual, androcentric best, to become a depersonalized signifier rather than an individual signified. In face of this phenomenon, Gölz adduces the possibility for feminine Jewish self-articulation to be virtually non-existent. There is no indication that for Biller the dilemma of self-definition is any less acute, however.

Indeed, it is no accident that Biller has conscientiously cultivated the image of an enfant terrible. His castigation and ridicule of what he perceives to be reactionary German politics and effete culture is equalled only by his repudiation of the ghetto mentality and the spinelessness of those whom he terms Nachmann's Jews.[2] Underlying the aggressiveness of this posture and reinforcing it are his responses to the perceived and real demands of the two very different social topographies—that is, minority Jewish and majority German—through which Biller moves.

On the one hand, Biller must contend with the secular and religious demands of the Jewish community. For the male, there is no guilt-free circumvention of his birthright: his Jewishness manifestly inscribed by circumcision, the son, unlike the daughter, bears the full weight of religious obligations, including saying kaddish for one year for deceased parents, participating in the congregational minyan, or founding a Jewish family and household. Small matter whether the author is observant or not: in a small community, the eyes and ears of the synagogue are watchful, particularly in a phase where religious observance is increasing, and where the *ba'al t'shuva*—the returnee to the faith—is a growing phenomenon. The strength of convention is such that even the most secularized Jews still retain the observance of kaddish and major holidays.

Nor do more secular Jewish communal demands and responsibilities offer respite from prescriptive models of the good son: the heavy-handed politics of Jewish German community leadership, especially vis-à-vis the postwar generations, have already been well documented elsewhere and need no elaboration here. The pressure to not disgrace the Jewish community by attracting adverse commentary from "outside" serves to muzzle criticism in the public arena and inhibits creative freedom by inducing self-censorship, especially if prominence in the wider community imbues an individual with increased representational value. Against this specifically Jewish cultural context, Biller's confrontational stance becomes more comprehensible, a coping strategy with which a buffer can be erected between individual needs for free self-expression and community expectations.[3]

This confrontational stance, moreover, must also be seen as a response to stereotyping processes in the non-Jewish world. To find such stereotyping, we need only turn to the dust jackets and book covers that grace Biller's works. By selecting evocative images and text sorts, the covers seek to construct a subtext that will lure the casual—and by demographic default, non-Jewish—browser into picking up and purchasing Biller's works. What fantasies, one may well wonder, are apparently so compelling in postunification Germany that they might succeed in achieving this goal? A comparison of three works—*Die Tempojahre* (*The Tempo Years*), *Wenn ich einmal reich und tot bin* (*One Day, When I'm Rich and Dead*) and *Land der Väter und Verräter* (*Land of the Fathers and Traitors*)—provides the basis for an answer.

The paperback edition of Biller's first collection of stories, *Wenn ich einmal reich und tot bin*, depicts a strutting child, presumably a portrait of the author as a very young man, jauntily wearing sunglasses while boldly aiming a gun drawn from a cowboy holster. The gun is aimed to the left, with the child's gaze meeting the target head-on. The spirit of aggressive confrontation conveyed by the photo is reinforced by the critical blurbs on the back cover, which, true to cliché, refer to Biller as a German Philip Roth, while extolling a wit capable of striking a raw nerve. Indeed, in a pique of creative conceit, even the doyen of literary critics, Marcel Reich-Ranicki, apparently alludes to the unprecedented nature of the volume when he is quoted as preferring not to say anything about "this type of literature."[4]

However, if the promise of belligerence, pain, and excitement is being actively marketed on the cover, so, too, is Biller's Jewishness. The reference to Philip Roth, with its connotations of Jewishness and American foreignness, is merely an opening move, immediately buttressed by the selection of the Jewish critic Marcel Reich-Ranicki. Furthermore, in order to drive the point home for even the most obtuse, a third critical imprimatur is sought from Michael Wise of *The Jerusalem Post*, a newspaper not usually cited on German dust jackets. Set against this heavily contextualized Jewishness, even an apparently neutral reference to Biller's wit evokes associations with Jewish wit, an ethnological topos with a long and durable history.

Moreover, when we read this textual evocation of Jewish identity against the bravura of the cover photo, a second and highly problematic thematic nexus emerges, namely the vulnerability of the Jew. The prophecy of wealth and death inherent in the title *Wenn ich einmal reich und tot bin* is juxtaposed with an image of childhood strongly suggestive of juniority, vulnerability, and American foreignness. Maxim Biller as a little cowboy evokes laughter but also discomfiture: the threat of the future, thanks to the association of Jewishness with wealth and death, necessarily elides to the past in a grotesque evocation of Holocaust-time-at-OKay-Corral. One may well wonder if consumers are not in fact being asked to interpret the photo as representing defiance in the face of perceived, and perhaps inevitable, victimhood. It is of no consequence to the browser that Biller selected the picture, that the balcony is probably in Prague, or that the person behind the lens is likely a family relative or friend: the chain of evocative associations is too long and too strong to allow a reflected response.

Not restricted to this one volume, the themes of victimhood, provocation, foreignness, and the Holocaust are expressed expansively in other cover art and documentation to Biller's works. On Biller's second release with the Deutscher Taschenbuch Verlag (dtv), *Die Tempojahre*, a stylistically 1930-ish linotype depicts a scene familiar to afficionados of the Weimar period: a chain-smoking reporter with dark, wavy hair and cigarette dangling, looks up from his old upright typewriter at an apparently Asian woman standing defensively in the middle of the room.[5] From the doorway, another man watches. The dynamics of the triangle are not established explicitly, but if the cigarette smoke billowing into the woman's purse is any indicator, a sexual attraction enhanced by difference links the reporter and woman. The campy background suggests an era of decadence and foreshadows an era of disaster. Reinforcing and elaborating the mood, blurb formulae describe Biller as a man "who prefers the [Oriental?] sabre to the light dagger," and praise him as "a talented and angry polemicist" and "possible intellectual grandson of Tucholsky." The comparison with Tucholsky strikes a particularly ominous chord in its evocation of the political circumstances impelling Tucholsky's suicide and in its fatal genealogy, which skips a generation in defining Biller as Tuchosky's intellectual *grandchild*.

For its part, the hardcover edition of *Land der Väter und Verräter* conjures up the sterotypically mysterious ambiance of the ghetto with its blurred, grey-toned depiction of an old iron-wrought lamp in a narrow alleyway. There is little doubt that this is the way of the Golem and the route to the traditional Jewish uncanny. Meanwhile, the back-cover promise of "stories about victims and survivors, conquerors and conquered, Holocaust and Stalinism, Germans and Jews, and other Europeans"[6] reveals a market strategy based on the perpetuation of Jewish and German as central, antithetical, nonoverlapping categories.

In all three works, references to Biller's birth in Prague and arrival in Germany at the age of ten convey a soupçon of his not quite belonging to the society in which he lives and for which he has written most of his adult life. It would seem that in spite of fifty years of postwar history in Germany, Jewishness, in the realm of the popular imaginary, is still as socially exceptional and exotic as it was immediately after the war.[7] As a self-identified Jew, Biller must confront a marketing process that portrays him as a threatening, sexualized, yet vulnerable and victimized Jew—a type, in other words, that is dangerous, but dead. In such a context, a politics of confrontation asserts his vitality, his presence rather than absence, and his determination to fight the mold in which the majority identity would cast him.

The question inevitably arises as to how, in his texts, the author negotiates the coercive inclusion of the Jewish side, and the equally coercive exclusion on the non-Jewish side. Inevitably, the detailing of Jewish identity begins with an evaluation of available models in German society. As an interviewer, Biller's contacts with "Jewish"—and I use the term loosely—intellectuals enumerate and implicitly reject established and traditional paradigms for Jewish life. A critical portrait of the eminent critic Marcel Reich-Ranicki, for example, reveals a man obsessively buried in the world of the aesthetic, incapable of really living in or acknowledging the German world where his body resides: "My homeland is literature" ("Reich-Ranicki,"*TJ* 46). Another Jewish German scion of Reich-Ranicki's generation, the emigré cultural historian Peter Gay of Yale University, is half-cynically, half-pityingly portrayed as a last exponent of apologetic literature for the German-Jewish symbiosis: "Peter Gay can't do anything else . . . he is a man of the dead German-Jewish past" ("Gay," *TJ* 163).

Nor does a move down a generation yield a more favorable portrayal of Jewish German identity. Songwriter and record producer Ralph Siegel, the conversion of whose father to Catholicism is subtly signalled, is portrayed as a superficial, neurotic, harmless, escapist, self-absorbed, and regrettably likable individual, totally disconnected from the major cultural and political vicissitudes of his own generation. Only iconoclastic Elfriede Jelinek fares astonishingly well, especially considering the manifest antifeminist prejudices Biller's narrative persona brings to the interview. Jelinek's vulnerability, unflappable integrity, and consistent maintenance of personal principles in face of Biller's premeditated and ruthless badgering invite Biller's open admiration, a response he reserves for other principled and uncomfortable outsiders discussed in the *Tempojahre*, such as *Zeit* columnist Fritz Raddatz, Czech writer Marek Hlasko, Second German Television producer Georg Stefan Troller, or German writer Werner Riegel. Jelinek's strengths, however, are balanced and offset by the awareness of the author—and interviewer—that in a consumer society preoccu-

pied with Jelinek's controversial image, her writings necessarily remain ineffectual and likely unread. "I can only imagine that people buy my books because
of the allegedly scandalous themes, but don't read them" ("Jelinek," *TJ* 180).

Biller's ability and desire to see past the marketing strategies that have created Elfriede-Jelinek-the-man-eating-feminist are manifestly fuelled by his own
need to circumvent marketing strategies similarly at odds with his own self-
understanding and writerly priorities. In rejecting the models and realities he
perceives in his interview subjects, Biller also chooses to repudiate the termi-
nally cynical and analytical monster, termed Dr. Biller ("Siegel," *TJ* 72, 73, 75,
76), within his breast. To analyze is to not participate: if Germany, as the author
asserts in his early text "Auschwitz sehen und sterben" ("See Auschwitz and
Die"), is the site of oblivion (*TJ* 116) and hence numbing in its incapacity to
tolerate or explicate Jewish life or death, then fiction and a distancing from
Germany become the inescapable vehicle for exploring these possibilities. Israel, America and Eastern Europe, as the heartlands of the Jewish past and present, as topographies of Jewish *life* in its rich variety, become the major sites for
the elaboration of Biller's search for Jewish self-identity. Thus, arriving in Budapest, Biller explains: "Like everyone else in a strange city, I sought nothing
other than a part of my Self" ("Lüge," *TJ* 19). The kaleidoscopic contestation of
multiple cultures, reflecting and deflecting off each other, engenders not just a
dialectical evolution of ethnic identities but also a process of interrogation of the
self. As sites of ongoing self-redefinition, Budapest—like New York, Prague, or
Tel Aviv—provides a portal of entry to the pre-Shoah "land of the fathers."

THE BODY OF HISTORY

Given the acknowledged stylistic brilliance of the author, Biller's depictions
of women are at first glance strikingly vapid, often skirting the realm of the cliché. The story "Hana wartet schon" ("Hana Is Already Waiting"), for example,
resonates with an apparently routinely pornographic display of narrative cunnilingus, while the nurturing, middle-aged wife in "Lurie damals und heute" ("Lurie Then and Now") exemplifies the soft side of the all-embracing Jewish
mother. By way of contrast, in "Aus Dresden ein Brief" ("A Letter from Dresden") the sadomasochistic fantasies of the male narrator structure a tormented
relationship in which the female protagonist is doubly silenced through her
death and the narrator's neurotic compulsion to have the last word. The very
discrepancy between these stereotypically androcentric characterizations and the
otherwise nuanced textuality of Biller's prose leads one to interrogate, rather
than prematurely dismiss, these troubling depictions of women. In fact, as I hope
to demonstrate, women are central to the narrator's wrangling with the angels
and demons of history and identity.

Quintessentially Jewish, the penis's search for (carnal) knowledge mediates
basic differences in its apprehension of Jewish and German women's bodies.
Almost stereotypically, the Jewish woman's body luxuriates in a rich corpu-

lence. Thus, Hana, in the story "Hana wartet schon," is squat, broad-hipped, buxom, and hirsute; yet it is this body, with its vulva exuding a mixed scent of urine and soap, which the narrator desires and consumes in ecstasy. In its refutation of conventional media constructions of female eroticism, Hana's body holds the promise of a vigorous fertility. Cunnilingus becomes an act of appropriation not just of the generic maternal but, more specifically, of the *Jewish* maternal, for within the context of traditional Ashkenazic recyling of the names of the *family* dead, Hana's name comes to signify not just herself but also her contemporary, the narrator's sister, and, reaching back to the time before the Shoah, the narrator's grandmother.[8] Conjoining with Hana is, by implication, tantamount to the predication of familial relationships, as well as to an integration into Jewish temporality, with the three Hanas evoking the Jewish past (the grandmother), present (the sister), and future (the Czech democrat).

Indeed, to read the union with Hana Jewishly, in line with halachic thinking, is to recognize the traditionally prescribed merger of the fractional male with the integral female in the founding of a Jewish household. The perceived immanence of the woman's Jewish identity serves to anchor the extrinsic—and hence more volatile—nature of male Jewish identity.[9] Indeed, interpreted more broadly, the woman signifies the nation, enabling a further reading of the narrator's coupling as his integration into the nation.[10] It is only appropriate that the narrator is drawn to Hana, for, as a leader of pro-democracy forces in the Czech Republic, she represents the same momentum to self-liberation and national redefinition to which the narrator himself aspires.

Reinforcing these aforementioned Jewish inferences and allusions is the deliberate juxtaposition of the couple's sensual pleasures with the celebration of the arrival of the Sabbath, illustrating what Daniel Boyarin observes to be the Jewish capacity to realize the epitome of the spiritual in the flesh. Sexual expressiveness on the Sabbath not only fulfills a religious injunction to observe with maximal joy a holy day perceived to be a harbinger of the pleasures of *olam haba* (the world to come), but also enables the actors to transcend the tawdry shabbiness of their immediate circumstances. It is thus the embodiment of hope for a better future.

Moreover, the woman's body not only reconnects the narrator to Jewish time, the Jewish nation and the messianic future of *olam haba*, but also mediates the lost patrimony of "the fathers." To "know" Hana is, patrilineally speaking, to link diagonally with Hana's reputed forebear, himself a wrangler with Jewish identity and Jewish rupture, namely, Kafka's friend and literary executor, Max Brod.[11] In addition—and more germanely—Hana brings to the narrator her grandfather's legacy, discovered, appropriately enough, in a dusty attic: a menorah, a tallis, tefillin, a yarmulke, shabbes candlesticks and silver kaddish cups.[12] Except for the candlesticks and menorah, Hana's patrimony cannot be used by her, for the cult objects are associated with religious responsibilities incumbent on the man. The objects serve to join Hana and the narrator: they elicit an exchange of family stories, and in their gender-specific uses, evoke the unity of the pair. In explaining and demonstrating the use of these objects as the Sabbath falls, the narrator complements and completes Hana's legacy, just as she does his.

At the same time, as a surrogate grandson, the narrator links himself symbolically to the vanished grandfather, thereby erasing, albeit revealingly, the cultural and psychological void left by the absent—and problematic—generation of fathers/survivors. It is surely no coincidence that in Biller's texts Jewish fathers are frequently depicted as deserters, as passive nonentities, as historical obstructionists, as cultural mediators and translators in the public, but never private, realm. Small wonder, then, that at the hands of such uncommunicative offspring, the grandfather's legacy is suppressed, the lines of direct descent broken. As a consequence, a sharp estrangement defines the relationship of the generation of knowledge-starved grandsons to these culturally dysfunctional fathers, a disconnection compulsively addressed and progressively redressed in Biller's most recent texts.[13]

Perhaps the sense of connectedness to the Jewish woman is most baldly stated by the narrator in "Aus Dresden ein Brief," who concedes, "As I listened to Ida, I felt how that mild, soft sentiment, came over me, which takes hold of me every time I find out that a woman I like is *amchu* " (*LV* 286). But perceptions, as this case demonstrates, deceive: the knowledge that Ida is Jewish is a misapprehension brought about by her own initial pious lies. Tall, slim, blonde, with the pallor of mortality, the aspiring Ida is physically a foil to the fecund, dark type represented by the Jewish woman. Like Hana, she follows a path parallel to that of the narrator, in this case the pursuit of a writing career. However, history intercedes to prevent the complementarity of interests manifest in the case of the Czech democrat and the narrator. Instead, the two authors compete to see whose narrative about the past will first reach the public and establish its authority. Ida prevails, with the narrator still awaiting acceptance of his manuscript by some publishing house. Shaping Ida's text, and in distinction to the narrator's situation, is the overwhelming presence of a monstrous father, whose Mengelesque attributes are capped by his duplicitous espousal of Jewish victimhood and saintliness in the Jewish milieu where he lives and works after the war.

The body of the woman is scarred by history: an incapacity to hear, occasioned by the narrative and physical blows meted out by a father intent on having his version of history prevail, at least in the domesticity of his German household. However, as the narrator shows, it is the spirit of the postwar generation that is more seriously deformed by the past. Ida representatively alternates between victim and accomplice, between acceptance and rejection of her father and his story/history, as well as the fictions of existence ("*eine spiegelverkehrte Marranin*," "a Marrano in reverse" ["Brief," *LV 287*]) he has invented to frame her own life. In persisting in a liaison with Ida, the narrator pursues a bundle of paradoxical motives: revenge on the father/history, liberation of the daughter from the father/history, reformation of the daughter's textuality, and, by extension, her political posture, in the hope their alternative texts will collude in their response to the past. However, even before Ida's ironic death at the hands of two neo-Nazis, it is clear that a long-term commitment—a reframed

German-Jewish symbiosis—is untenable.[14] The juxtaposition of the truth—the revelations about Ida's father and her relationship with him—before coition with Ida results in the postcoital knowledge that the narrator "simply cannot love someone like that" ("Brief," *LV* 294). Instead, the narrator seeks another body with another history and set of prospects: the dusky Frankfurt Jew Ilona, whose belly will soon bear the narrator both a Jewish child and a Jewish future.[15]

Elsewhere in this volume, Diana Orendi points to the relationship of Biller's portrayal of Ida to the contemporary Jewish/Catholic/German/American writer Irene Dische.[16] In patently and violently rejecting Dische's polyvalent model of Marrano existence, the narrator advocates the moral necessity of a dichotomy between Germans and Jews, even unto the third generation.

SPEAKING DIFFERENTLY

If narrative treatment of carnal relations reveals a cleft between German and Jewish, so, too, does another form of social intercourse, namely language. Though writing in German for a German-speaking public, Biller consistently—and increasingly—breaks the monovocality of the German narrative text with the interspersion of other languages. This is especially true of his anthology *Land der Väter und Verräter*. We need only recall, by way of example, the nontranslated Czech phrases in the short story "Ein trauriger Sohn für Pollak" ("A Sad Son for Pollak"), the invention of a Germano-Slavic language by the two fleeing German-Jewish children in "Wie Cramer anständig wurde" ("How Cramer Became Honorable"), the Germanicized-Anglicized Yiddish of the American Liberators in "Mannheimeriana," or the original composition in Czech of the final text of the anthology, "Der Anfang der Geschichte" ("The Beginning of the Story"). What, we must wonder, is the tactical strategy underlying these conspicuous forays into the terrain of linguistic—and hence cultural—dissonance? Indeed, the preceding discussion of the body in history may arouse suspicions that the narrative use of language is linked to the historical problematics of communal identity.

An initial distancing from German culture and the German community occurs in the first selection of Biller's anthology. In the story "Ein trauriger Sohn für Pollak," the Jewish German/Czech narrator interviews a famous Czech intellectual in the hope of discovering the truth behind the termination of his parents' friendship with the man. The sporadic use of Czech phrases at the beginning of the narrative deliberately strikes an alienating chord, particularly since no translation is given. It is clear, however, that in these interchanges, both men are retreating into a world and into a time removed from those of the contemporary reader. In the course of the ensuing discussion, the issue of betrayal is displaced from Germany onto Czechoslovakia and Russia, the time shifts from the Holocaust to Cold War Stalinism, the culpability is transferred from the Czech writer onto the author's father. In this context, the use of the Czech language fatally links the men, underscoring the commonality of a shared historical space and venture. The aggressive defensiveness of Pollak, the narrator, and the defensive aggressiveness of the Czech writer over the twists of betrayal braiding their self-consciously formulated narratives have an unexpected linguistic correlate: in the midst of a heated debate and explosive animosity, both Czech speakers suddenly switch to the German language, a move that patently signals their distance and antagonism.

This reading of the German language as marking a moment of negative distance is reinforced in a subsequent story, "Wie Cramer anständig wurde." This time, two Jewish boys—one of Eastern European, one of German background— are on a transport from Hamburg to a concentration camp in Poland. The desire for comfort and culture leads them to immerse themselves in the reading of the German Jewish boy's patriarchal legacy: a costly first-edition copy of Thomas Mann's novel *Buddenbrooks*. Even their alternate reading of the Hagenstroms cannot prevent their realizing the internal contradictions of humanistic idealism in Mann's depiction of Jews, or the hollowness of humanistic tradition in their current peril. Faced with the brutal behavior and language of SS officer Cramer, they precipitously pull out of the self-described language of *Dichter und Denker* (poets and philosophers), relying instead on a "nonsensical" Germanic creole with Slavic elements. Not surprisingly, the impetus to invent this imaginary language emanates not from the *Ostjüdisch* youngster, but from the outwardly and culturally more assimilated "German" Jew. The reinvention of Yiddish opens up a Jewish space over which the children can exercise some measure of control, even as they face existential peril. A Jewish language, and with it a Jewish articulation of the world, sets, at the very least, a psychological buffer between the two boys and their SS tormenter. As a defensive shield, this linguistic strategem is not impregnable, however, for Cramer, too, can pursue the children into the linguistic realm. Nonetheless, the language continues to serve as a point of opposition and self-assertion, preventing the final degradation of being murdered in and by a language that they fatally considered representative of their lives and values.

As a would-be writer and aspiring literary failure, their captor/destroyer/ author Cramer systematically bankrupts the German language of authenticity and moral stature. The language of the problematic humanistic idealism represented by Mann is transmuted into the market value of a limited edition, while Cramer's own use of the German language reveals it to be the instrument of petty bourgeois self-aggrandizement. In the killing fields of Poland, it can, when accompanied by the gift of the "German" boy's body, curry favor from a commanding officer whom the soldier dispassionately knows to be a sadistic pedophile. In the realm of the imaginary, the German language becomes the vehicle for a modest literary success predicated on Cramer's ability to retell the boys' story as schematically and melodramatically as possible. Either way, the literal and metaphorical disappearance of the boys, and their view of events, is assured. Not just biography but by implication historiography itself is ultimately linked to Cramer's corruptive German. If the boys and/or their narrative are to survive, a linguistic safe haven is required, even if that haven—crypto-Yiddish—is a shadow of its earlier glories.

The Yiddish of "Mannheimeriana," on the other hand, shows that the possibility of self-preservation in that language exists only for those who deserve it. In Italy, arriving Jewish American GI's seek to enfold a figure—the poet Mannheimer—who morally, religiously, and intellectually is no longer capable of such well-meant integration. Mannheimer has crossed the Pale: an opportunistic convert to Catholicism, he has betrayed his sister to the Italian fascists and surrendered her to certain death, only to epitomize her poetically as a symbol of femine perfection in what subsequently—and ironically—becomes widely acclaimed as his masterpiece. The recurrence and inversion of the sister motif present in "Hana wartet schon," when combined with the renunciation of faith, serve to convey Mannheimer's dissociation from the Jewish community and people. Small wonder, then, that he is unable to respond to the cocoon of Anglicized Yiddish with which his liberators seek to welcome and absorb him, for their idiom cannot be his.

BACK TO BEGINNING

"Der Anfang der Geschichte" ("The Beginning of the Story"), at the very end of Biller's anthology, marks the beginning and the illusory end of the narrator's intellectual search for identity. Ensconced in his parents' former apartment in Prague, the journalist son takes moral stock of his life's work up to that point: "I was like somebody who continuously had to justify and prove himself, and in the end, my own people, rather than the Germans, had taken the rap: there it was—the secret of my success" ("Anfang," *LV* 376). Congruent with his dichotomization of Germans and "my own people" is the narrator's retreat from the German language, back to his mother tongue of Czech: "German slipped away from me like the memory of some unromantic, meaningless situation; evidently, the language had never struck roots in me, and I had no strength to struggle for them" ("Anfang," *LV* 368).

Thus, the road to cultural reconnection follows a circuitous route, leading at first into the realm of the imaginary, where suturing of the lacerated roots of Jewish culture and history is achieved by severing ties to the symbolic German father and reconnecting to the symbolic Jewish mother. As a closing shot and opening salvo, "Der Anfang der Geschichte" plays a critical transitional role in reversing this process. The author leads us back out of fictionality by transposing the problematics of the story into the textuality of social reality. Written in Czech, and mediated by an outside translator, this text reproduces the very strategies of linguistic withdrawal articulated from the beginning of the anthology, thus bringing the reader back to "the beginning of the story."

Will the reader follow the tempting fictional cue of separating German from Jewish? Certainly that could be read as one possible behavioral consequence suggested by the models established in Biller's text. And yet this conclusion seems strangely facile, given the circumstance that this anthology is written in German for a German and largely non-Jewish reading public, by an author still living in German and Germany. What is the reader to make of the contradiction between the separation of Germans and Jews predicated by the stories and the bridging status of the anthology as a work in its role of cultural mediation? Would it even be meaningful to write if one believed the "oblivion" of the land was an inalterable given? Unless we are to accuse the author of the crassest cynicism, some other motivation must impel his writing project.

It is significant that in one of his journalistic essays, Biller asserts that the return to public worship at the synagogue is "one way to laugh in the face of the anti-Semites" ("Gay," *TJ* 159). Provocation, by extension, becomes an act of asserting presence where none is publicly desired. Arguably, Biller's writing must be read in light of this notion of the necessity for *public* attestation of vitality. The streams of Russian refuseniks, Czech intellectuals, shtetl villagers, upbeat Frankfurt Zionists, venomous reporters, and even anti-Semites of various stripes streaming across Biller's texts create a vision of Jewish life that refutes the necrological containment of the oblivious centrist eye. Moreover, the polyvocal incursions of Biller's foreign-language usage erode the homogeneity of "German" by superimposing upon it the long-recognized linguistic pluralism typical of Yiddish, itself a function of the influences of many tongues and cultures.

In flaunting what otherwise would have been repressed, forgotten, ignored, or overlooked, Biller has engaged in a politics of confrontation that strikes at the heart of moral, ethical, and historical revisionism, and that seeks to open up new existential spaces for Jewish life in texts as in reality. Moreover, by this act of public testimony, Biller obstructs what might have been an inevitable tendency in postunification Germany to direct moral circumspection away from the Holocaust to victimhood as experienced by former East Germans. Now this elision—and with it, consideration of how the Shoah still affects the relations of postwar generations of Germans and Jews—is no longer possible.

NOTES

1. See "Hovering over the Pit," *Hasidic Tales and Legends of the Holocaust*, ed. Yaffa Eliach (New York: Vintage, 1988), 3–4.

2. See for example "Die Nachmann-Juden," *Die Tempojahre* (München [Munich]: Deutscher Taschenbuch Verlag, 1991), 171–74. A biting indictment of the passivity of the Jewish community, the piece ends with a rallying call for Jews to leave the *Judengasse* (Jews' Street, that is, ghetto) and charge into the worlds of politics, culture and scholarly (*wissenschaftlich*) discourse, and into the vitality that they represent.

3. Public pugnaciousness is scarcely unique to Biller: fellow writer Rafael Seligmann and historian Michael Wolffsohn also demonstrate a proclivity for acerbic confrontation. The relationship between these formulations of a public persona and the pressures exerted by competing community claims merits separate investigation.

4. "Ich möchte mich zu dieser Art von Literatur lieber nicht äußern." See the citation on the back cover of Maxim Biller, *Wenn ich einmal reich und tot bin* (München [Munich]: Deutscher Taschenbuch Verlag, 1993).

5. From the back-cover blurbs on *Die Tempojahre* (München [Munich]: Deutscher Taschenbuch Verlag, 1990?). The lithograph by Jill McElmury dates from 1987.

6. From the back cover blurb of *Land der Väter und Verräter* (Köln [Cologne]: Kiepenheuer & Witsch, 1994). Presumably, the Israelis are also among those to be considered "other Europeans."

7. Jewishness as an abnormal, exceptional status in post-Holocaust Germany was first extensively treated in the late 1970s and early 1980s by Henryk Broder and Lea Fleischmann. See the latter's 1980 book, *Dies ist nicht mein Land: Eine Jüdin verläßt die Bundesrepublik* (München [Munich]: Heyne, 1992).

8. The positive attitude toward union with the Jewish body is reflected, too, in the story "Lurie damals und heute," in which a visiting Israeli academic and survivor is cajoled by a politically suspicious German professor to participate in a round-table discussion on the Holocaust. Distrustful and agitated, Lurie returns to his bed after finally dispelling the unwanted early-morning call. In the meantime, his wife Ella is sitting up in bed, looking "old and beautiful and Jewish" ("Lurie," *LV* 302). As the embodiment of Jewishness, her power of attraction in a moment of high insecurity is intense. Once more, the need to bury himself in the security of the Jewish maternal body overwhelms a narrator, who in this instance is received, childlike, by a wife with open arms whispering, "Come to me, my little one, come on already" ("Lurie," *LV* 302).

9. If Jewishness is extrinsically signified on the male body, it is immanent in the female. Indeed, religious notions of male fractionality and female wholeness underlie the injunction that without a spouse, the male is incomplete.

10. The theme of the nation is thematized explicitly in the author's use of the term *amchu*, referred to elsewhere in this chapter.

11. For a discussion of rupture in Max Brod's generation, see the contributions on Kafka in this volume by Iris M. Bruce and Scott Spector.

12. The stress on the religious rather than secular heritage is no aberration: Biller consistently places religious observance at the core of his understanding of Jewish identity. Indeed, the return to tradition is "the only way to laugh in the face of the anti-Semites" ("Gay," *TJ* 159). Public religious observance not only defies centrist perceptions of or desires for Jewish invisibility, but its more important function is to unify the residual Jewish community from within. Seemingly cajoled into attending Friday night services at the Budapest synagogue, the author confesses: "I had planned it in advance, because for days I'd been thinking, "Where, if not there, can I find what I'm looking for?" ("Lüge," *TJ* 21–22). Nor is this yearning for community disappointed: the faces Biller sees in Budapest belong to Munich, to Haifa, to Tel Aviv, and to Prague as well. Synagogue attendance and religious observance become a mechanism for bonding with what Biller frequently terms *amchu*, his secularized version of the *b'nai Yisroel*: the peace of the Sabbath, in his texts, unites Jews everywhere.

13. Though Biller's journalistic forays paint the paternal generation in bleak tones, there are signs that a slow understanding of and compassion for the psychodynamics of that generation is taking hold. Thus an omniscient narrator marks the end of a long feud between two survivors by having one figure think that "when it comes down to it, everyone wants to make it through somehow and in his own way, and, when looked at from this angle, both of them had acted wrongly and yet correctly" ("Roman," *LV* 275).

14. The story, as biographical and thematic allusions make clear, is in fact a vehement attack on Jewish/Catholic/German/American writer Irene Dische's amphibian sense of identity.

15. The phonetic twinning of Ida/Ilana, in the context of Ida's mimetic identity, points not just to similarity but to intrinsic difference. The linking of the names and the physical attributes of each woman evoke and revoke Celan's juxtaposition of Shulamith and Margarete. Not Jewish death but the beginning of Jewish life is the promise held before the reader.

16. See Diana Orendi, "The New Expatriates," in this volume.

WORKS CITED

Biller, Maxim. "Der Anfang der Geschichte." In *Land der Väter und Verräter (LV)*, 356–78. Köln [Cologne]: Kiepenheuer & Witsch, 1994.

———. "Aus Dresden ein Brief." In *Land der Väter und Verräter*, 281–94. Köln [Cologne]: Kiepenheuer & Witsch, 1994.

———. "Auschwitz sehen und sterben." In *Die Tempojahre (TJ)*, 115–31. München [Munich]: Deutscher Taschenbuch Verlag, 1991.

———. "Die große Budapest-Lüge." In *Die Tempojahre*, 9-22. München [Munich]: Deutscher Taschenbuch Verlag, 1991.

———. "Hana wartet schon." In *Land der Väter und Verräter*, 167–78. Köln [Cologne]: Kiepenheuer & Witsch, 1994.

———. "Hat Gott Humor, Herr Raddatz?" In *Die Tempojahre*, 23–30. München [Munich]: Deutscher Taschenbuch Verlag, 1991.

———. "Kennen Sie einen guten deutschen Witz, Herr Reich-Ranicki?" In *Die Tempojahre*, 44–49. München [Munich]: Deutscher Taschenbuch Verlag, 1991.

———. "Mannheimeriana." In *Land der Väter und Verräter*, 179–214. Köln [Cologne]: Kiepenheuer & Witsch, 1994.

———. "Der perfekte Roman." In *Land der Väter und Verräter*, 229–79. Köln [Cologne]: Kiepenheuer & Witsch, 1994.

———. "Peter Gay: Ein enttäuschter Jecke." In *Die Tempojahre*, 157–63. München [Munich]: Deutscher Taschenbuch Verlag, 1991.

———. "Sind Sie lesbisch, Frau Jelinek?" In *Die Tempojahre*, 178–85. München [Munich]: Deutscher Taschenbuch Verlag, 1991.

———. "Sind Sie noch zu retten, Herr Siegel?" In *Die Tempojahre*, 70–76. München [Munich]: Deutscher Taschenbuch Verlag, 1991.

———. "Ein trauriger Sohn für Pollak." In *Land der Väter und Verräter*, 13–66. Köln [Cologne]: Kiepenheuer & Witsch, 1994.

———. "Wie Cramer anständig wurde." In *Land der Väter und Verräter*, 93–116. Köln [Cologne]: Kiepenheuer & Witsch, 1994.

Boyarin, Daniel. *Carnal Israel: Reading Sex in Talmudic Culture*. Berkeley: University of California Press, 1993.

"Hovering above the Pit." In *Hasidic Legends of the Holocaust*, ed. Yaffa Eliach, 3–4. New York: Vintage, 1988.

Fleischmann, Leah. *Dies ist nicht mein Land: Eine Jüdin verläßt die Bundesrepublik* 1980. Reprint, München [Munich]: Heyne, 1992.

Nolden, Thomas. *Junge jüdische Literatur. Konzentrisches Schreiben in der Gegenwart*. Würzburg: Königshausen & Neumann, 1995.

Part 3

Redrawing Borders: Redefining Jewish Identity

Chapter 9

"My Ears Repeat": Interpretive Supplementarity in Esther Dischereit's Novel *Joëmis Tisch: Eine jüdische Geschichte*

Sabine Gölz

Esther Dischereit's book *Joëmis Tisch: Eine jüdische Geschichte* (*Joëmi's Table: A Jewish Story*)[1] engages the complexities of a Jewish German "identity" through a series of highly unusual narrative strategies. Using deconstructive techniques, contributor Sabine Gölz identifies pivotal elements in the narrator's search to become a Jew after being what she terms an "Unjew" for twenty years. However, it becomes clear that crossing the boundaries of identity harbors its own perils. The narrator's Jewishness emerges as a swiveling positionality, caught between (male) representational identity—the official Jewish community—on the one hand, and the vacuum of un-Jewishness on the other. Moreover, the legacy of the Holocaust, with its perceived imperative to take on a portion of the pain, threatens to overwhelm the narrator's evolving Jewish identity by turning her into a mere signifier of Jewish suffering. By skillfully associating and analyzing key images, Gölz demonstrates how the narrator seeks to circumvent the limitations of what she perceives to be a cultural textuality incapable of expressing her identity. Only by submerging herself beneath the surface of what she terms a Dead Sea of meaning can the narrator discover new possibilities of expressing her identity. A deliberate obfuscation of feminine identities in Dischereit's text—reflected in a confounding of narrative perspectives as well as names and their referents in the "real" world—seeks to assert feminine Jewish identity against the perceived domination of the androcentric ONE-ness of the Jew as signifier.

I am writing this chapter in translation. The sentences I am writing are in English, yet there is a strangely definite sense in which my response to Esther Dischereit's book *Joëmis Tisch: Eine jüdische Geschichte*, is *in German*. In the encounter with Dischereit's text, my customary exile turns into a *writing in translation*. In response to her text, the vector yielded by the conflicting inter-pellations by German, Jewish, and gender identities shifts direction. When I read Kafka or Celan, the vector drives me *away*. When I read Dischereit, it points me back. But this does not result in a simple return to a linguistic or ethnic "home." Even if this text were ever to appear in a German-language version, it would still only do so *in translation* as well. The trace of that distance will not be erased, nor would I want to erase it: if I have a home at all, it is in that trace and in that distance.[2]

BECOMING A JEW

"At the border, I draw a breath of relief. Made it, got through" (Dischereit 35).[3] This sentence appears about one third of the way into Esther Dischereit's novel. For a moment, it seems to suggest that a border could be crossed into safety, to an "other" side, where the breath of relief can be drawn ("*Ich atme auf*"), where the danger has been left behind.

In one sense, Dischereit's whole novel is situated on the "other side" of danger. Just like the author, the protagonist—"Hannah's daughter"—was born after the war. She has not experienced the persecution herself, she has "never been there" ("*bin niemals dort gewesen*" 35). She has, however (or so we gather from the elliptical and fragmentary narrative), grown up in the awareness of "Han-nah's" escape from a transport and her survival of the Nazi persecution in hid-ing, but also with the knowledge that there was a younger sister who failed to escape. She has grown up among the traces that these experiences have left on her mother. Although situated herself on the far side of physical danger, then, the narrator nevertheless continues to be surrounded by the effects of those ex-periences. These traces exert a claim on her that, for most of her life, she has resisted.

The novel begins with a turnabout that acknowledges the failure of that re-sistance: after a twenty-year-long effort to ignore the pull of that past, the nar-rator has decided to turn back to it: "There I sit on this silly swivel chair. After twenty years of Unjew I want to become a Jew again" (Dischereit 9).[4] The nar-rator is situated on a "swivel chair" *between* identities, rather than squarely within one or the other. With the inaugural turn toward "becoming a Jew," she acknowledges that she cannot merely ignore the Jewish part of her heritage and the link to the past that it carries. To be a Non-Jew is not an option for her.[5] The best she can do is become an *Unjew*—someone who is marked by the effort of denial. She may be on the other side of physical danger, but there is still no place for her to "hide" in Germany.

But what does it mean to "become a Jew"? For twenty years, the narrator had been an Unjew—had been trying to un-Jew herself, to put herself at a dis-tance from that legacy. The novel begins with the moment when she reverses direction. But if being an Unjew never was the same as being a Non-Jew, this swiveling into the other direction also does not simply transform her into a

"Jew." Instead, it brings her face to face with a man behind a desk, with a *representative* of the Jewish community. His first reaction to her expressed desire to rejoin is to demand twenty years' worth of back taxes.

The distance that was unattainable in the struggle to get *away* asserts itself instantly with the decision to *return*.

THE PROBLEM OF NAMING

The question of what it could mean to "become" a Jew concerns the relation between *self* and *representation*, between the world of names (and of the communities formed in those names) and an individual subject. The world demands an answer in response to questions such as the one posed casually by an unsuspecting comrade: what is her nationality? The inquiry plunges her into a conflicted and inconclusive search for a *name* that would adequately answer the question: "Neither proudly nor self-confidently, and most certainly not indifferently . . . shall I say German? German one would probably have to say; BUT would then follow . . . what BUT? But Jew. There it is, thick and heavy, the word, which was affixed to the lapel, hung around my neck with cords. These cords are cutting my neck" (Dischereit 9).[6]

The comrade has no idea of the conflict stirred up by his question: "My comrade . . . does not know that. And what is it to him, after all?" (Dischereit 9).[7] How, indeed, is she to name herself? The word "German" is only part of the answer. "One" would probably have to say it, but it is insufficient, it leaves a lacuna that is too significant to ignore. It misses something essential. The word "Jew," on the other hand, does (at least in Germany) much more than answer a question of mere "nationality." It is too heavy, its impact too great. Once such a question has been asked, that word acts as a dead weight around her neck. Spoken or not, it thwarts any attempt to ignore it, or to find a casual and ordinary answer to the "innocent" question.

Nor does the narrator succeed in dodging the issue of "nationality" altogether by joining a community that is differently defined, more generically oppressed—by immersing herself, for example, in the class struggle and becoming "a normal left-winger": "They caught up with me, the dead of history, and let me have my share. I did not want my share, stubbornly I wanted to be a normal left-winger—oppressed in the repertoire of the classes, class struggles, of the rulers and the ruled" (Dischereit 9).[8]

The attempt to immerse herself in the cause of those "oppressed in the repertoire of the classes" fails as well. The vectors of oppression do not all point in the same direction, and a generic union of the *oppressed in general* is not a possibility. This becomes clear in one of the scenes later in the novel, which recounts a regional meeting of the General Trade Union (*Einheitsgewerkschaft*). There, the Jews are voted off the list of those who are to be included in (what the narrator calls) the "ritual enumeration" of "suffering in history" (Dischereit 66).[9] Insofar as the Jews are workers, according to the argument of the assembly's leader, they are to be considered subsumed (*mitgedacht*) under the rubric of Communists and Socialists (66–67). Representation is thus denied with the argument that it is already implicitly granted under a different rubric. If the word "Jew" was too heavy, its impact too great for it to be spoken, the suppression of the word constitutes the opposite problem: a lack of representation that results in an exclusion through simple invisibility. The complete absence of the name *Jude* leaves a lacuna in the order of representation, which is felt only by those who have disappeared into it.

But the alternative to the lacuna—the decision to declare herself a Jew, to perform *in that name* in contemporary Germany, also does not result in a representation of *self*. What happens is actually the inverse: insofar as she tries to "wear" the link to *the dead of the past* which that name imports, she is converted from a signified into a *signifier*. Her connection to the dead inscribes itself in her face and makes *her* represent something which, as a living human being, she does not care to represent: "I am sick of wearing suffering incarnate on my face" (Dischereit 68).[10]

What she needs to be able to live is a connection with the order of representation—a foothold that prevents complete invisibility without, however, turning her into a signifier. She needs a way to mark her presence as a subject, and she needs to find a place for the share she has received, a place that will accommodate what is significant for her without overwhelming her with that significance at the expense of her own life.

"Hannah's daughter" eventually declares herself a singularity that *refuses* itself representation. This declaration is made against the background of the realization that she cannot find herself represented in and by the generalized social entity of "society": "Hanna's daughter is not society, is only one, I,—just as all Jews ultimately were only one" (Dischereit 91).[11] This sensation of being "one" ("*eins*") is the opposite of the sense of being a "representative" part of a community that stands (in the idiomatic expression) *as one man*. Such a singularity has no recourse to community and thus to representation, and its life remains indiscernible to those who still have faith in representation. Unlocatable in the existing repertoire of identities, such a "one" becomes a ghost to the world of names—alive, right here, even embodied, yet somehow unperceived, weightless, silent, and invisible.

The narrator's choice is a reaction to the fact that the "share" she has received from the dead of history remains unrepresentable. That share, that connection, has singled her out, it cannot be deleted from her self-perception and it thwarts her attempts to immerse herself in "society." In response, she herself assumes the position of an unrepresentable singularity—of one, *eins*, I—situated on a swivel chair *between* named identities, none of which she can fully embrace, because, whenever she tries, something crucial goes missing. She breaks with the logic of naming and instead embarks on the process of writing this novel—a text that makes its home, as I will argue, in a space of a self-conscious interpretive supplementarity.

The interpretation of herself as *eins* turns out to establish a link with "all Jews." They, too, were *eins* in this sense. Here we must pay attention to two things: the tense of the verb, and gender. The Jews who were "one" are situated in a *past* temporality: "just as all Jews ultimately *were* only one" ("wie alle Juden letztlich eins nur *waren*" [my emphasis]). What her decision to become a singularity connects her to is precisely the share she has received from the "dead of history." Secondly, the nonnames that "Hannah's daughter" chooses for herself and that bring about that connection with "all Jews" in that past temporality sidestep the opposition between male and female gendering: *eins* is grammatically neuter, while the small Roman numeral "ı" is unmarked in terms of gender. The connection between such singularities, past and present, eludes what is representable to and as "society." Therefore, it cannot form the basis for a community in whose name one could collect taxes.

Indicative of the narrator's characteristic indirectness in relation to names is also her refusal to make the predictable pilgrimage or *hadj* (10) to Israel:

> Hannah's daughter cannot be found on any list of travelers to see the
> Promised Land. Doesn't she want to see her land?
> One land is no land. (Dischereit 102)[12]

One name is no name. "Hannah's daughter" lives in the diaspora of representation. Her decision to "become a Jew" does not lead to the mandatory trip to Israel. Rather, two sections of her text detail journeys to Morocco and Spain respectively, where the narrator explores the contemporary life and the history of the diaspora Jews there. A third section returns us to Hannah's life in postwar Germany.

THE DEAD SEA

The narrator's withdrawal from representation and naming we can find allegorically represented in the following sentence, which erupts as something of a non sequitur at the end of the section that contains the narrator's stated decision not to make that pilgrimage, or *hadj*: "—and the Dead Sea, it buoys. It buoys so wonderfully that nobody can go under. But nevertheless it is dead, and perhaps nobody can live who cannot go under" (Dischereit 10).[13]

The "Dead Sea"—the surface created by the world of names—remains dead as long as we continue to float on it. For life to become possible, we must "go under." That world very quickly ceases to explain anything when it comes to the types of traces that Dischereit's novel sets out to explore. As long as a Jew *is* a Jew, a German *is* a German, and as long as that is the only way we know how to recognize each other, all we do is throw names at each other. Neither our life nor our connection with the dead can be accommodated by that tautological and sterile discourse. The language of names is a Dead Sea in which we have to *go under* in order to find both our connection with the dead *and* a space in which to live.[14]

Nevertheless, it would be very misleading to think that all names are therefore the same—that they have the same properties. For each of us, there are some names that affect us more than others. For the narrator of Dischereit's novel, there is the indifferent and dead surface of names, which means nothing and cannot accommodate her because it leaves out something essential. The word *Jude* is different. It has different properties, it will not float on the surface of that sea, but exerts a force that pulls her "under"—into silence, indirectness, solitude. It is the word that hangs heavy around her neck (see Dischereit 9, quoted earlier). The leaden "weight" that this name (specifically in its German version) has acquired through the historical events associated with it gives it properties that distort the surrounding social and signifying space. Such a word one prefers not to pronounce, prefers not to hear. In the German language especially, its impact is too great, it creates a pause, a hole in the conversation that becomes only more apparent when one tries to cover it up with more words—words that quickly signify nothing but their own helplessness. The trace left by the historical events is that distortion itself, which affects what can or cannot be said without itself becoming representable. That is why the narrator's decision to "become a Jew" is not a decision to settle in her own "land" on the continent of representation, but the choice to *go under*. She decides to cease resisting that pull, and instead to give way to it and explore its implications. The decision to "become a Jew," then, is no act of naming. Rather, it is the moment that initiates the process of *writing* that generates the novel.

With the decision to go under, the perception of names changes. In Dischereit's text, names acquire the properties of *stones*—a metaphor that (for example) in Paul Celan's vocabulary connotes a word that no longer functions as an ordinary signifier but has "stepped out of the mountain" of language.[15] In Dischereit's text, the word "Jew" becomes a *stone* that is hung around her neck, pulling her under.

But this is only one aspect of the shift in her relation to names. On the other side, there is the narrator's experience as an "ordinary left-winger," which has taught her the dialectics of throwing stones—and of being *thrown out* in return. Her decision to "become a Jew" and to go under is also a decision to stop throwing stones: "But this time—this time I don't have a stone in my hand. The stone around my neck the others cannot throw" (Dischereit 54).[16] To take around her neck a name that disrupts the surface of the world of names has not only the consequence that she can no longer name herself, but also that she cannot name others—or be named by them.

Even when made into a project rather than repressed, the name "Jew" does not lead the narrator into representation. It still does not make her the member of a community. Instead, it leads her into a position of singularity and unnameability. But the invisibility of that position differs decisively from that of one who is merely the victim of an exclusion, for by taking the stone around her neck and going under, she has reclaimed her initiative relative to the order of representation. Her invisibility becomes her work.

YOUR EYES

A new relation to the "dead of history" comes about insofar as the narrator is a singularity, *one*, just like the Jews were only *one*. There are moments where this text reaches out and lets the reader *have a share* in this relation, as well. The following passage flashes up into my eyes as I read. It has an impact, it has me participate:

> Your eyes are so big, so black. They would have given you away. Even just because of these eyes. You are a meat, not a child. Your wriggling, chuckling, bursts of laughter stuck into your throat. Loaded onto the car. Not fast enough did you run. You peeked through the crack in this car. The sun flashed in. You wanted to take hold of it. It burned you. And when the car was standing and the motor was still running, you looked at me. I know, I feel your eyes.
>
> We are on no car. Are standing here in a room, with bed and wardrobe, and your eyes, they are looking at the dreidel.
>
> Forty-five years ago, I had a sister. She was as old as you. Who tells me that you are not my sister.
>
> Or the years would not have gone forward at all, but back. (Dischereit 18)[17]

In this passage, the eyes looking into and the eyes looking out of that car, the eyes of a doomed child, of a sister, a mother, a daughter, of the narrator, of the reader, become inseparable. The collapse of the inside-outside distinction happens in a *flash*, it burns, and it reverses the flow of time, because it transports *me* into the past, and *you* into the present, and vice versa. *Who tells me that you are not my sister.* The flash and shock of this moment are almost tactile, and the connection that they establish between the reader and the text (and between past and future) is something altogether different from a relation between names and their referents. It is a moment when I am "touched" by what I read. It reverses time and establishes a link between one who was a singularity *then* and one who, struck by this moment, becomes one *now*. It imparts a share in the past that perforates the sense of relief at being on the other side of danger.

MY EARS REPEAT

The one who is touched in this way, who receives such a share imparted by the dead, becomes a certain kind of reader—what Michel de Certeau calls an "absolute" reader. For such a reader, the practice of reading, the activity of the reader as a desiring and responsive subject, take precedence over any exegesis of what might be "contained" in the text.

The narrative strategies of Dischereit's novel can be interpreted as being not so much as a mode of *narration* than as a particular practice of *reading* and *listening*. For example, there is a passage in the novel where the narrator listens to someone who became a fugitive at the end of the war, whose family left behind a large estate, and who now tells the narrating "I" about the experience of being displaced, of being transported west by train, of having to start a new life. The narrator echoes selected details with variations that translate the retold scenes into the variant in which they would have applied to Jews at the time, and to Hannah in particular:

> "[. . .] and were then loaded onto stock cars."
> My ears repeat: Hannah loaded onto stock cars.
> "I was twelve years old at the time, I have to add. For us at that age there was even a sense of adventure about it."
> She was six years old.
> "Until harsh reality set in and we had to stand in line for food in the camp."
>   . . .
> "The only thing I have not forgotten. It was a beautiful day in May. We had a big dog at home, and it came running after us."
> The sister came running after her . . . and tripped.
> ". . . when we had to get up onto that truck."
>   . . .
> "We had to leave everything behind. [. . .]" (Dischereit 60)[18]

The ears repeat *with a difference* what they hear, and thus the narrative of the other person is continuously supplemented with reminders of the missing story of the sister who did not escape. Twice, however, that already silent commentary is elided completely. Two times, ellipses mark a "nothing" in the text, which requires that we as readers supply something that the narrator cannot or will not put into language: the knowledge of what happened in the camp, or in that truck—". . .". Toward the end of this section, the issue of the *connection* with the past, with what has been lost, is explicitly thematized, first in the nostalgic account of the refugee, then again in the narrator's silent supplementation:

> "You can tell your children a lot about home [*Heimat*]. But the connection is missing all the same."
>   She told me nothing, almost nothing. Oh—if only I had no connection. (Dischereit 34)[19]

Where narration has taken place, then, the connection goes missing. For the narrator, on the other hand, the connection with the past is not established by narration, but on the contrary, by silences and elisions, by the places where something was not told, not talked about, and thus by the very nothing that reasserted itself in her silent commentary. Hannah—she "told me nothing, almost nothing." This *nothing* is the share that the narrator has received, that now drives her repetitions, the share that she imparts to her readers in turn.

HANNAH, META, ESTHER . . .

A reader who relies on the characters' names to identify them will not get very far in reading Dischereit's novel. A number of names appear and reappear in Dischereit's novel, but they seem to have come off the people they would name. The narrator never names herself. Large segments of the book are narrated in the third person, with the central figure not named except indirectly via her mother: she is "Hannah's daughter." There are sections of first-person narration, and if we identify that narrating "I" with "Hannah's daughter," this is already a decision for which we as readers have to take responsibility. Moments like the one cited at the beginning of section four make it clear that sometimes there is more than one "I" in this text, and that the reader's "I" is irreducibly one of them. What produces the cohesion of this narration is not accessible via names. Rather, it is located in the cohesion of a specific *way of reading* as we have traced it in the previous section.

Nevertheless, there is a moment when the "I" does accept a name. She is in an office to make an application, when the man behind the desk confesses a certain bewilderment because the applicant reminds him of a classmate of his, back then, whose name was Ruth Deretz. After this, the application procedure continues, and the applicant's name, address, and so forth are properly inserted into the form. The scene comes to the following conclusion:

> "Well, let me read the whole thing to you one more time, to make sure everything is in order. Mistake in the spelling [literally: in the mode of writing; *Fehler in der Schreibweise*]? I don't understand."
> First rays of sunlight flash through the dusty office window and take hold of a corner of my application. I, Ruth Deretz—I am hungry. (Dischereit 55–56)[20]

A "mistake" or "lack" (*Fehler*) appears in writing when the official reads out the written application to make sure that everything is correct. This *Fehler*, this place where something is missing (*fehlt*), is something the bureaucrat does not understand and cannot read. As if in response to that *Fehler*, the sun flashes into the room, indicating a moment of opening, but also recalling the scene when the sun flashed into that truck. The scene concludes with the one moment when the narrating I names herself by accepting the moment of *mistaken identity* which returns as a lack in writing, and which, as such, remains unreadable to the bureaucrat as a moment of her naming: *I, Ruth Deretz—I am hungry.*

Apart from this moment of naming by means of a *Fehler*, the figures in this book remain in hiding, withdrawing from names. The characters keep changing names, they do not answer to their "proper" names. Names are *changed* by marriage, changed to sound more or less Jewish or German, they are changed to

provide cover in the effort to go into hiding (*untertauchen*). Who was the "real"
Ruth Deretz? Was she the same person as the "Ruth Walter" with whom "Meta,
Heidi, Elke" is said to have left? Or is it even Hannah herself, in a different
guise, speaking to someone to whom she is "Ruth"? ("'Excuse me,' says Ruth,
and Hannah quickly leaves the store." "Hannah-Ruth," "Hannah Walter," see
Dischereit 26–27.) Who is "Meta, Heidi, Elke" (26)? Who is mother, sister,
daughter in this carousel of names, where the persons change their names to hide
in and from a hostile world that persecutes them, but also adopt them, embracing
a mistake to express a relation of affinity ("I, Ruth Deretz")?[21] Names are
adopted when something touches the "I," when relation surfaces or is established by mistake, when an unspoken affinity is confirmed in a flash of sunlight.
But they do not give us access to the person, they do not establish a bureaucrati-
cally legible hold over a living being. Short of such moments, the names are
roles to be played, simulacra that may facilitate rescue by hiding, not by revealing the person: "Her daughter kisses *as Elke* a woman with a hairdo" (see Dischereit 26; my emphasis.). "*As Esther*, she saved her people" (Dischereit 111;
my emphasis.). When she is little, "Hannah's daughter" performs the role of
Esther in a play for Purim: "With dignity she is supposed to approach her king,
serve a beverage without a word, and silently tell her suffering with her eyes.
For she shall forfeit her life if she addresses him—without having been told to
speak" (Dischereit 101).[22]

The role of "Esther," which is played by "Hannah's daughter," and which
cannot leave the novel's author indifferent, since she herself must "walk around
with the allusion" to the story of Esther "for life" (*zeitlebens mit der Anspielung
herumgehen*; Bachmann 4, 239), is the role of a woman who on pain of death is
not allowed to speak except when she is asked to, and who therefore must "silently tell her suffering with her eyes." Her eyes and silences must make themselves felt, they must find a way to touch by means of the *nothing* that reaches
out to *your eyes*, and that gives you your share.

WRITING

When reading subjects cease to invest names with reality, the latter become
inert. The world separates into two: a realm of signifiers, or stones, and a performative realm of live interpretation. What changes is not the signs but our
relation to them. We are reading a novel, a collection of signifiers that have been
arranged in certain ways by a writing self that clearly resists the names she is
offered by the available language and society, but who also is not willing to accept simple invisibility as her fate. *Writing* can accommodate the *Fehler*, it offers a way to combine presence and absence and to straddle oppositions that
otherwise remain unmanageable.

In a passage that reads like a complement to the passage on the Dead Sea, we
encounter the only other appearance of the small Roman numeral, the sign for
that singular self that is "not society," but "*eins,* I." The passage is introduced as

"Example I "—yet there is no "Example II." "Example I" remains singular, a numeral without any enumeration. One count is no count. The example narrates the story of a sailor's disappearance, which, as a whole, is set in quotation marks and framed by a first-person introduction. *Example I* is adduced to introduce You (*Sie*) to the *survival syndrome*: "I will introduce you to it." I cite the section at length, since it is one of the key passages in Dischereit's book:

> Do you know the survival syndrome? No? I will introduce you to it. A pathology you don't come across every day. Example I:
> "(Sailor—through ship's accident)
> One day, he was cut off from the shared content of human life. It happened in one fell swoop, with one slash of the knife, from that day on he stood outside of humanity, he lost his reality, he became a false pretense [*Vorspiegelung falscher Tatsachen*, a simulacrum]. Are these words too strong? Why? Hasn't he been annihilated? Please, examine him once more. There is an unusual flawlessness [*Fehlerlosigkeit*] in his emptiness [*Leerheit*]. It [*Diese*, she/this one] is particularly perfect. Misfortune has raised it [her] to a higher power [*potenziert*], has turned the former sailor into something which is nothing. He has gone under. His going under is a masterpiece. It has been brought about with unheard-of skill and performed on purpose.—Since he is alive, he has not been completely extinguished. He is a remnant that spreads itself between a crutch and a wooden leg. One can form a rune with him, a Hebrew letter. . . ." (Dischereit 33)[23]

The passage describes the condition of one who has "gone under," who, with one slash of the knife, has moved to a place "outside of humanity," who has lost his reality (*Wirklichkeit*), and who has become a fraud, a false pretense, a mere simulacrum. And yet, this disappearance is not a victimization, but a *masterpiece*. It has been "performed on purpose." Disappearance is claimed as *strategy*. Someone in that passage claims the credit of initiative and intention, inviting us to study that emptiness, to investigate it *again*.[24]

This strange creature, this mere remnant, then, can do what the narrator failed to accomplish. Insofar as he is not there, one can turn him—with the help of two prostheses—into a letter that makes Germanic and Hebrew writing coincide: *One can form a rune with him, a Hebrew letter*. The *masterpiece* of going under, the disappearing act by which someone turns from something into nothing—from I into 0?—is possible only in *writing*, and only in such writing can the two crutches on which such a nothing has to walk be made to coincide as *Hebrew runes*: as German-Jewish writing. Only such a *nothing* is capable of spreading itself between two names, between "a crutch and a wooden leg," to straddle a divide that remained unbridgeable for anyone who remained on the surface of the Dead Sea of names.

But how exactly is this feat of bridging the otherwise irreconcilable opposition between those names achieved? Who is that "nothing," the "one" that can form that Hebrew rune with him?

GENDER AND ANTINOMOUS READING

Another dimension at play in this disappearance from the language of names is gender. Only a reading that is also conscious of the dimension of gender can give the requisite force to the critique of representation deployed in Dischereit's novel.

The "sailor" in "Example I" is referred to in the third person masculine: "he." But that masculine gendering is introduced as the marker of a lack and emptiness. The sailor, too, must be read as a non-name, or anti-nome, that marks an empty space on the surface of the Dead Sea, merely reserving a place for something or someone neither named nor represented by the word "he." The "unusual flawlessness [*Fehlerlosigkeit*] in his emptiness [*Leerheit*]" is due to the fact that "[m]isfortune has raised it [her] to a higher power [*potenziert*]." The "one" who can form the crutches into a writing in which German and Hebrew cohere must read itself as *not "he."* Required for bringing about the transformation that turns the pronoun "he" from a representation into a simulacrum is a readerly presence that recognizes the marker of the masculine gender as the point of cohesion between the words "*Jude*" and "*normaler Linker.*"[25]

Dischereit's book explores the survival syndrome of a specifically feminine subject. The communities that the narrator found it impossible to join failed to accommodate her either as a Jew or as a woman, or both, and we will not understand the complexity of the issues she addresses unless we take that second aspect into account. All of the potential identity goals that the narrator takes on as projects and fails to reach are given in the masculine: her project is to become "a Jew"—*Jude*—once she has failed to become "a normal left-winger"—*ein normaler Linker.* The norms that she is offered at every turn, the communities she attempts in vain to join, are always already gendered, and they are gendered in such a way that "she" fails, once more, to find herself represented. This male gendering of "national" and other group identities repeats and doubles the problem of representation or lack thereof that we have studied before: insofar as she considers herself "subsumed" under the male gendered name, she disappears into invisibility. Insofar as she insists on naming herself as feminine, she loses the generalizing effect that the masculine form imparts: the name "woman," too, will not float. It is not a name that the generic subject "one" ("*man*") would use. What remains is the possibility to read herself as unrepresented, to perform the *slash of the knife* that cuts her off from the shared content of human life *in general.* With that slash of the knife, however, *he* loses his reality, since that reality exists only as long as I read myself as *himself.*[26]

The issue of gender takes our considerations to a *higher power*, it forces us to recognize the word "he" as the very name of flotation. By doing so, by practicing an antinomous reading, we turn the Dead Sea as a whole into stone and subtract ourselves from it. This practice can be found among women writers precisely because for "her" the *general* problem of representation, as well as the specific problem of a specific ethnic community, is exacerbated by the cultural role of gender in creating community: *Das Unglück hat sie potenziert*—"Misfortune has raised her to a higher power" (Dischereit 33).[27] The pronoun *sie* in that sentence refers to the feminine deictic *diese* (this one, fem.), which in turn points back to either one of the two feminine nouns *Fehlerlosigkeit* and *Leerheit* (flawlessness, emptiness) in the sentence before that one. Dischereit (as well as I as a reader) thus makes use of the practice—widespread in twentieth century literature—of letting the "nothingness" of grammatical gender take on a life of its own. In the sentence intervening between these nouns and "her" being raised to a higher power, we encounter another point of contact between text and reader, another moment where the reader is *touched* by the deictic power of language: *Diese ist besonders vollkommen* (This one is particularly perfect.). "This one" is either the flawless emptiness of the sailor or it is a feminine readerly presence who has been *potenziert* by the misfortune that haunts any feminine subject in a Western literary space: her inability to find a livable arrangement with representation short of "this one"—the decision to cut herself off with one fell swoop from that which considers itself representative of "humanity."

The survival syndrome is discussed as "his" disappearing act. Yet to be put into effect, "his" going under must be matched by "her" *Potenzierung*. The subject that has disappeared from the world of signifiers returns into language as an unrepresented reader. The order of representation separates, like oil and water, into at least two layers: the layer of the signifier (*he*) and that of a reader who remains unsignified in order to recover the initiative in signification, and thus the ability to make her own sense. The "going under," the purposefully engineered disappearing act, then, does not merely avoid the opposition between Jewish and German. The representational homelessness at issue in Dischereit's book is specifically that of a feminine subject who—short of raising herself to the *higher power* of an "ab-solute" (cut-off) reading—can find no viable way of relating to *his* order of representation.

Potenziertes writing does not form a tradition in the usual sense of the term because it does not rely on signifiers that go from hand to hand, that are handed down. Rather, it relies on the repetition of the flash of self-consciousness and recognition, on the moment of mistaken identity, when *your eyes* become mine, when each of us in turn is *this one*. If such a writing is to be rescued from oblivion, we need to learn how to read it—and we can only learn to read it by becoming part of it.[28]

THE STAR

The section that contains "Example I" is immediately succeeded by the section "at the border" that begins with the sentence I quoted at the outset: "At the border, I draw a breath of relief. Made it, got through" (Dischereit 35).[29] However, the relief is almost instantly supplanted by self-conscious paranoia and terror. The narrator's contemporary reality is doubled by an imaginary repetition/anticipation of the very past that she thought finally to have left behind. At the border, at the moment when identity is checked, a flash of extreme self-consciousness does (does not, yet does) burn a *star* onto her skin: "But if they were to ask me to undress—why should they ask that—if they were to ask me to undress, and I were to undress. And one would see the star, through the clothes—does not see it [him]—burned onto my skin through the clothes—is not burned, have never been there—burned onto my skin, and the dogs would be drawing near" (Dischereit 35).[30] This happens whenever such a crossing of a border is performed: "Always this happens to me when I cross the border, even if I were merely to cross the Rhine into Alsace" (Dischereit 35).[31]

How do we interpret this moment of "inscription," and the "star" that it imprints—or does not imprint—on her body? Is it (as it was read by some during the seminar out of which this volume arose) straightforwardly the return of the repressed—the moment of authentication when the narrator's inescapable Jewishness is finally inscribed on her body?

The star recalls, of course, the yellow star that Jews were forced to wear under Nazi rule (and that Hannah designed to be detachable, see Dischereit 90). But it is also a trace left by a panicked moment of self-consciousness that erupts at the border, under scrutiny, when identity is being checked. This self-consciousness with regard to the moment of identification seems to collapse the difference between then and now, between here and there. And as such, the impetus of the moment is to elude identification: it is directed against the process of checking identities *as such*. Furthermore, "star" is also a translation of the name Esther—of the author's first name as well as of the role played by "Hannah's daughter" for Purim, when, "as Esther," she saves her people. And last but not least, the star is also a frequent cipher for literary canonicity. Yet as such it can function only as long as it remains a distant point of orientation rather than an imprint on one's body. The moment that imprint occurs, we are back in the gendered regime that this book (and this reader) resists: her body is once more claimed as a signifier, while "he" retreats into invisibility ("does not see him" *sieht man ihn nicht*). The violence of that identification/inscription denies the undecidability that is indispensable both for life as a subject and for the life of a literary work. The star "would be" there only if "one" (*man*) would ask the text to undress.

The moment *at the border*, then, is a complex moment in which all of the strands that we have been tracing converge. Here, the breath of relief can be drawn, here the share of the past is imparted, and here the future of the work we have been reading will be decided as it is read, but here, too, it reads us in turn. The moment we cross over, we enjoy the relief of having escaped the gaze that checks identities. But simultaneously with that event, we encounter the sudden awareness that there is no other side to cross over to. Instead of arriving at the "other side of danger," we arrive in the position of what Julia Kristeva calls the position of the "victim/executioner," where the border runs *through* the subject rather than between subjects (Kristeva 34).[32]

On the other side of the border we greet the non-German uniform. To greet the next uniform as though it could guarantee freedom requires—as the narrator self-ironically suggests—a certain blunting of one's critical abilities: "Ganz blöde grüße ich die undeutsche Uniform wie den Vorboten der Freiheit" ("Stupidly, I greet the non-German uniform like the harbinger of freedom"; Dischereit 35). The word *blöde* (silly, dull, stupid) hearkens back to the moment at the very first sentence of the book: "There I sit on this silly [*blöden*] swivel chair. After twenty years of Unjew I want to become a Jew again" (Dischereit 9).[33] The swivel chair and the border are both sites *between* identities, between uniforms, neither of which the narrator ultimately wears. The stupidity (of which probably none of us is free) is located in the act of greeting one as though it could promise delivery from the other. Delivery is needed not by the right uniform, but from uniforms.

The moment of border crossing differs, however, decisively from that initial swiveling. It opens a vertical dimension that simultaneously brings back the panicked memory and claims the freedom of the subject. The mere swiveling between identities remains inconsequential unless it is accompanied by this tearing open of a vertical[34] in a moment of self-consciousness in which each of us registers the complex impact of the force fields of historical and personal memory and of our interpellations by a whole set of names, identities, and uniforms (including the "naturalized" uniform of "the body") in the very same moment that, with one slash of the knife, we sever ourselves from the world of signifiers and reclaim our initiative as readers and subjects.

POSTSCRIPT

Yet there is an "other" side to this border, nevertheless. Self-consciousness erupts on the side of the one who becomes "text" to be read by the gaze that scans for signs of identity (Is the star there or is it not there? What shines brighter—its presence or its absence?).[35] But the same may happen on the side of a reader hesitant to be dressed up in the uniform of those who do the checking at that border, a reader hesitant to ask the text to "undress" and to deliver itself in its naked essence. In order to ask the text to undress, the reader must dress. Only in a world of uniforms and bureaucrats can the marks of identity be inscribed on the body. Those marks become undecidable again in the opening of the "vertical"—in the intervention or the "going under" of a subject at home in its singularity.

We can ask no proof from this textual moment—not the proof that the writing subject has truly received the imprint of the yellow star, nor that she will truly escape from *them*. Rather, the moment I insist on such proof, I become one of *them*. To avoid that, I have only one choice: to take in the border myself, and to ask for no other proof than the one whose burden I bear myself. In a world where meaning is an event, we must each receive our share of the past and supplement what we read—but *without* inscribing identities on each other's bodies. We must relate to each other not as names and identities, but as unrepresentable singularities. That is the only way to keep the border open.

I swivel around in order to face the task—after twenty years of being Un-German—of becoming German again. German without a uniform—German in translation. As it borders on the English language, the little Roman numeral reads as a first person pronoun: I. *Who tells me that you are not my sister?*

NOTES

1. Esther Dischereit, *Joëmis Tisch: Eine jüdische Geschichte* (Frankfurt: Suhrkamp, 1988). References will be to the German edition. Translations are my own.

2. For a text that is in a sense a companion piece to the present one, see my "How Ethnic Am I?" *PMLA* 113 (Jan. 1998): 46–51.

3. "Ich atme auf an der Grenze. Geschafft, durchgekommen."

4. "Da sitze ich auf diesem blöden Drehstuhl. Nach zwanzig Jahren Unjude will ich wieder Jude werden."

5. The helpful suggestion to clarify the implications of Dischereit's word "Unjew" ("*Unjude*") by juxtaposing to it the word "Non-Jew" I owe to the editors of this volume, Linda E. Feldman and Diana Orendi.

6. "Weder stolz noch selbstbewußt, gleichgültig schon gar nicht . . . soll ich Deutsche sagen? Deutsch müßte man wohl sagen, ABER käme dann . . . was ABER? Aber Jude. Da steht es dick und schwer, das Wort, das ans Revers geheftet war, mit Kordeln um den Hals mir hing. Diese Kordeln schneiden mir den Hals."

7. "Mein Mitgenosse . . . weiß das nicht. Was soll er auch damit?"

8. "Sie holten mich ein, die Toten der Geschichte, und ließen mich teilhaben. Ich wollte nicht teilhaben, partout ein normaler Linker sein—unterdrückt im Repertoire der Klassen, Klassenkämpfe, der Herrscher und Beherrschten."

9. "rituelle . . . Aufzählungen" "[der] Leiden der Geschichte."

10. "Ich habe es satt, das inkarnierte Leiden im Gesicht zu tragen."

11. "Hannahs Tochter ist nicht die Gesellschaft, ist nur eins, I,—wie alle Juden letztlich eins nur waren."

12. "Hannahs Tochter steht auf keiner Reiseliste, nur einmal das Gelobte Land zu sehen. Will sie ihr Land nicht sehen? Ein Land ist kein Land."

13. "—und das Tote Meer, es trägt. Es trägt so wunderbar, daß niemand untergehen kann. Aber trotzdem ist es tot, und vielleicht kann niemand leben, der nicht untergehen kann."

14. Ingeborg Bachmann's sentences about reading without relying on names applies to Dischereit's novel as well (4:252): "[W]ir sollen die Figuren ja gar nicht an ihren Namen erkennen. Die Namen muten wie Fallen an. Sondern erkennen sollen wir sie an etwa ganz anderem. An einem Flor, der jede Person umgibt, an einer in sehr zarten Stimmungen bezeichneten Konstellation, in der sie stehen." ("We are not supposed to recognize the figures by their names. The names seem like traps. But we are to recognize them by something entirely different. By a halo which surrounds each person, a constellation in which they stand, and which is indicated by very tender moods.")

15. See for example Paul Celan's poem "Was geschah?" (1:269).

16. "Aber diesmal—diesmal habe ich keinen Stein in der Hand. Den Stein um meinen Hals können die anderen nicht werfen."

17.
> "Deine Augen sind so groß, so schwarz. Sie hätten dich verraten.
> Allein schon wegen dieser Augen. Du bist ein Fleisch, kein Kind.

Dein Zappeln, Prusten, Lachen dir in den Hals gesteckt. Verladen auf den Wagen. Nicht schnell genug bist du gelaufen. Durch den Spalt in diesen Wagen hast du geguckt. Die Sonne hat hineingeblitzt. Du wolltest nach ihr greifen. Da hat sie dich verbrannt. Und als das Auto stand und trotzdem noch der Motor lief, hast du mich angeguckt. Ich weiß es, spüre deine Augen.

Wir sind auf keinem Wagen nicht. Stehen hier in einem Zimmer, mit Bett und Schrank, und deine Augen, die schauen auf den Dreidel.

Vor fünfundvierzig Jahren—da hatt ich eine Schwester. Die war so alt wie du. Wer sagt mir denn, daß du nicht meine Schwester bist.

Oder die Jahre wären gar nicht vor-, sondern zurückgegangen."

18.
" '[. . .] und wurden dann in Viehwaggons eingeladen.'

Meine Ohren repetieren: Hannah in Viehwaggons eingeladen.

'Ich war damals zwölf Jahre alt, muß ich dazu sagen. Für uns war in diesem Alter sogar ein bißchen Abenteuer dabei.'

Sie war sechs Jahre alt.

'Bis dann die rauhe Wirklichkeit kam und wir anstehen mußten um Essen im Lager.'

. . .

'Das einzige, was ich nicht vergessen habe. Es war ein wunderschöner Maientag. Wir hatten einen großen Hund zu Hause, der lief uns nach.'

Die Schwester ist ihr nachgelaufen . . . und dabei gestolpert.

'. . . als wir auf diesen Lastwagen raufmußten.' . . .

. . . .

'Wir mußten alles dalassen . [. . .]'"

19. "'Man kann den Kindern von der Heimat viel erzählen. Aber die Beziehung, die fehlt doch.'

Sie hat nichts, fast nichts erzählt. Ach—fehlte mir doch die Beziehung."

20. 'So, ich lese Ihnen das Ganze noch einmal vor, damit auch alles stimmt. *Fehler* in der Schreibweise? Versteh' ich nicht' [my emphasis].

Erste Sonnenstrahlen blitzen durch das verstaubte Bürofenster und erfassen eine Ecke meines Antrags. Ich, Ruth Deretz—ich habe Hunger.

21. For a discussion of the issues of names and authorship in the writings of German Jewish women writers, see also Hahn.

22. "Würdig soll sie sich ihrem König nähern, sprachlos ein Getränk servieren und stumm ihr Leiden mit den Augen forterzählen. Denn des Todes soll sie sein, spricht sie ihn an—ohne dazu aufgefordert zu sein."

23.
"Kennen Sie das Überlebenssyndrom? Nein? Ich werde es Ihnen vorstellen. Eine nicht alltägliche Pathologie. Beispiel I:

'(Matrose—durch Schiffsunfall)

Eines Tages wurde er von dem gemeinsamen Lebensinhalt der Menschen losgelöst. Es geschah in Bausch und Bogen, mit einem Messerschnitt, von dem Tag an hat er außerhalb der Menschheit gestanden, er verlor seine Wirklichkeit, er wurde eine Vorspiegelung falscher Tatsachen. Sind das zu starke Worte? Wieso—ist er nicht

vernichtet? Bitte, untersucht ihn noch einmal. Es ist eine
ungewöhnliche Fehlerlosigkeit in seiner Leerheit. Diese ist besonders
vollkommen. Das Unglück hat sie potenziert, hat den früheren Ma-
trosen zu etwas gemacht, was nichts ist. Er ging unter. Sein Untergang ist ein Meisterwerk. Er ist unerhört gut bewerkstelligt und mit
Absicht ausgeführt. —Da er lebt, ist er doch nicht ganz ausgelöscht.
Er ist ein Rest, der sich mit einem Stelzfuß und einer Krücke
ausspreizt. Man kann mit ihm eine Rune bilden, einen hebräischen
Buchstaben.'"

24. For a discussion of the strategic disappearance of the object, which turns representation into a simulacrum, see also Baudrillard (for example, 86).

25. For a discussion of woman as antinomous, see Meyer 103.

26. For a more detailed discussion of the crucial role that the willingness of readers to
read themselves as "himself" plays in establishing a "connection" between the scenes of
writing and reading, see chapters two and five of my forthcoming *The Split Scene of
Reading: Nietzsche/Derrida/Kafka/Bachmann.*

27. The word *potenziert* recalls, of course, the famous definition of Friedrich
Schlegel's "Romantic Poetry" in his 116th *Athenäums Fragment* (1:205): "Und doch
kann auch sie am meisten zwischen dem Dargestellten und dem Darstellenden . . . auf
den Flügeln der poetischen Reflexion in der Mitte schweben, diese Reflexion immer
wieder potenzieren und wie in einer endlosen Reihe von Spiegeln vervielfachen. Sie ist
der höchsten und der allseitigsten Bildung fähig—nicht bloß von innen heraus, sondern
auch von außen hinein—, indem sie jedem, was ein Ganzes in ihren Produkten sein soll,
alle Teile ähnlich organisiert, wodurch ihr die Aussicht auf eine grenzenlos wachsende
Klassizität eröffnet wird. . . . Andre Dichtarten sind fertig und können nun vollständig
zergliedert werden. Die romantische Dichtart ist noch im Werden; ja das ist ihr eigentli-
ches Wesen, daß sie ewig nur werden, nie vollendet sein kann."

28. Her positioning as a subject who has been *potenziert* marks a point of contact
between Dischereit's poetic strategies and those of Ingeborg Bachmann. Bachmann, too,
constructs her texts around an unrepresented, "unnameable" subject in a similar double
move of "going under" and "raising to a higher power." Her disappearing act, too, is
motivated by the desire for a position of subjecthood, which for her remains unattainable
within the given symbolic order, and by a refusal to efface the difference between herself
and the male subject whose absent presence forms the heart of that order. Bachmann, too,
is not willing to consider herself simply *mitgedacht* (subsumed) under the masculine
pronoun, and she, too, is aware that the decision to embrace the feminine gender in representation thwarts her ability to achieve accreditation as a subject. Bachmann, too, frequently uses the masculine as an antinomous name, a mere placeholder. The change
called for by this strategy is a change in how we read. The *Potenzierung* will only have
happened if the erasure of the name is reenacted in and by reading. Then, however, she
can use the third person masculine to not name herself, but rather to speak about her inability to give herself a name. What unites Bachmann and Dischereit is the use of the
male gender as a means for turning the very sentence in which the possibility of representation is negated into an example of what it speaks about. The moment a *potenziertes*
subject constitutes itself as such and in relation to such an example, a mode of access to
language has been established that differs decisively from representation. Take, for instance, the moment when Bachmann (at the beginning of her "Frankfurt Lectures on Po-
etics") says (4:184): "Nur das Stichwort fehlt für den, der im Augenblick selbst vorzu-
treten hat und alle die Werke, die Zeiten, hinter sich liegen fühlt." ("Yet the keyword is
missing for him who at the moment has to step on the scene and who feels that he is

leaving all the works, the times, behind."). Here, too, we can observe the separation between the past temporality of the representational order—the works, the times—and the performative of the "moment" when a woman steps on the scene as reader and finds herself in the position for which the keyword (*Stichwort*, literally: stab-word) is missing: in the position of the performer—the speaker or reader—rather than the named or signified. The strategy of antinomous naming is a way of reclaiming initiative from such a position of exclusion. It is the strategy of those who cease reading themselves as victims.

Insofar as Dischereit employs this strategy just as consciously as Bachmann, we can place them both in an emerging tradition of a writing by women who find remarkably similar solutions to the problem of how to survive the representational order in which they find themselves, an order centered on creating the conditions of possibility of a male subject. Relative to that order, these women writers embrace the flawless unrepresentability of the nothing, which forms signs without being signified by them, and where writer and reader can succeed each other without losing the consciousness of their singularity.

29. "Ich atme auf an der Grenze. Geschafft, durchgekommen."

30. "Aber wenn sie verlangten, ich solle mich ausziehen—warum sollen sie das verlangen—wenn sie verlangten, ich solle mich ausziehen, und ich zöge mich aus. Und man sähe den Stern, durch die Kleider hindurch—sieht man ihn nicht—durch die Kleider hindurch auf meine Haut gebrannt—ist nicht gebrannt, bin niemals dort gewesen—auf meine Haut gebrannt, und die Hunde kämen heran."

31. "Immer geht mir das so beim Grenzübertritt, und führe ich bloß über den Rhein ins Elsaß."

32. "This process could be summarized as an interiorization of the founding separation of the sociosymbolic contract, as an introduction of its cutting edge into the very interior of every identity whether subjective, sexual, ideological, or so forth. This happens in such a way that the habitual and increasingly explicit attempt to fabricate a scapegoat victim as foundress of a society or a countersociety may be replaced by the analysis of the potentialities of victim/executioner which characterize each identity, each subject, each sex."

33. "Da sitze ich auf diesem blöden Drehstuhl. Nach zwanzig Jahren Unjude will ich wieder Jude werden."

34. Bachmann 4:195: "Es gibt in der Kunst keinen Fortschritt in der Horizontale, sondern nur das immer neue Aufreißen einer Vertikale."

35. See Dischereit 90: "Der fehlende Stern beginnt zu leuchten."

WORKS CITED

Bachmann, Ingeborg. *Werke*. Ed. Christine Koschel, Inge von Weidenbaum, and Clemens Münster. 4 vols. München [Munich]: Piper, 1982.

Baudrillard, Jean. *Fatal Strategies*. Trans. Philip Beitchman and W. G. J. Niesluchowski. New York: Semiotext(e), 1990.

Celan, Paul. *Gesammelte Werke in fünf Bänden* [*Collected Works in five volumes*]. Ed. Beda Allemann and Stefan Reichert. Frankfurt: Suhrkamp, 1986.

Certeau, Michel de. "The Absolute Reading: A Practice of Texts." Trans. Victor Aboulaffia. Typescript.

Dischereit, Esther. *Joëmis Tisch: Eine jüdische Geschichte*. Frankfurt am Main: Suhrkamp, 1988.

Hahn, Barbara. *Unter falschem Namen: Von der schwierigen Autorschaft der Frauen.* Frankfurt am Main: Suhrkamp, 1991.

Kristeva, Julia. "Women's Time." *Signs: Journal of Women in Culture and Society* 7, 1 (1981): 13–35.

Meyer, Eva. *Zählen und Erzählen: Für eine Semiotik des Weiblichen.* Wien [Vienna]: Medusa, 1983.

Schlegel, Friedrich. *Werke in zwei Bänden.* Berlin: Aufbau, 1980.

Chapter 10

Zapping Jews, Zapping Turks: Microchip Murder and Identity Slippage in a Neo-Nazi Hate Game

Linda E. Feldman

The growing popularization of the computer in the late 1980s inevitably led to the adoption of the new medium by all political shadings, including the far right. In this chapter, Linda E. Feldman examines KZ Manager, a freeware neo-Nazi game that postulates the Holocaust of the Turks in 1944. Circulated in Austria and Germany in 1988, the game offers little excitement in terms of action, sound, or graphics. Feldman argues that the allure of the game necessarily lies with its appeal to player fantasies.

An examination of the structure of KZ Manager reveals that deliberate slippage underlies the construction of space, place, time, and character in the game. Thus, traditional discourses on the Jews here signify the Turks, the referentiality of 1944 reaches into the future as well as into the past, and the location of Treblinka/Treplinka points to events past, future, or nonexistent. In addition, the game constructs its player ego in similarly slippery terms. Though male, the player's sexuality, ideology and class affiliation are deliberately left open.

Feldman argues that as a consequence of the postmodern polyvalence underlying the construction of the game, historical knowledge becomes an act of arbitrary interpretation by a weak and decentered Self. The dissolution of historical facticity through this revisionist psychodynamic ultimately places into question the possibility of moral accountability.

In 1988, a neo-Nazi computer game entitled KZ Manager began to circulate as freeware in Austria and West Germany.[1] The appearance of the German-made computer game, according to the Simon Wiesenthal Center of Los Angeles, was scarcely anomalous, for survey results indicated that in both countries an estimated 20 percent of all youth aged 18 or younger had previously used similar racist materials. Indeed, almost 40 percent of young people were aware of the existence of such hate-mongering games.[2]

According to published reports, interviewed youths attested to their satisfaction with KZ Manager. While conceding that a prohibition against hate games enhanced their appeal, one eighteen-year-old high school interviewee went on record as saying that the game was "exciting," and had been copied not only by his classmates but even by his father, who played it during breaks or slow periods at work. Given KZ Manager's rather primitive graphics and lack of animation and fast-moving action, this positive response is at first surprising. A bookkeeping simulation that is only occasionally interspersed with snippets of racist and scatological "humor," the game provides screen images far more closely resembling the accountant's record book than the rock video frame.

KZ Manager, then, despite its computerized environment, is at first glance scarcely representative of media theorist Derrick De Kerckhove's vision of a postmodern and postliterate electronic aesthetic, in which the viewer's body and physical responses to advanced media act as the first, and often only, arbiter of the scanning contents of the screen.[3] No anarchic sensuality, multimedia bombardment, or psychedelic imagery characterizes this computerized simulation. Rather, the scrolling and often stodgy linearity of the written text, with its disciplining of the viewer's mind and body to the confining possibilities of the simple preset script, would seem to hearken back to the pre-postmodern reading behavior of an earlier generation. If user satisfaction is somehow nonetheless procured, then it follows that the scripting, rather than the imaging or presentation, of KZ Manager in some way responds to and/or evokes user fantasies. The remarks that follow, then, represent an attempted meditation on the nature of these fantasies and their textualization in the game. In the process, I will argue that ontological and epistemological slippage, as manifested in the construction of sliding concepts of identity and alterity in KZ Manager, and as reflected in the game's striking spatial, chronological, and linguistic elisions, constitute a deliberate and consistent strategy that serves, appropriately enough, to give subjectivity, and with it memory, facticity, and moral accountability, the slip. But before embarking on a more detailed discussion of individual structural elements in the game's polyvalent script, it might be useful to review the broad outline of the game, as seen from the player's point of view.

KZ Manager begins as a programmed film-cum-slide presentation. After an up-beat musical interlude and sundry greetings and antigreetings,[4] a black-and-white banner in English identifies the Missionaris—misspelled—as the producers and advertises the upcoming release of an English-language version of the game. Following a predetermined interval, the screen clears and is replaced by a largely orange-and-black frame, ostensibly depicting Treblinka concentration camp, and naming additional sponsors of the game (Fig. 10.1).

The Treblinka graphic is subsequently replaced by an image of the West German flag, followed by a Nazi banner. The next sequence of frames administers what could be termed an Aryan test, explicitly designed to assess the player's political and racial reliability. Whoever survives this selection process

Fig. 10.1
Depicts the Gothic topography of Treblinka in KZ Manager

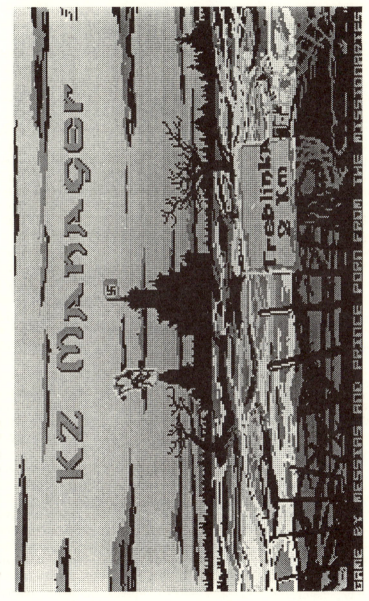

proceeds on to the game itself. The politically and/or racially ineligible, on the other hand, are confronted with a purloined icon of the grim reaper announcing that the would-be players are parasites who will shortly be dispatched to Buchenwald and Treblinka. Finally, after displaying an adapted version of Himmler's 1943 speech in Poznan calling on German troops not to let moral scruples interfere with the eugenic imperatives of genocide, the screen states the objectives of the game as follows—and I quote—"Your task is to eliminate all parasites by the end of the war. You begin in 1944 and have exactly 300 days in which to complete your task."[5]

At this point, a menu-driven accounting phase ensues, which presents the players with such options as buying and gassing victims; purchasing crematoria, gas, and gas chambers; burning corpses; dispatching slave labor to labor camps; and profiting from the sale of looted articles. Promotions within the camp hierarchy are linked to the player's murderous success, which is ensured by censorious or laudatory feedback from the game's sponsors. As a sign of extreme favor, for example, "excellence" is rewarded with congratulatory messages delivered by Hitler personally.

CONSTRUCTING TURKISH DIFFERENCE

Describing KZ Manager to its Viennese readers, the newspaper *AZ* notes that the objective of the game is to discover "how many Jews have to be gassed daily in order to achieve the quota,"[6] while another Austrian paper, *Die Presse*, states that the aim is "to build as many gas chambers as possible and to gas as many Jews and Turks as possible."[7] But these journalistic summations underscore the conundrum of the game: 1944 though it may be, it is not the Jews but rather the Turks who are the primary object of KZ Manager's explicit annihilatory intentions. How and why, one may well wonder, could the reporters have failed to observe that Jews are not the explicit targets of the game? The answer, as we shall see, lies in the scripting of the Turk as Other—as Jew, as sexual deviant, as proletarian, as nonhuman, a process that begins with the selection procedure preceding the game proper and continues through to the Himmler excerpt initializing the game.

Far from being a diversionary adjunct, the introductory Aryan test is crucial in establishing the identity and power parameters that govern the game. Indeed, the questionnaire sets in place a model of Turkish alterity, or Otherness, which is subsequently contrasted in the game with the identity of the envisaged player, whom I shall term the ludor Self. As a means of ensuring that potential players adopt the desired construction of Turkishness, the questionnaire utilizes a multiple-choice format. Respondents must accept as a consequence basic premises on the nature of Turkish identity or else forfeit their chance to "play" and "win." All but one of these premises contribute to the formation of a highly negative connotational complex for Turks and Turkishness.

The first question of the test, for example, asks where one finds Turks—on discarded park benches, under manhole covers, at the bottom of garbage heaps, in the whorehouse, at the social welfare office, or in the concentration camp. Implied in these "choices" are the presumed penury and rootlessness of the park bench occupant, the filth of the sewage conduit or garbage dump and its slithery scavengers, the sexual and moral depravity of bawdy house transactors, and the parasitism of the welfare recipient. As portrayed in these answers—all of which are considered to be "correct" by the program—the social milieu of the Turks constitutes a threateningly dirty, dissolute, degenerate, and destitute Pale, reflective of the middle-class prejudices and, above all, middle-class anxieties of the auctorial interlocutor. The reference to the concentration camp, at this point, functions as an auctorial promissory note, a soon-to-be-realized consequence of the social transgressiveness believed to be inherent in the perceived alterity of the Turks. At the same time, the reference to the camp is more than an anticipatory promise: it is a signpost pointed toward the past and the terrible punition of the Jews, and explicitly eliding the identity of the two minorities.[8]

The second question, for its part, endeavors to establish difference as being the constitutive element of the Turkish body and its daily activities. How, the question asks, does one recognize Turks? The alternative responses include: by their smell (cumin), by their appearance (rags), by their accommodation (overflowing garbage containers), by their foods (garbage), by their wealth, and, finally, by their chic clothing. The inherent assumption that existential difference imprints the body in physically discernible ways is striking. The true German body, in other words, recognizes the Other instantly and instinctively; the body of the Turkish Other is marked with the signs and sights and, above all, the smell of its alterity.

For the auctorial interlocutor, the scent of danger literally and figuratively hangs in the air: reminiscent of garlic in the case of the Jews, Turkish cumin threatens the auctorial centrist ego, simultaneously underscoring both Turkish difference (the perception of cumin as an Oriental spice) and, most dangerously, Turkish similarity (the outward similarity of "Turkish" cumin and "German" caraway). The implication is that the resemblance of the two seasonings must be offset necessarily by an insistence on underlying innate difference. As in the case of the Jews, stereotypical difference serves as the mechanism to define, and abject, a minority perceived to be non-German.

The hypothetical wealth and chic clothing of the Turks referred to in the final two alternatives, as the earlier reference to rags in option 2 makes clear, mark a deliberate inversion of the perceived and actual socioeconomic status of Turkish workers and their families, reflecting not just middle-class contempt of the working poor but also apprehension lest this situation change in the future. Will the Turks, the game seems to be asking and/or suggesting, at some point acquire wealth and thereby become Germany's new Jews? Will they, too, otherwise become indistinguishable to the nondiscerning eye?

The final question seeks to identify Turks as gypsylike beings existing outside the law and Christian propriety. Which cheerful, colorful people, the question inquires, makes toys for good little children on Christmas eve? This time, players choose from only two possible responses, one of which is blatantly inappropriate: the seven dwarfs or illegal *Gastarbeiter* (foreign workers). Castigated as rootless aliens in the implied comparison with the Sinti, the Turks are now shown to be desecrators of one of the holiest days of Christendom, ironically purveying and controlling the spirit of the most elaborately observed holiday in Germany with their production of toys for the guileless young. This presentation of Turks as non-Christian defilers of Christmas holidays and as economic lawbreakers thus seeks to criminalize as well as damn them.[9]

Striking in these proffered responses is the survival and transfer of residual discourses on the Jews. Indeed, a straight line links medieval and modern anti-Semitic theories to KZ Manager's construction of Turkish Otherness. In the second question, for example, the construction of Turkish physical difference, with its emphasis on olfactory distinctiveness, derives from the theologically postulated *foetor judaicus* of the Middle Ages, which attributed to Jews an evil stench as a sign of their bedevilment. Nor, as Sander Gilman has demonstrated, did this belief in a special smell die with the onslaught of the modern era: reformulations and elaborations in 19th- and 20th-century racial theory on Jews led to the incorporation of smell as a distinctive Jewish marker in Nazi racial theory.[10] For its part, the third question revives and revises a medieval discourse on religious difference, which posits a cosmological dichotomy between the innocent Christian, here represented by the believing children, and the diabolical non-believer, as represented by the profiteering Turkish desecrators of the faith. In addition, in the first question turn-of-the-century sociobiological theories of criminality and social Darwinism tinge the depiction of the Turks as potentially dangerous, antisocial elements.

The familiarity of these various clichés, when combined with graphics incorporating the most noteworthy features of the *Stürmer* Jew—the pronounced nose, hunched posture, bowed legs, small stature, and innate ugliness—serves to present today's Turks as yesterday's Jews, rekindling the racist hypothesis that, as perceived Semites, Turks and Jews share a common biological heritage, here reflected in their comparable physiognomies.[11] Small wonder, then, that the Austrian journalists, confronted with a familiar construction of existential alterity adapted from Nazi propaganda, failed to notice the little difference of ethnicity, or, as we shall see later, its big implications.

THE CONSTRUCTION OF THE LUDOR SELF

Lest the elisions of these portrayals seem fortuitous, an examination of the strategies underlying the identity markers of the centrist authority of the game, the ludor Self, provides a useful basis for comparison. The first marker provided by the game is that of a masculinist sexual orientation. The homophobic anti-greetings in the film-cum-slide show preceding the game seek to enforce heterosexuality. Indeed, as the reference to AIDS ("[Y]ou are dead?") makes clear, deviation from the perceived sexual norm marks the realm of fatal disease. Furthermore, the ludor Self, as indicated by the exclusively masculine forms given to the various roles held by the player throughout the game, is clearly male. Indeed, there is no space for women in the world of KZ Manager, be it as saints or sinners, as "white" women or "red."[12] This gender exclusivity is intimated in the opening sequences, when the list of "sponsors"and the names of high scorers are provided. This fictional cast includes Adolf Hitler, Heinrich Himmler, the messiah, the missionaris [*sic*], Pussy Doc, Prince Porn, and Long Dong Silver.

The combination of messianic fervor and pornographic narcissism is striking; indeed, the exaggerated phallocentrism and cult of charisma suggest, if anything, a lack of sexual self-assurance and self-definition in the ludor Self and/or the producers of the game and/or its players. No alluring woman figures in the system of rewards and punishments, thus restricting the expression of potency to the realm of verbally exhibitionist fantasy. In KZ Manager, as in Theweleit's analysis of *Freikorps* leaders, individual male powerlessness before female sexuality seeks redress in the solidarity of men and reassurance in the comparison of phallic stature within the group. Together, their phallic desire intermeshes yearnings for power, potency, and redemption.

But unlike Nazism under Hitler, the power dynamic within KZ Manager's *Männerbund* (confederacy of men) is diffuse. Though Adolf Hitler is nominally still the symbolic core of the game, a decentering process is manifest. Himmler, for example, is quoted more extensively, while Prince Porn and Messias head the high-score lists and provide the more numerous commentaries on the performance of the player. The player's allegiance, or interest, slips by the moment from one figure to another, with no one charismatic enough to embody the yearned-for unity of power, potency, and salvation. Weak though the individual player ego may be at the onset of the game, it gains only marginal strength and focus in a *Männerbund* without strong leadership.

The second key marker framing the player's assumed identity is nationality. Through a display of the emblems of nationhood, Germanness is established as the natural foil to an elaborately defined Turkishness. However, the unfurling of two very different German banners—the flag of the Federal Republic and subsequently that of the Third Reich—designating contradictory conceptions of national identity points to an intrinsic and deliberate ambivalence. The paradoxical suggestion proffered to the aspiring player is that the ludor Self can be a loyal, constitutionally observant federal German, while at the same time adhering to the values and political structures of Nazi Germany. The ludor Self is thus free to negotiate the liberalism, egalitarianism, and individualism guaranteed by the Federal Republic on the one hand, and the illiberalism, authoritarianism, and totalitarianism of the Reich on the other. The implied continuum of *Bundesdeutsch* and *Reichsdeutsch*, suggested by the juxtaposition of the Federal German flag to the Reich's banner, allows the player to slip at will toward whatever pole is politically or psychologically more expedient at a given moment. Thus, the ludor Self, in a clever recruiting strategy by the game's author(s), can enter the value system of a racist worldview without compromising fealty to the existing political order.

If the delineation of German nationality is thus opaque, so, too, are indicators of the ludor Self's class identity. Certainly, the fantasy peddled by the game—the ability to convert living subjects into abject objects and accumulate the material coefficient of power, namely, wealth—would seem to reflect middle-class aspirations, especially as espoused by those young people who see themselves as disenfranchised. But the development of the liberal economy after World War II, the rise of media influence in the shaping of popular values and myths, and the growth of consumerist values have tended to level many of the divisions creating separate class cultures. The unemployed youth, the underemployed laborer, the out-of-work lawyer or auto machinist, by way of example, may all very well share the fantasy of political, sexual, and financial power promised by the game.

Thus, in contrast to the specificity, vigor, and clarity of detail observed in the depiction of the Turkish Other, a marked ambiguity in the sexual, social, and political spheres characterizes not just the ludor Self, but even the relationship of the auctorial to the ludor identities.[13] These apparent discrepancies, however, are only partially attributable to the recruiting function of the text and the corollary need to accommodate a broad-based public. Instead, the ambiguities of the ludor Self can be viewed as a conceptual pendant to the slipperiness of Turkish/Jewish identity and point to a deliberate strategy of slippage that carries over to the game's treatment of space and time.

DETERRITORIALIZING HISTORY

KZ Manager, it will be recalled, situates its fable in Treblinka;[14] that is, a directional caption in the bottom right-hand quadrant of the Treblinka frame informs the viewer that Treblinka is two kilometers distant. But the pictorial frame does not depict the historical Treblinka. If anything, it is inspired, in all its uncanny garishness, by the world of the Gothic novel, with its lonely moor and forbidding castle/fortress/watch tower. Unlike the conventional Gothic venue, however, no light has been left on to promise the new arrival ultimate salvation. Treblinka, viewed from this distant and distancing perspective, comes to represent a shift out of real space, time, and historical consciousness. It is Treblinka, but also not-Treblinka, and, given the two-kilometer distance still remaining to the camp, it can even be construed as not-quite-Treblinka or not-yet-Treblinka.

The space occupied by this "Treblinka" is thus not purely geographical: by alluding to acts past, present, and future, space serves as a temporal signifier as well. This, in turn, has ramifications for the player's attempt to "make sense" of the year in which the ostensible action of the fable occurs, namely, 1944. If in KZ Manager a temporal space can simultaneously reach backward as well as forward in history, so, too, must the concurrent time. As a necessarily equally imaginary construct, "1944" is also torn from its historical moorings, a rupture signaled by the nominal function of the camp as a death factory for the extermination of the Turks.

If the objective of the game is in fact the announced extermination of the Turks, then the temporal expression "1944" represents not the past, but rather an indistinct point in the future; if, however, the slaughter of Jews is being referred to by the year, then the referral to Turks is, historically speaking, anachronistic. We have already seen how, on a symbolic level, Turks form part of a sliding continuum with Jews. Given these repeated discrepancies and slippages between fact and allusion in the game, extermination becomes an activity that can simultaneously reach back into the past (the massacre of the Jews), or extend into the future (the annihilation of the Turks), or even, in the case of the more scrupulous players, not occur at all (the fable is not historically real).

Ultimately, annihilation is no longer a function of historical circumstances and chains of events, but rather of interpretation, as the player behind the ludor Self assigns contextually possible meanings to the now slippery terms "Treblinka," "1944," and "Turks." This hermeneutic freedom, moreover, by disallowing fixed meanings, adeptly undermines principles of accountability and responsibility, a point particularly well illustrated by a further example of slippage. Thanks to the use of *ihr* (her/their) rather than *Ihr* (your), Himmler's opening injunction to genocide at the beginning of the game can be interpreted variously as meaning "You have 300 days' time to complete [their][her][your] task." In this way, the crimes of the ludor Self can, if so desired, be attributed to the player's predecessors, or charged to the account of faceless others.

Moreover, underscoring this refashioning and revisioning of history is not just a rejection of historiographical facticity and causalities but also, if the script of KZ Manager is a reliable indicator, the decline of memory. Several times, for example, "Treblinka" is typed "Treplinka," an error induced surely as much by historical ignorance as by possible dialect interference.[15] Similarly, "Himmler" on at least two occasions is rendered "Himmeler," involuntarily in keeping with the game's transfigurative promises—*Himmel* means heaven—but sorely out of touch with facticity. Taken together, anamnesis and slippage enable a consumerist approach to the past, which, should it continue, will increasingly consign history to the realm of the imaginary.

CONCLUDING REMARKS

The unhinging of facticity from history; the symbolic slippage of Jew and Turk, of past, present, and future, of Treblinka and Gothic venue; the deferral of individual culpability and accountability to external agency all constitute a psychological dynamic of revisionism in KZ Manager. Historically, these elisions appeared at a critical juncture in West Germany's wrangling with the past. The ongoing controversies surrounding the Bitburg incident, the Kohl visit to Israel, the use of concentration camp experimental data in ongoing scientific research, the deployment of preserved body parts of camp victims in medical school laboratories, as well as the vehemence of the historians' controversy—the *Historik-erstreit*—all tended in 1988 to discredit a right-wing movement that was in the process of re-forming and expanding.[16] In this context, the slippages contained in KZ Manager are able to deflect criticism and disarm player resistance, where necessary, by positing a historical past that never happened.

However, the leveling of the Berlin Wall in 1989 and subsequent unification of the two Germanys can only have compounded an identity crisis reflected in the weakness of the ludor Self and, by extension, in those players identifying closely with him.[17] The need to radically redefine German identity and reevaluate history under steadily deteriorating economic circumstances, by weakening the perceived strength of the centrist ludor Self, may well have had a compensatory reinforcement in perceptions of alterity. Thus, the xenophobic violence in Germany in the wake of unification represents a slippage from the realm of the symbolic to that of the historical, reversing a process of partial repression that necessarily followed the Holocaust. This relationship between game and deed, it must be stressed, would seem to be one of conjuncture rather than simple causality, since both respond to an underlying psychological dynamic.[18]

Despite the apparent linearity of KZ Manager's viewing screens and set-up, we see the beginning of a postmodern aesthetic in the game's construction of space, time, agency, and sphere of performance. In apparent defiance of De Kerckhove's linking of postmodern sensibility with advanced technology, KZ Manager transcends the linearity imposed by the limitations of its technical resources. Moreover, in proffering a recipe for a psychological dynamic of revisionism, the game emulates the rewriting of history as portrayed in George Orwell's *1984*, where the protagonist erases the past with a flick of technology. It is discomfiting to think that in the encroaching brave new world of virtual reality, where, according to De Kerckhove, bodies learn from far more sophisticated scanning and imaging processes, biomimetically practiced mass murderers walk the streets, waiting consciously or unconsciously for the arrival of a catalytic leadership and an opportunity for mass murder.

NOTES

1. I would like to thank Saul Litman, Canadian director of the Simon Wiesenthal Center of Toronto, as well as the Research Department of the Simon Wiesenthal Center of Los Angeles for their cooperation in making available to me a copy of KZ Manager. Thanks also go to Rick Dumala of the University of Windsor Computing Center, who provided me with on-campus use of his Atari computer and generated the printouts used in this chapter, and to Torrey James, who photographed and enhanced the computer printouts.

2. For Austria, the Center cites an Austrian survey suggesting that 39 percent of Austrian youth know of the games, while 22 percent had actually encountered them. See "Computer Games Catapult Neo-Nazi Hate into European Homes," *Response* 12, 2 (1991): 2.

3. Derrick De Kerckhove is past Director of the McLuhan Center of Media Studies at the University of Toronto. For his view of the postmodern aesthetic of the multimedia era see "Notes for an Epistemology of Television," *Currents in Modern Thought* (June 1992): 474–94 .

4. With the term "antigreeting" I refer to the ill wishes directed at those perceived to be hostile to the political priorities of the producers of KZ Manager.

5. "Ihre Aufgabe ist es alle Parasiten bis zum Kriegsende zu Eleminieren (Tuerken). Sie beginnen im Jahr 1944 und Sie haben genau 300 Tage Zeit um ihre Aufgabe zu erfu-ellen!!" Note the misspelling of "*eleminieren*" instead of "*eliminieren*," "*ihre*" instead of "*Ihre*," and the lacking punctuation.

6. The original states the player must discover "wie viele Juden müssen täglich ver-gast werden, um das Plansoll zu erreichen." See Albert Kaufmann, "Is nur a Jud, sagte das Kind [It's only a Jew, the child said]," *AZ*, 22 May 1991, 12.

7. The original German states the goal is "möglichst viele Gaskammern zu errichten und möglichst viele Juden und Türken zu vergasen." See Norbert Rief, "Spiele, in denen die NS-Zeit verherrlicht wird, verseuchen den Heimcomputermarkt [Games glorifying the Nazi period contaminating home computer market]," *Die Presse*, 21 May 1991, 5.

8. Until this point, the comparison is implied, in that the young might not recognize the recurrent themes of Nazi propaganda. The reference to the KZ would presumably be familiar to most young players, however. The question of elision is discussed more fully later in this chapter.

9. Unlike the Jews, the Turks cannot be faulted with entrepreneurial manipulation of the German economy. Hence, the game never poses the critical question as to which em-ployers own the factory and allow their workers to toil away on Christmas eve.

10. For a discussion of the *foetor judaicus*, see Sander Gilman, *Between Jew and Anti-Semite: The Secret Language of the Jews* (Baltimore: The Johns Hopkins University Press, 1986); *The Jew's Body* (London: Routledge, 1992); Harold Eilberg-Schwartz, *The People of the Book* (Berkeley: University of California Press, 1990).

11. This equation of Jews and Turks is even more compelling when one compares these depictions with those of Turks in the early modern period. The modifications in the stereotype are striking.

12. The differentiation of "white" and "red" women is drawn from Klaus Theweleit's *Männerfantasien* (Reinbek bei Hamburg: Rowohlt, 1979).

13. Given KZ Manager's rather distinctive programming script—a variant of BA-SIC—and the discrepancies in writing and especially spelling skills between nonvisible programming instructions and on-screen texts, it might well be easier to deduce the cul-tural and educational background of the game's programmer(s) than those of the envis-aged ludor Self. Indeed, the know-how and technology required to produce the game are more suggestive of economically and/or educationally privileged origins in a country where, at this point in time, hardware and software costs had contributed to a signifi-cantly lower public use of computers.

14. The term fable is used here in its literary meaning of a plotline.

15. The erosion of memory is not restricted to Germany! In 1988 the campus news-paper of the University of Western Ontario carried an interview with a Holocaust survi-vor, who was described as having been incarcerated in the Madonna (*sic*) concentration camp.

16. The Bitburg incident, involving Chancellor Helmut Kohl and President Ronald Reagan, erupted when it was revealed that a planned wreathlaying to commemorate the memories of German and American soldiers killed in the Second World War was to take place in a cemetery containing the remains of several SS officers. See Bark and Gress 2:

425–27. Kohl's visit to Israel, intended as a conciliatory gesture, exploded into controversy when he referred to those who were children in the Third Reich as having had the "grace of a late birth" (*"die Gnade der späten Geburt"*), a remark interpreted as a flight from responsibility. See Bark and Gress 2: 423–25. The historians' controversy, unleashed by Nolte's argument that the model for the concentration camp system was in fact an Asian invention, resulted in a debate about historical relativism, the ramifications of which can still be felt in the current furore over Daniel Goldhagen's work, *Hitler's Willing Executioners*. For a cursory summary of the *Historikerstreit* see Bark and Gress 2: 416, 432–40, 446–47.

17. The fragility of the centrist self is further pronounced with the ambivalent 300-day limitation to the game. Must the annihilation of the Turks/Jews be accomplished before the German defeat of 1945?

18. Precisely the transition from "normal" to "pathological" behavior characterizes much of the debate on Christopher Browning's *Ordinary Germans* and Daniel Goldhagen's *Hitler's Willing Executioners*. It would seem that what distinguished the transition from the realm of the symbolic to that of material history is not so much the presence of a different pyschopathology as the collapse of a restraining mechanism. Why that mechanism fails is, of course, the unresolved issue.

WORKS CITED

Bark, Dennis L., and David R. Gress. *A History of West Germany*. 2 vols. 2nd edition. Oxford: Blackwell, 1993.

Browning, Christopher. *Ordinary Germans: Reserve Battalion 101 and the Final Solution in Poland*. New York: Harper Collins, 1992.

"Computer Games Catapult Neo-Nazi Hate into European Homes," *Response* 12, 2 (1991): 2.

De Kerckhove, Derrick. "Notes for an Epistemology of Television." In *Currents in Modern Thought* (June 1992): 474–94 .

Eilberg-Schwartz. *The People of the Book*. Berkeley: University of California Press, 1990.

Gilman, Sander. *Between Jew and Anti-Semite: The Secret Language of the Jews*. Baltimore: The Johns Hopkins University Press, 1986.

——. *The Jew's Body*. New York: Routledge, 1992.

Goldhagen, Daniel. *Hitler's Willing Executioners*. New York: Alfred Knopf, 1996.

Kaufmann, Albert. "Is nur a Jud, sagte das Kind [It's only a Jew, the child said]," *AZ*, 22 May 1991, 12.

Rief, Norbert. "Spiele, in denen die NS-Zeit verherrlicht wird, verseuchen den Heimcomputermarkt [Games glorifying the Nazi period contaminating home computer market]," *Die Presse*, 21 May 1991, 5.

Theweleit, Klaus. *Männerfantasien*. Reinbek bei Hamburg: Rowohlt, 1986.

Chapter 11

The New Expatriates: Three American-Jewish Writers in Germany Today

Diana Orendi

This chapter explores the rather curious phenomenon of the presence of American-Jewish expatriate writers in postwar, post-Holocaust Germany. Specifically, Orendi examines the autobiographical works of three American-Jewish women writers: Jeanette Lander, Jane Gilbert, and Susan Neiman. As point of departure for her analysis, Orendi uses a thesis formulated by philosopher Isaac Deutscher in a 1958 essay. The notion of the assimilated "Non-Jewish Jew" (Deutscher) as having been a major force in propelling Western culture during the last five hundred years is contrasted here with the opposing force: the pull of a more conservative, more traditionally defined and more comforting Jewishness to which all three American Jews resort as something of a haven after their German sojourn.

If one can talk of fashions in an area as sturdy and unfrivolous as *Germanistik* (German Studies), the present vogue undoubtedly is a focus on multiculturalist concern and specifically "minority literature" in Germany. The recent increase in acts of xenophobia and anti-Semitism has called forth—on the cultural scene, if not within the political realm—the much-needed opening of a dialogue between minority writers and German mainstream critics. This enterprise having furthermore been legitimized by prominent theoreticians such as Deleuze and Guattari (*What a Is Minor Literature?*), critics have of late lavished attention on a body of literary works considered heretofore unworthy of much attention. In 1989, a whole issue of *New German Critique* was devoted to *Ausländerliteratur*, works created by foreign immigrants living in Germany. But while due mention was made of the numerous authors hailing from Italy, Turkey, Greece, and Yugoslavia, one group of writers—tiny but vocal nonetheless—was not included in the discussion. There was, to be sure, Cilly Kugelmann's article in *New German Critique*, entitled "Tell Them in America We're Still Alive!," which disclaimed the extinction of a Jewish community in Germany. But even among the small group of German-born Jews in Germany, few today are aware of the minute but growing number of American Jews who have made their way to Germany to work, live, and write.

I would like to present a brief introduction to some members of this school of writers, concentrating on several American-born Jewish women writers who have lived and worked in Germany, have published works in German and/or English, and in autobiographies and fiction have documented and reflected upon the experiences made during their individual travels and travails. The writers I will deal with are Jeanette Lander, Jane Gilbert, and Susan Neiman.

In the realm of American literary history, the word "expatriates" immediately evokes the names of other Americans who lived and worked in Europe—in Paris that time—during the twenties. But Ernest Hemingway, F. Scott Fitzgerald, Katherine Anne Porter, and Dorothy Parker never perceived their exile to be permanent, and returned to the United States after exhausting their youthful vigor and their need for the exoticism of Europe. The present generation of writers may differ dramatically in this respect. Two of the three authors have elected to stay in their chosen exile. The reasons for this decision will tell as much about Jewish-German relations as it will about the quest on which these Americans embarked: to search for an identity by exploring the roots of their religious and cultural heritage. There is, thus, much more at stake for this new flock of American emigrés who urgently seek the sort of answers from their host country that the "lost generation" never had to concern itself with: whether and how these pilgrims feel welcomed or rejected, admitted or antagonized, is of consequence above all to them personally. Conversely, their presence in Germany presents a challenge and a testing ground for a society severely in flux, a nation still battling the effects of the Holocaust while facing a thorny path towards multiculturalism. In their study "Kafka: Toward a Minor Literature," Deleuze and Guattari claim that in the arena of minority literature the personal becomes the political, the private applies to the larger public realm. And thus these Jewish writers' situation, as it is reflected in their writings, in some small degree also bears witness to the success or failure of a newly emerging German society.

When Isaac Deutscher formulated his thesis about the "Non-Jewish Jew" in an essay of 1958 (25–41),[1] he used the term to apply to the great Utopian thinkers of Jewish descent whose ideas shaped and changed Western culture from the time of Spinoza to Freud. Deutscher defined the concept for those forward-looking thinkers who transcended the narrow confines of their orthodox Jewish identity to become cosmopolitan in their intellectual reach, their ideas grappling with matters of universal rather than national or communal concern. Only by rejecting the restrictions imposed by religious and cultural traditions, Deutscher claims, were Heinrich Heine, Karl Marx, Rosa Luxemburg, Leon Trotsky and others empowered to cast their revolutionary visions. The image of the Jew who has to assimilate in order to be a politically active intellectual has dominated much of the discourse about Jewish identity—particularly German-Jewish identity—in this century. The fact that Deutscher formulated his argument after the Holocaust speaks for his unbroken faith in humanity's capacity both to transmit and to receive what he calls the "message of universal human emancipation" (41). Nonetheless, it also speaks of a certain naïveté or disdain on the philosopher's part for the survival of Jewry.

In his later essay "Who Is a Jew?"[2] Deutscher calls Auschwitz the cradle of a new Jewish consciousness created by the very extermination of six million Jews. He concludes that he "would have preferred six million Jews to survive and Jewry to perish" (50), instead of seeing it rise out of the ashes phoenixlike. But since this is not a choice, history's severe lesson is a mandate contemplated and understood by many modern Jews. To them this lesson has signaled a renewed determination to wrestle with a self-definition along traditional religious and cultural modes. It is a search in which Jews all over the world are engaged today. It also served as point of departure for the artists I want to consider here.

Jeanette Lander, born in 1931, has lived in Germany since 1960. At the center of her novelistic and lyric work is the exploration of the theme of Otherness. Her largely autobiographical novel *Auf dem Boden der Fremde* (*On Foreign Soil*), published in 1972, details the midlife crisis of Yvonne, an American-born Jew. Having grown up in the American South during the thirties and forties in a warm and loving Jewish environment in which Yiddish was spoken, Yvonne, like so many American Jews, had conceived of herself as a member of one of several ethnic minorities, all of which coexisted more or less peaceably within mainstream American society. She had followed Friedrich, a German ex-soldier sent to the United States for denazification, to his home country and had adapted over the years to what seemed to her a cold and harsh sphere compared to "*der Heem*" ("home"), of which she thinks often and lovingly. With her marriage faltering, Friedrich's latent racist and sexist traits emerge and drive Yvonne to intense soul-searching and a redefining of her roles as mother of an adolescent son and as leftist-liberal artist in a world exploding with the student rebellion of the late sixties. Despairing of her German escapade, Yvonne flees back to the refuge of *der Heem*, but the American South she grew up in has vanished, to her shocked dismay. The Jewish-Black symbiosis, as she remembers it fondly from her childhood, has given way to a society defined by segregation and racism. She finds that those who had escaped death in Europe have in their turn become instruments of oppression. While her parents and their friends chide her for living "in the house of the hangman," she has to assess their role as complicitous with a racist and imperialist government. Sadly, the visitor concludes that the idealism of her parents' generation, those who had wanted to engineer a society of peaceful coexistence, has succumbed to consumerism and a wide-eyed fascination with technological progress. Yvonne's realization that racism and class warfare are universal rather than just German phenomena prepares her to accept the fact that she is a stranger both in the United States and in German society. Leaving her son as messiah to spread the gospel of the New Left, Yvonne herself returns to Germany, the country of her voluntary exile.

"I'm at home on foreign soil. Only as a foreigner do I really feel good. I enjoy the advantage of not being easily categorized. The necessary risks provoke
my sense of adventure. It is freedom not to be safe" (*Fremd im Eigenen Land*
[*Strangers in Their Own Country*], 258), Lander has said. With the feeling of
dwelling safely in the diaspora, she proclaims that her sense of self has become
strong and independent in the isolation from her origins. As she admits in this
same essay, the author regrets today the often shrill tones with which she pro-
tested her victim status in her early years abroad. Looking back, she characterizes her initial clash with German culture as violent. In the last thirty years,
however, rebellion has given way to a gradual emancipation from an exclusively
and belligerently Jewish identity. She cherishes her sense of Jewishness as a
"final inner reserve" to which she can return at will. Thus, she seems at peace
today with her role at the margin, which permits her to represent alterity while
harboring the secure knowledge of an inner sanctum to which she can withdraw.

If Jeanette Lander derives a mellow sense of well-being from resting protected in an awareness of her selfhood, there is no sanctuary in which Jane
Gilbert finds solace. The differences start with the way the two women writers
were brought up. Born in New York in 1947, Jane Gilbert was raised by a generation of Jews Isaac Deutscher would have classified as Non-Jewish Jews. So
fearful and conflicted about their identity were the older Gilberts that every detail of their educational guidance instilled confusion and anxiety in Jane and her
siblings. Not only were the children given Christian names, their surname was
changed, and speaking Yiddish was strictly taboo. Jane remembers her mother
uttering in relief, "I'm so glad [our Jewishness] does not show" (23), as she
glanced sympathetically at African-Americans. But even if all visible traces of
the postwar generation's Jewishness had been erased, the children were nonetheless intrigued by the mystery of their all-too-Jewish grandparents. No identity
crises for these examples of "real Jews" (14)—these were Jane's words later in
memory of the older generation—whose heavy Polish accents, eating habits, and
adherence to religious rules the children found hard to integrate into their assimilated home environment. To Jane's parents, being Jewish merely entailed
the obligation to excel in the cutthroat competition of school, university, and,
ultimately, life. This was a race in which the late-born ones were ultimately
meant to prove themselves worthy of being survivors of the cataclysm that had
swallowed most of their relatives.

By the time Gilbert left for Germany and university studies there, to the absolute horror of her parents, she had been so heavily indoctrinated against this
country that her decision can only be understood as an act of rebellion. Propelling her must have been the desire to revolt against what she saw as the hypocrisy of her parents' generation. Coupled with this, one detects a nostalgic admiration for the unbroken sense of self exhibited by the shtetl-Jew grandparents.
Not surprisingly, the book Gilbert wrote about her seven years in Germany is
entitled *Ich mußte mich vom Haß befreien* (*I Had to Liberate Myself from Hatred*), and it does not make for pleasant reading! The reader is asked to follow
Gilbert on a quest, during which, as often as not, she finds herself misinterpret-

ing well-meant gestures as genuine examples of anti-Semitic sentiments. For years she insists that no one besides her, the intended victim, has the right to suffer, and she does not relent from this sadomasochistic pursuit of misery until she has dealt her parents the figurative death blow: she applies for, and is eventually granted, German citizenship. There is no release in the closure of this book, on whose jacket we find the author's words: "I have become German precisely because I am Jewish. That has nothing to do with reconciliation, but it is my way of working through the past." Touted by her editor as "a confession made by someone who today understands those who cannot confess," this avowal—as much as the whole treatise—fails to move. There is a lack of sincerity coupled with an absence of warmth, elements that could have arisen only out of understanding her parents' anxieties and pain. Gilbert remains unforgiving because she does not concede their deprivation. The daughter fails to acknowledge or even see the premise from which her parents started out: the older Gilberts acted as Non-Jewish Jews, Deutscher's definition for the assimilated Jew who has emptied his consciousness of the cultural heritage and who thus has none to transmit to the next generation. Where Lander is comforted by the memories of her *Heem* and all the magic this experience entailed, Gilbert sadly is forced to turn to a void impossible to fill.

Susan Neiman, today professor of philosophy at Yale, wonders sometimes if perhaps she gave up on Germany too easily. She spent the years 1982 to 1989 in Berlin writing a dissertation on Enlightenment philosophers, learning German, and learning to cope with the daily frustrations of life as a foreigner, as a Jew in Germany. She also fell in love with the city, with its multicultural inhabitants, and with the man whom she married midway through her stay. In her memoir *Slow Fire: Jewish Notes from Berlin*, published in the United States in 1992, she details the frequently stinging, often exhilarating events of her sojourn, which ended just before the wall fell. Neiman grew up in Atlanta in another diaspora home, where Jewishness was less an issue, however, than the emerging civil rights movement and other liberal causes that punctuated the stages of her childhood. Like the other Americans switching cultures, she was unprepared for the precariousness of the situation of Jews living in Germany today: the fearful attempts to hide or minimize their presence, the constant attendance of policemen in synagogues and schools, the bomb threats, the disguising of Jewish stores as "Oriental grocery" stores, all of which testify to the tentativeness and highly unstable conditions of Jewish life in Germany. She found Germans eerily anxious to practice *Vergangenheitsverarbeitung* (working through the past) with or on her. But she insists today that it was more the fascist elements of the past that interested them, more their own rather than Jewish history. "Every time I see you I think of Dachau, baby" (cited on dust jacket), she quotes a German boyfriend, whose perverse fascination with her origins stood in stark contrast to his pro-Nazi family background. It also doomed their affair. Notwithstanding pained relationships and a sense of dejection, Neiman is soon captured by Berlin's unique aura, which is irrepressibly upbeat and life affirming. In this mood she turned to reflect on her ethnic origins, and she defiantly started to celebrate her Jewishness. "Being Jewish was not to be reduced to being a possible victim of anti-Semitism" (230). That would have seemed to her the "final fascist triumph" (231). And thus she and her half-Jewish, half-German husband have their newborn son circumcised; this life-affirming, faith-affirming celebration is described in the book as a scene that is both touching and humorous as the two assimilated Jews show their ignorance of many of the traditions surrounding the highly ceremonial *bris*. Asked in 1988 to organize an event commemorating 750 years of Jewish contributions to Berlin culture, Neiman concluded sadly: "It was impossible to celebrate contemporary Jewish culture because there was nothing to celebrate" (274).

"A Jew—a mensch—can't live here without going crazy" (286), was Neiman's ultimately resigned explanation for her little family's departure to the United States in 1989. Upon her return for a visit in 1993, though, Neiman was "positively astonished" to find that the impact of reunification had produced in its wake increased signs of survival of Jewry in Berlin. "More *Kneipen* (pubs), more stores, better access to synagogues" (speech at Cornell University, 1993). She and her family remain firmly convinced that their decision to leave was the right one, particularly in light of the events in Rostock and other German cities and what Neiman perceives as a more and more sophisticated xenophobia of the West. Nonetheless, the scholar pleads today for moral and material support for those Jews who choose to live in Germany. Her appeal, voiced strenuously during a March 1993 visit to a Cornell University graduate seminar on "Reemerging Jewish Culture in Postwar Germany," is directed at international Jewry. Instead of condemning Jews for wanting to keep a presence alive in Germany, they should be made to feel secure. Instead of looking toward the past and paying tribute to dead cultural artifacts, the world should try to cope with living Jews. And though the task requires, in Neiman's words, a good dose of Utopian thinking, it also has an excellent chance of success.

Neiman's words probably best summarize the position all three authors discussed here would subscribe to today. They insist on their selfhood as representatives of a minority, of the Other in Germany, but they appeal to the humanity of all to sustain them in their enterprise. Each one of these writers is defiantly proud of having arrived at a juncture in her project of self-definition. There is Lander's irreverent celebration of difference, Gilbert's hard-won admission that there is much worthy of redemption in Germany, and finally Neiman's discovery that there is hope for a renewal of her culture's imprint on that of the majority. Even though she declined to take an active part in this rejuvenation, her venture has caused her personally to reembrace her Jewishness. They all disclaim—at least for the time being—Deutscher's thesis that this is or should be the age of the Non-Jewish Jew.

NOTES

1. Isaac Deutscher, "The Non-Jewish Jew," *The Non-Jewish Jew* (London: Oxford University Press, 1968), 24–41.
2. Deutscher, 42–59.

WORKS CITED

Broder, Henryk, and Michael Lang, eds. *Fremd im Eigenen Land: Juden in der BRD.* Frankfurt am Main: Deutscher Taschenbuch Verlag, 1979.

Deleuze, Gilles, and Felix Guattari. "What Is a Minor Literature?" In *Kafka: Toward a Minor Literature*, 16–27. Minneapolis: University of Minnesota Press, 1986.

Deutscher, Isaac. "The Non-Jewish Jew." *The Non-Jewish Jew.* 24–81. London: Oxford University Press, 1968.

Gilbert, Jane. *Ich mußte mich vom Haß befreien.* München [Munich]: Deutscher Taschenbuch Verlag, 1991.

Kugelmann, Cilly. "'Tell Them in America We're Still Alive!' The Jewish Community in the Federal Republic." *New German Critique* 46 (1989): 129–140.

Lander, Jeanette. *Auf dem Boden der Fremde.* Frankfurt am Main: Insel, 1972.

———. "Unsicherheit ist Freiheit." In *Fremd im Eigenen Land: Juden in der BRD,* Broder and Lang, ed. 258–64. Frankfurt am Main: Deutscher Taschenbuch Verlag, 1979.

Neiman, Susan. *Slow Fire: Jewish Notes from Berlin.* New York: Schocken, 1992.

Chapter 12

An Entrepreneur of Victimhood: Jewish Identity in the Confessions of a *Stasi* Informant

Denis M. Sweet

"Hep Hep . . . Hierosolyma est perdita."

The central question that Denis M. Sweet's chapter tries to resolve is whether Andreas Sinakowsi was a GDR gay man forced to commit espionage by the Stasi to save his skin or whether he was a GDR Jew whom the Stasi rescued from anti-Semitic attacks. Sinakowski's controversial 1991 autobiographical account, *Das Verhör* (*The Interrogation*), however, confounds the mystery of the author's true identity and motivation. By portraying his life as a hell of sexual, physical, and mental abuse, Sinakowski tries to negotiate a release from guilt with his readers, but his "true confession," as Sweet argues, rings of compromise and co-optation, wish fulfillment and denial, rather than truth and the potential for absolution. In the process, Sweet demonstrates that for Sinakowski, Jewish identity is stripped of any cultural, religious or philosophical signification, serving instead as a blank category that subsumes all auctorial suffering.

Following on the heels of the massive street protests in East Germany in the fall of 1989, a flood of publications began to appear—most notably interviews with former secret police agents or their informants—that set out to document one of the more notorious agents of oppression of the former regime, that of the East German state security apparatus, the *Stasi*. At first glance, Andreas Sinakowski's *Das Verhör* (*The Interrogation*) appears to be one such documentation in the form of a personal narrative or confession. But what was most striking about this publication, what set it apart, what made it quite sensational even, were not revelations of high crime and complicity, but quite simply the multiple identities of the author. Andreas Sinakowski was gay and had been an informant for the *Stasi* between the ages of 19 and 26. Rather than being unknown to them, or a matter of no concern, his homosexuality was instrumentalized by the *Stasi* for its own intelligence-gathering purposes. This young gay man who had worked as an informant for a Communist secret police organization bedded his prey, following orders from on high. That was the sensation. But another identity plays a key role in this narrative as well, without which all the events narrated would never have transpired: Andreas Sinakowski is a Jew.

That Jewishness is central to Sinakowski's narrative. Without it, *Das Verhör* would be an altogether different kind of work; it would simply be the autobiographical and sexually nonmainstream and therefore—for some—scandalous narrative of a former *Stasi* informant now grimly informing on himself, as John Tagliabue put it in his review of the work in the *New York Times*.[1] With Sinakowski's Jewishness, however, comes not one more cumulatively added identity, but a whole new construction. The narrative of confession is transformed into one of accusation, the guilt of the informer turns into the self-righteousness of the victim. It is for this reason that *Das Verhör* is a deeply disturbing work that raises fundamental questions of moral argument, an argument that itself is inextricably imbedded in a much larger social discourse of purported guilt and professed innocence that has surfaced since the collapse of the GDR: the Communist perpetrators bearing all the guilt lined up on the one side, confronted by their innocent victims on the other. With his informant's confession, Andreas Sinakowski stands on the one side but claims that his identity allows him the rights and prerogatives of the other.

Jewishness is constructed here not merely as a fact of identity but as an overarching moral argument. It explains how the teenaged Sinakowski came to be a *Stasi* informant in the first place, thus providing an initial alibi that gradually grows in the course of the work into something much different: Jewishness—in post-Shoah Germany—as exculpation in itself. The book begins with a witch hunt. The teenaged Sinakowski is hunted down by his classmates at the school where they are being trained to be cooks. They threaten him. Hep, hep, they chant in the school corridors. "In the school corridor they hissed 'hep, hep.' They didn't have any classical education, but the hep that the Romans had cried out after the destruction of Jerusalem, *Hierosolyma est perdita*, Jerusalem is destroyed, has belonged to the minor battle gear of amateur Nazis since the 30s" (15).[2] What they will do to him is left unclear. They tell jokes. How many Jews fit into a Trabi? Answer: thirty, four on the seats and twenty-six in the ashtray.

It is not the details of this narrated event, or even its correspondence with the facticity of real events, the resurgence of anti-Semitism in East Germany, that is so telling. It is rather that this event has the function of a central myth. It describes the most sensitive place of origin, the motor that propelled the teenaged Andreas Sinakowski into the hands of the *Stasi* in the first place. Namely: Andreas Sinakowski is a Jew whom the *Stasi* rescued from anti-Semitic attacks. This is the font of persecution and deliverance from which all the ensuing narration takes its cue. It was his Jewishness that led him to the *Stasi*, or rather that brought the *Stasi* to him.

But what was Jewishness, who was a Jew, when was a Jew a Jew, in the former German Democratic Republic? Chaim Noll, another young Jewish East German writer who left for the West in the mid-1980s as did Sinakowski, describes his family, a family that could stand for many others, in a memoir of his childhood and youth that thematizes Jewish identity in the GDR and the obstacles to it, where religious identity, even Jewish cultural identity, had been eclipsed by a new ideological, Marxist identity. Jewishness, as Noll describes it in this memoir, had become in all its manifestations merely an undesirable inheritance and incumbrance from the past, a detrimental holdover, not something Marxists, secular, hopeful, and building a career in the new order, might want to identify themselves with. The way these Jews posed the question was as an option—for Marxism or for Judaism— and for this family, as for many others, the foregone conclusion was for Marxism (with the exception of the narrator/son, whose choice was to leave East Germany in order to live his life as a Jew.)[3]

According to the (formerly East) Berlin sociologist, ex-*Stasi* informant, and Jewish activist writer Irene Runge, only a practicing member of the religious community officially counted as a Jew. "In the GDR," Runge writes, "the same rule applied as in the rest of Germany: a Jew is whoever is a member of a religious community. . . . Jewish secularity had, up to the very end, no place in our atheistic fatherland" (69). And the practicing members of the religious communities in the GDR were scant in number.[4] Eclipsed by the new ideological order, recognized only as practicing members of the official religious community, all the others who had other connections with Jewishness were left to their own devices.

When was a Jew a Jew under these conditions? There is no easy answer. And the answer might vary in different times and circumstances in the life of the same individual. Andreas Sinakowski mentions the complications of what it means to be a Jew in another account entitled "Zwischen Tabu und Trauma" ("Between Taboo and Trauma"), a brief essay he had written for the German gay magazine *magnus* about the Jewish gay organization L'Chaim.[5] The experience of Jewishness in the German context that he depicts here I take to be his own. He describes a kind of constant inner flux in motion throughout one's life having to be subjectively re-negotiated, but bounded by two absolutes impinging from the outside: the Holocaust and the contemporary German reaction to Jews in Germany, whether anti-Semitic, philo-Semitic, or, rather commonly, as if to distant and unfamiliar museum relics. Within that space the nonreligious Jew must negotiate an identity— or abandon one, as Chaim Noll described—an identity personally negotiated in the constrained space between the shadows of Nazi genocide and the uncontrollable behavior of others. It is just that Sinakowski's narrative in *Das Verhör* has little to do with such a negotiation. Quite the contrary, Jewishness appears here as a kind of talisman, an external signifier without subjective correspondance, a sign hung about the author's neck not so much for elucidating identity as for another purpose.

Despite the punctilious recounting of his childhood, there is no mention of Judaism or Jewishness, no inkling of Jewish identity or Jewish observances, neither in his own life nor in that of any of the relatives by blood or marriage around him. The single mention, the rather vague allusion during a visit to Israel of belonging to "this people" by virtue of "more than several percent of my blood" (63), might not even suffice for the blood laws of the Nazis. Andreas Sinakowski claims to be a Jew but has no recognizable Jewish identity. At the same time he is someone for whom being a "Jew" is essential. For this is the spring that propels his narrative.

A Jew as victim: this "Jew" can only be a victim. The ensuing narration of Sinakowski's childhood and youth is one of victimization, a vortex of victimization so profound that it relentlessly multiplies from the initial anti-Semitic incident in the school to encompass ever more manifestations, ever more victimizations that grow ever more grotesque. His entire family is dysfunctional. Abandoned by her husband, Sinakowski's mother attempts to abort the fetus Andreas, but "the quinine showed no effect, at least no visible effect, and so it became a normal pregnancy and hell for my mother" (32). This child grows up amid the ravages of a violent and abusive, alcoholic stepfather and a masochistic, drunken mother.

> I caught a glance of her on the demolished sofa, wooden slats poking through the lacerated upholstery. Her head hung to the floor, her knees were pressed against the wall. She had pulled a corner of the white table cloth over her naked body—both splotched with blood. I bent over her and tried to wake her up, but all I could get out of her was babbling and a deep sigh. Once she tried to open her swollen eyes before turning on her side. "Go buy some ice cream," she groaned. (35)

Left alone by his mother for weeks on end, the five-year-old, in another repulsive scene, is groped by his uncle after he has told the boy he can sleep in uncle's bed. This same uncle has sex later on with the teenaged Sinakowski who breaks it off when the uncle pathetically suggests a ménage à trois. All of these recounted events from his childhood and youth reinforce in scene after scene one theme: an ineluctable victimization, one so all-encompassing that there is no part of Sinakowski that is not abused, misused, broken. Under the ever-present onslaught, even his body parts corrode.

> After my first bad middle-ear infection my soul finally had found a protector against the voices, against the sounds of the beatings, but above all against the buzzing silence that followed those nightly beatings. The passages of my ears filled again and again, week by week, with rampant growths that had to be torn out with minute pliers in over ninety out-patient operations over the years or were burned off with diluted acid, culminating in one last final operation, during which half of my auditory canal as well as a piece of my skull were removed. (35)

This autobiography, which in memory after memory, scene after narrated scene, details how others abuse or neglect without stint, enslave or are inflamed by the child and youth Sinakowski, reaches its grotesque crescendo after Sinakowski is left in the care of his step-grandparents. His mother had been put in prison for murdering one of her drunken, abusive lovers, and his stepfather takes the boy to his own parents for upbringing. There the sight of Sinakowski's young body kindles the crazed, lecherous gaze of his step-grandmother. The more her lust swells, the more her aged body decomposes, literally:

> Oozing scabs and boils filled with pus spread over her body. Day after day she heaped tar and zinc salves on this landscape of craters. . . . While other children walked on soft carpets, scraps of skin from her psoriasis glued themselves to the soles of my feet. Taking strange paths they crept into the china and the linen, even into the refrigerator. (47–48)

Thus his upbringing ends. This story of abuse, of a stolen childhood, has a narrative function—that of accusation. "They had stolen twenty years of my life. Whatever might be sacred to a child became filth and lies under their mere breath" (62). Here is a wild, thrashing-about kind of accusation, aimed not only at specific people like the step-grandma, mother, stepfather, uncle, boys in school, but also at Germany as a cultural entity, and, repeatedly, woven in and out of the text like so many glittering icons of evil, the names of the butchers of the Nazi period and the geographic place names that signify their destruction of European Jewry: Wannsee, Vilnius, Auschwitz.

It is a strategy of accusation buoyed up by a peculiarly literary kind of grotesquerie that allows no quarter, that is absolute: here the victim, there the perpetrators, unmasked and vile. Here the helpless, hapless child and there the lecherous, drunken, abusive adults; here the Jew and there his tormentors, both then and now. A constellation that endorses unmitigated accusation, a rhetorical strategy that preordains only one kind of guilt: that of the others. This is the story, then— and the strategy of its narration—of Andreas Sinakowski's childhood and youth that prefaces, frames, and introduces the other story of this text, the truth-telling story the title *Das Verhör* suggests, the story of an informant's complicity with the *Stasi*.

But this second story parallels the model of the first, and is one in which the question of personal guilt cannot even be posed. Complicity and any guilt attendant upon it have been displaced. Andreas Sinakowski's co-optation by the *Stasi*, as in the many familial co-optations preceding it, is—also—sexual. Explaining his deep-seated revulsion at the sight of the naked female body by the memory of the elderly, lecherous female wiles that his step-grandmother employed against him, the teenaged Sinakowski's libido has nowhere else to turn but to his own sex. It is a refuge, a hiding place from women, but it is not a place where the refugee feels at home. On the contrary, he despises men too, at least the gay ones with whom he has sex.

The men to whom he is drawn, the men from whom he seeks approval, the men he wants to resemble, are the "real" men, the macho men, the powerful and manly men, the men of the state security organs. For them he keeps his own organ at the ready. His tool becomes a tool of the intelligence trade. Not to have sex with *them*, of course, but with the prey they assign him. It is an exercise in self-hatred from which there is no exit. He beds those—like himself—whom he despises for the sake of affirmation from those who despise him because of it. A vicious circle. He wants approval; they want information. He wants them; they want the others. He betrays the others—the function of the informant is to betray the confidence of others—down to every detail, down to the senseless minutiae that distend intelligence files everywhere, only to proclaim, again and again, that he is their victim.

The multiple victimizations, in this text, are worn as a kind of identity armor that encloses and constricts—and protects him. His role is that of tool, and through a chink in the armor he extends his tool, a periscope of conspirative observation, to observe for his masters, who misuse him. Is it Faust's pact with the devil, as he claims? Or is this claim—like other claims in this text—simply an attempt to stylize, to invoke a literary tradition, to erect a calculated monument to victimization? Faust as Mephistopheles' victim, Andreas Sinakowski as victim of a diabolical organization? But this formula does not add up. Faust was not a victim, but a keen player well aware of his moral transgressions. Nonetheless, Andreas Sinakowski insists on his victimhood. He is a victim who hates himself—"He only hates, and in each one of the others, himself" (93)—who has internalized widespread social hatreds: "'You only want to get fucked in the ass by them,' they screamed after me in the stairwell. . . . 'Assfucker,' rained down on me from all sides. This doll's house was ruled by terror" (55).

Such terror, internalized, can, from the viewpoint of state security, be usefully employed. It can help subvert, for example, the emancipatory forces of gay men and lesbians then just beginning to organize under the auspices of the Lutheran church. The self-hating gay man and *Stasi* informant Andreas Sinakowski played a part not only in attending, recording, and informing, but also, following *Stasi* guidelines on undermining (*zersetzen*) the human rights groups in the church, in sowing seeds of suspicion, noting conflicts, fissures that might be conveniently widened. His homosexuality is useful in maintaining state order not only by combating political "dissidents," but also by regulating the more self-assertive homosexuals organizing to claim civil rights for those marginalized in the "actually existing socialism" of the GDR. The "working circles on homosexuality" within the church were massively infiltrated. After the *Wende*, the group in Zwickau, for example, estimated that over 60 percent of its members had been *Stasi* informants.[6]

What recourse does such a gainfully employed victim have? Is there no way out of following orders? Powerless and caught in the grips of a seemingly all-powerful state security apparatus, he might seek to undermine the confidence in the confidence man he is. He might blow his cover. And this he attempted to do, avowedly at length:

> Proud and naive, I told Peter Edel of my work for the *Stasi*. "It's late, let's bring the evening to an end," he said and carried the cups and glasses into the kitchen. . . . Doris, in whose apartment I had first met Scholz, didn't register my questions and signals. In 1990 she said, "I didn't know, that's not what I wanted." . . . M., who not only said he was my friend, never once spoke to me after our nightly prowls in the onethousandfourhundredandsixty days that I still had left in the GDR about that which he knew but didn't want to know about. Jan Koplowitz decided, after I had turned the topic of conversation in our fireside chat

> to my sleeping partners and me, to get up and go make tea. . . . Dirk, to whom I told my story in twenty minutes, didn't react either. Sometimes he stayed over at my place, we saw each other several times a week. "You are a good story teller," he laughed. (80–81)

A passage of foiled attempts, of repeated tries. Actual names are named (names that appear in this text here for the first and last time), a kind of minidocumentation of frustrated attempts at truthfulness: My aim was to confess, they just did not want to listen. But this text can be read in another, more telling way, namely as the narration of guiltlessness. It is not the *Stasi* informant who is guilty of having committed conspirative acts, but the others who are guilty for refusing to listen when the truth is told. Whatever he undertakes, this victim cannot free himself because the others cowardly refuse being implicated. They refuse to see and hear even when they see and hear. Although deftly alluded to by the author in this passage, deliberate deafness is never proved. It is more convenient to suggest cowardice or cover-up on the part of his interlocutors.

That the informant is left to his own devices, or rather hangs by a conspirative umbilical cord from his *Führungs-Offizier* (controlling officer), who binds him to him for psychological recognition as well as for every other aspect of his life—in a world of all-encompassing calculated prevarication, he is the one familiar and receptive audience from whom future assignments and money depend—all this is part and parcel of the conspirative job description. These are means by which dependency in a relationship of exploitative power is constructed. They do not occlude responsibility for the informant's own actions. "I leafed through the album, I saw life: long hair, short hair, little hair, glasses, shirt with tie, wire-rimmed glasses, turtleneck sweater, narrow shoulders, broad nose, beautiful, for him a bestiary. Get rid of all of them, they are all dangerous, annihilate everyone" (71).

Even here in one of the few passages in the entire narration that details the informant's day-to-day routine of identification and denunciation, a concrete, telling passage all the more valuable because of the framework of dependency, even passivity it adumbrates, the informant, here quite literally in the backseat of a Trabi, takes a backseat to the driving eager, greedy, destructive will of his Mephistophelian *Stasi* officer driver. In his recounting, the informant devolves into passive spectator, the information squeezed out of him for hour after hour by an active and capable and culpable solicitous other. While the photographed faces of the spied upon disappear into an insatiable black bag, it is the *Stasi* that is doing the disappearing, not their observing, observant tool.

This text employs multiple victimizations, all leading to one prestabilized result: guiltlessness, innocence, not guilty by virtue of overwhelming historical and developmental mitigating circumstances. Unsparing literary grotesquerie is put to good use to attain this aim. It is not only the strategy a clever trial lawyer might take to get his or her client off, but in an age of competitive victimhoods, it presents a moral dilemma with far-reaching ramifications: victimhood as armor to make the victim impervious to all guilt, victimhood that protects the guilty.

The one victimization among all the other victimizations brought to bear on this text—the one that plays the role of linchpin—is the victimization of the Jew, the

Jew as victim. This is a Jew under a very particular historical constellation. A Jew in an officially antifascist, post-Holocaust German state. A protected Jew. A species.

Such Jewish identity, in this particular text, is employed as a sign that stands for something else: the author who is now relating his story could not have been guilty because—despite being an informant for the *Stasi* who caused hurt, harm, and misery to the arbitrarily assigned others he betrayed—he belonged to the victims par excellence of twentieth-century history. All of the multiple victimhoods of this author are inscribed on the plus side of the ledger and add up to an enormous credit that nothing on the debit side can wipe away.

Victimhood and helplessness, self-hate and righteousness form an unwieldy agglomeration here. The activities for the *Stasi* (ostensibly this text is a true confession of those activities)—his betrayal of friends, his identification of "enemies of the state," his infiltration of dissident artists' circles—all of these real and concrete activities are outweighed by previous victimhoods, cancelled out, morally suspended. In this confession mea culpa is transfigured into *j'accuse*.

If the "truth" of this life lies in a string of evasions, complicity, co-optation and subjugation, one afterward literarily concretized by means of a highly rhetorical strategy of avowing innocence by reason of overarching prior victimizations, Jewishness first and foremost among them, then this confessional narrative, *Das Verhör*, at its end, after the GDR has ceased to exist as a state, is not an end but merely a continuation under new management. Constructed in the name of truth, it is a monument to evasion. Supposedly written to the end of finally confessing, of no longer holding it in after all these years, of elucidating one's life and actions in a hearing, *Das Verhör* constitutes only elaborate denial. In this confession, all the others are guilty.[7]

Andreas Sinakowski's *Das Verhör* had spun out of an earlier, larger interview project with GDR writers who had emigrated to the West, suggesting that this confessional narrative was meant as part of a process for discovering, uncovering the hidden historical events of the GDR period: a personal confession of complicity as contribution to a critical elucidation of the past. Is it that?

A true confession written in postunification Germany that sensationalizes discovering "the truth" of a gay, Jewish *Stasi* informant, written in a genre suggestive of the unmitigated truthfulness that it will convey to the reader and expressly recommended in the foreword for that very reason, this work by an author from East Germany does indeed convey a truth: a truth of compromise and co-optation, of wish fulfillment and denial. This author displays his life in the GDR, perhaps unwittingly so, if one reads against the grain in which his confession was written, as inextricably mired in the qualities just listed: compromise and co-optation, wish fulfillment and denial.

The Jewish identity to which he alludes, one that he allocates to himself by virtue of an anti-Semitic incident, is a rhetorical Jewishness first and foremost, not a personal negotiation of actual identity, but a device of argument for the purpose of absolution in advance, a device not of truth but of avoidance.

NOTES

1. John Tagliabue, "Game Is Up, So Informers Inform on Themselves," *The New York Times*, 30 Jan. 1992: 4.
2. This translation and the others that follow are my own. The pagination corresponds to the original text: Andreas Sinakowski, *Das Verhör* (Berlin: Basis Druck, 1991).
3. Chaim Noll, "A Country, a Child, but Not the Country's Child," in *Jewish Voices, German Words: Growing Up Jewish in Postwar Germany and Austria*, ed. Elena Lappin, trans. Krishna Winston (North Haven, CT: Catbird Press, 1994), 44–64.
4. "In 1981 there still lived 600 Jews in the GDR and East Berlin, of whom only 30 were under the age of 35," estimated Inge Deutschkron in her study *Israel und die Deutschen* (1983), 188, as quoted by Erica Burgauer, *Zwischen Erinnerung und Verdrängung: Juden in Deutschland nach 1945* (Reinbek bei Hamburg: Rowohlt, 1993), 155.
5. Andreas Sinakowski, "Zwischen Tabu und Trauma," *magnus: das schwule magazin* 2, 6 (June 1990): 31–34.
6. See Denis M. Sweet, "The Church, the Stasi, and Socialist Integration: Three Stages of Lesbian and Gay Emancipation in the Former German Democratic Republic," in *Gay Men and the Sexual History of the Political Left*, ed. Gert Hekma, Harry Oosterhuis, and James Steakley (New York: Haworth, 1995), 349–65.
7. In this respect, Andreas Sinakowski's "confessions" are no different from the mass of interviews with former official and unofficial members of the GDR state security apparatus that were appearing at the same time. They point without exception to someone else as the guilty party. Members of one *Stasi* department typically point to another department, or to higher-ups. Those in higher positions reserve guilt for the party. See Christina Wilkening, *Staat im Staate: Auskünfte ehemaliger Stasi-Mitarbeiter* (Berlin: Aufbau, 1990).

WORKS CITED

Burgauer, Erica. *Zwischen Erinnerung und Verdrängung: Juden in Deutschland nach 1945.* Reinbek bei Hamburg: Rowohlt, 1993.

Noll, Chaim. "A Country, a Child, but Not the Country's Child." In *Jewish Voices, German Words: Growing Up Jewish in Postwar Germany and Austria*, ed. Elena Lappin, trans. Krishna Winston , 44–64. North Haven, CT: Catbird Press, 1994.

Runge, Irene. *"Ich bin kein Russe": Jüdische Zuwanderung zwischen 1989 und 1994.* Berlin: Dietz, 1995.

Sinakowski, Andreas. *Das Verhör.* Berlin: Basis Druck, 1991.

—— "Zwischen Tabu und Trauma." *magnus: das schwule magazin* 2, 6 (June 1990): 31–34.

Sweet, Denis M. "The Church, the Stasi, and Socialist Integration: Three Stages of Lesbian and Gay Emancipation in the Former German Democratic Republic." In *Gay Men and the Sexual History of the Political Left*, ed. Gert Hekma, Harry Oosterhuis, and James Steakley, 349–65. New York: Haworth, 1995.

Tagliabue, John. "Game Is Up, So Informers Inform on Themselves." *The New York Times*, 30 Jan. 1992, 4.

Wilkening, Christina. *Staat im Staate: Auskünfte ehemaliger Stasi-Mitarbeiter.* Berlin: Aufbau, 1990.

Further Reading

The following bibliography makes no claims to completeness. The editors have chosen to focus on materials that have appeared since 1990. For the benefit of those readers who are not fluent in German, English-language materials have been suggested whenever possible. This list contains no titles cited in the bibliographies following each essay.

Baader, Meike Sophia. "Grenzgängerinnen zwischen den Welten: Jüdische Frauen in Geschichte und Gegenwart." *Babylon* 13/14 (1994): 177–82.

Baioni, Giuliano. *Kafka—Literatur und Judentum*, trans. Gertrud Billen and Josef Billen. Stuttgart: Metzler, 1994.

Bechtel, Delphine. "Sur une terre étrangère': la littérature juive féminine de langue allemande depuis 1970.' *Germania*. 17 (1995): 79–100.

Benz, Wolfgang, ed. *Zwischen Antisemitismus und Philosemitismus: Juden in der Bundesrepublik*. Berlin: Metropol, 1991.

Berger, Alan. "Bearing Witness: Second–Generation Literature of the Shoa." *Modern Judaism* 10, 3 (1990): 43–63.

Bodemann, Y. Michal. *Out of the Ashes: The Vicissitudes of the New German Jewry*. Jerusalem: Institute of the World Jewish Congress, 1997.

———. ed. *Jews, Germans, Memory: Reconstructions of Jewish Life in Germany*. Ann Arbor: University of Michigan Press, 1996.

———. ed. *Gedächtnistheater: die jüdische Gemeinschaft und ihre deutsche Erfindung*. Hamburg: Rotbuch, 1996.

Bormann, Alexander von. "Wir sind nicht, was wir sind.' Nichtidentität als Erzählkonzept im deutschjüdischen Roman nach 1945." In *"Wir tragen den Zettelkasten mit den Steckbriefen unserer Freunde": Das Osnabrücker Symposion zur deutschen Literatur jüdischer Autoren nach dem Holocaust*, ed. Jens Stüben and Winfried Woesler, 31–52. Darmstadt: Häusser, 1994.

Boyarin, Daniel and Jonathan Boyarin. "Diaspora: Generation and the Ground of Jewish Identity." In *Identities*, ed. Kwame Anthony Appiah and Henry Louis Gates, Jr., 305–37. Chicago: University of Chicago Press, 1994.

Brenner, David. "Promoting East European Jewry: *Ost und West*, Ethnic Identity, and the German–Jewish Audience." *Prooftexts* 15,1 (1994): 5–32.

Brenner, Michael. *After the Holocaust: Rebuilding Jewish Lives in Postwar Germany.* Princeton: Princeton University Press, 1997.

———*Nach dem Holocaust: Juden in Deutschland 1945–50.* München [Munich]: Beck, 1995. The German original of the preceding title.

Broder, Henryk M. *Erbarmen mit den Deutschen.* Hamburg: Hoffmann und Campe, 1993.

Brumlik, Micha. "The Situation of the Jews in Today's Germany." Bloomington: Jewish Studies Program, Indiana University, 1991.

Burgauer, Erica. *Zwischen Erinnerung und Verdrängung: Juden in Deutschland nach 1945.* Reinbek bei Hamburg: Rowohlt, 1993.

Cohn, Michael. *The Jews in Germany 1945–1993: The Building of a Minority.* Westport, CT: Praeger, 1994.

Feinberg, Anat. "Abiding in a Haunted Land. The Issue of Heimat in contemporary German-Jewish Writing." *New German Critique* 70 (Winter 1997): 161–81.

Friedman, Michel. *Zukunft ohne Vergessen: Ein jüdisches Leben in Deutschland.* Köln [Cologne]: Kiepenheuer und Wietsch, 1995.

Frakes, Jerold C. "The Names of Old Yiddish." In *The Politics of Interpretation: Alterity and Ideology in Old Yiddish Studies*, 21–104. Albany: State University of New York Press, 1989.

Geller, Jay. "Of Mice and Mensa: Anti-Semitism and the Jewish Genius." *Centennial Review* 38, 2 (1994): 361–85.

Gerstenberger, Katharina and Vera Pohland. "Der Wichser. Edgar Hilsenrath—Schreiben über den Holocaust, Identität und Sexualität." *Deutschunterricht* 44 (1992): 74–91.

Gilman, Sander L. *Jews in Today's German Culture.* Bloomington: Indiana University Press, 1995.

———. "Jewish Writing in a Reunified Germany: Questions of Gender and Identification." In *The Jewish Experience of European Anti-Semitism*, 45–111. Burlington, VT: Center for Holocaust Studies at the University of Vermont, 1995.

———. "Jewish writers in contemporary Germany: the dead author speaks." *Studies in Twentieth Century Literature.* 13. (1989): 215–43.

——. "Male Sexuality and Contemporary Jewish Literature in German: The Damaged Body as the Image of the Damaged Soul." *Genders* 16 (Spring 1993): 113–40.

———. *Smart Jews: The Construction of the Image of Superior Jewish Intelligence.* Lincoln: University of Nebraska Press, 1996.

———. "Sounding Too Jewish: The Discourse of Difference." In *Brücken über dem Abgrund: Auseinandersetzungen mit jüdischer Leidenserfahrung, Antisemitismus und Exil*, ed. Amy Colin and Elisabeth Strenger, 113–33. Munich: Fink, 1994.

———. "Zwanzig Mark oder: die sichtbare Unsichtbarkeit der Juden im 'neuen' Deutschland," trans. Claudia Mayer-Iswandi. In *Zwischen Traum und Trauma—die Nation: Transatlantische Perspektiven zur Geschichte eines Problems*, ed. Claudia Mayer-Iswandi, 167–94. Tübingen: Stauffenberg, 1994.

Haas, Aaron. *In the Shadow of the Holocaust: The Second Generation.* London: Tauris, 1990.

Hamburger, Michael. "Gedanken zur Identitätsfrage." In "Wir tragen den Zettelkasten mit den Steckbriefen unserer Freunde": *Das Osnabrücker Symposion zur deutschen Literatur jüdischer Autoren nach dem Holocaust*, ed. Jens Stüben and Winfried Woesler, 23–30. Darmstadt: Häusser, 1994.

Heenen-Wolff, Susann. *Im Haus des Henkers: Gespräche in Deutschland.* Frankfurt am Main: Dvorah, 1992.

Herzog, Todd. "Hybrids and Mischlinge." *German Quarterly* 70, 1 (Winter 1997): 1–17

Hutton, Christopher: "Freud and the family drama of Yiddish." In *Studies in Yiddish Linguistics*, ed. Paul Wexler, 9–22. Tübingen: Niemeyer, 1990.

Jacob, Jessica, Claudia Schoppmann and Wendy Zena-Henry, ed. *Nach der Shoa geboren: Jüdische Frauen in Deutschland*. Berlin: Elefanten, 1994.

"Juden und Deutsche." [Themenheft] *Spiegel Spezial* 2 (1992).

Kauffmann, Uri, ed. *Jüdisches Leben heute in Deutschland*. Bonn: Inter Nationes, 1993.

Kluger, Ruth. *Katastrophen: Über deutsche Literatur*. Göttingen: Wallstein Verlag, 1994.

Köppen, Manuel. "Von Versuchen, die Gegenwart der Vergangenheit zu erinnern. Rafael Seligmanns Roman *Rubensteins Versteigerung* und die Strategien des Erinnerns in der zweiten Genheration." *Sprache im technischen Zeitalter* 33 (1995): 250–259.

Lamping, Dieter: "Gibt es eine neue deutsch–jüdische Literatur?" *Jahrbuch der finnisch–deutschen Literatur* 26 (1994): 221–25.

Lappin, Elena, ed. *Jewish Voices, German Words: Growing Up Jewish in Postwar Germany and Austria*. North Haven: Catbird, 1994.

Leventhal, Robert S. "Versagen: Kafka und die masochistische Ordnung." *German Life and Letters* 48 (2): 148–69.

Loewy, Hanno, ed. *Holocaust: die Grenzen des Verstehens: Eine Debatte über die Besetzung der Geschichte*. Reinbek bei Hamburg: Rowohlt, 1992.

Lorenz, Dagmar, ed. *Insiders and Outsiders: Jewish and Gentile Culture in Germany Since 1989*. Detroit: Wayne State University Press, 1994.

Mattenklott, Gert. *Über Juden in Deutschland*. Frankfurt am Main: Jüdischer Verlag, 1992.

Nechama, Andreas and Julius H. Schoeps, ed. *Aufbau nach dem Untergang: deutsch–jüdische Geschichte nach 1945*. Berlin: Argon, 1992.

Nolden, Thomas. "Contemporary German Jewish Literature." *German Life and Letters* 47.1 (January 1994), 77–93.

———. *Junge jüdische Literatur: Konzentrisches Schreiben in der Gegenwart*. Würzburg: Königshausen und Neumann, 1995.

Noll, Chaim. *Nachtgedanken über Deutschland*. Reinbek bei Hamburg: Rowohl, 1992.

O'Doherty, P. "German-Jewish Writers and Themes in GDR Fiction." *German Life and Letters* 49, 2 (April 1996): 271–81.

Ostow, Robin. "From the Cold War Through the Wende: History, Belonging and the Self in East German Jewry." *The Oral History Review* 21, 2 (Winter 1993): 59–72.

Paucker, Henri. "Chocolate, Cheese and Judaism: Xenophobia and Anti–Semitism in Switzerland." *In The Jewish Experience of European Anti–Semitism*, ed. Hazel Kahn Keimowitz and Wolfgang Mieder, 117–42. Burlington: Center for Holocaust Studies at the University of Vermont, 1995.

Petersen, Vibeke Rutzou. "The Best of Both Worlds? Jewish Representations of Assimilation, Self, and Other in Weimar Popular Fiction." *German Quarterly* 68,2 (Spring 1993): 160–73.

Rabinbach, Anson and Jack Zipes. *Germans and Jews since the Holocaust: The Changing Situation in West Germany*. New York: Holmes and Meier, 1986.

Rapaport, Lynn. *Jews in Germany after the Holocaust: Memory, Identity and Jewish–German Relations*. New York: Cambridge University Press, 1997.

Reich–Ranicki, Marcel. *Die verkehrte Krone. Über Juden in der deutschen Literatur*. Wiesbaden: Reichert, 1995.

Remmler, Karen and Sander Gilman. *Reemerging Jewish Culture in Germany*. New York: New York University Press, 1994.

Saalmann, Dieter. "Guest Literature in the Federal Republic: German as a Means of Literary Articulation." *Language Quarterly* 28, 3–4 (199?): 70–80.

Schneider, Richard Chaim. *Zwischenwelten: Ein jüdisches Leben im heutigen Deutschland.* München [Munich]: Kindler, 1994.

Schoeps, Julius. *Leiden an Deutschland: Vom antisemitischen Wahn und der Last der Erinnerung.* München [Munich]: R. Piper, 1990.

Silbermann, Alphons and Herbert Sallen. *Juden in Westdeutschland: Fremdbild und Selbstbild einer Minorität.* Köln [Cologne]: Wissenschaft und Politik, 1992.

Speaking Out: Jewish Voices from United Germany. Chicago: Editions Q, 1995.

Stern, Frank. *Im Anfang war Auschwitz: Antisemitismus und Philosemitismus im deutschen Nachkrieg.* Gerlingen: Bleicher, 1991.

————. "Jews in the Minds of Germans in the Postwar Period." Bloomington: Jewish Studies Program, Indiana University, 1993.

Sternheim-Goral, Walter L. Arie. *An der Grenzscheide: Kein Weg als Jude und Deutscher?* Münster: Lit, 1994.

Stüben, Jens and Winfried Woesler, ed. "Wir tragen den Zettelkasten mit den Steckbriefen unserer Freunde": *Das Osnabrücker Symposion zur deutschen Literatur jüdischer Autoren nach dem Holocaust.* Darmstadt: Häusser, 1994.

Taylor, Jennifer. "Writing as Revenge: Jewish German Identity in Post-Holocaust German Literary Works: Reading Survivor Authors Jurek Becker, Edgar Hilsenrath and Ruth Kluger." Diss., Cornell University, 1994.

Traverso, Enzo. *The Jews and Germany: From the Judeo-German Symbiosis to the Memory of Auschwitz.* Lincoln: University of Nebraska Press, 1995.

Winkler, Willi. "'Wie funktioniert ein Dosenöffner?' Irene Disches Erzählungen." *Merkur* 45 (1991): 157–59.

Wistrich, Robert. 'Belonging to a normal Nation: The uneasy revival of the Jewish community in Germany.' *Times Literary Supplement.* June 7, 1996. 14–15.

Wolffsohn, Michael. *Die Deutschland-Akte: Juden und Deutsche in Ost und West: Tatsachen und Legenden.* München [Munich]: Ferenczy bei Bruckmann, 1995.

Wroblewsky, Vincent von, ed. *Zwischen Thora und Trabant: Juden in der DDR.* Berlin: Aufbau, 1993.

Index

About the Editors and Contributors

David Brenner is Assistant Professor of Germanic and Slavic Languages and Literatures at the University of Colorado at Boulder, CO. His first book, *Marketing Identities: The Invention of Jewish Ethnicity*, was published in 1997 with Wayne State University Press. His articles have appeared in *German Quarterly, Prooftexts*, the *Women in German Yearbook* and the *Yearbook of the Leo Baeck Institute*, as well as in volumes with Stanford University Press and Berghahn. His research crosses traditional disciplinary lines, combining cultural, film, and media studies with German and Jewish history. His latest project is a book about the reception of *Schindler's List* in the US, Germany, and Israel.

Iris M. Bruce is Assistant Professor of German at the University of Western Ontario in London, Ontario. Her research focus is on Kafka's position within the tradition of Hassidism, Zionism and Yiddish culture. With publications on Kafka in the *Kafka Yearbook*, Bruce is currently revising a manuscript entitled "The Reluctant Zionist: Franz Kafka and the Jewish (Con)Text."

Linda E. Feldman is Assistant Professor of German at the University of Windsor in Ontario. She has published on portrayals of Jews and women in the writing of H. J. C. von Grimmelshausen, and is currently completing a monograph on the memoirs of Glückel von Hameln.

Sander L. Gilman is Henry Booth Luce Professor of Human Biology at the University of Chicago. The author of over forty books and numerous articles, he is past President of the Modern Language Association. His most recent book publication is *Franz Kafka: The Jewish Patient*.

Sabine Gölz is associate professor of German and Comparative Literature at the University of Iowa in Iowa City. She has published articles on critical theory, especially on Derridean and feminist readings on Ingeborg Bachmann, Franz Kafka and Paul Celan. A book entitled "The Split Scene of Reading: Nietzsche/ Derrida/ Kafka/ Bachmann" is forthcoming.

Sonja M. Hedgepeth is associate professor of German at Middle Tennessee State University in Murfreesboro. The author of a recently published book on Else Lasker-Schüler, *Überall blicke ich nach einem heimatlichen Boden aus: Exil im Werk Else Lasker-Schülers*, Hedgepeth has also written on Holocaust issues and pedagogical and methodological concerns.

Christopher D. Kenway is a doctoral student in history at the University of California in Los Angeles. He has worked as a historian and research assistant at the Survivors of the Shoah: Visual History Foundation as well as the National

Center for History in the Schools, both in Los Angeles. His dissertation deals with the *Körperkultur* movement.

Diana Orendi is associate professor of German and Comparative Studies at Cleveland State University in Cleveland. Besides pursuing research interests in Holocaust studies, film studies, and issues of German-American literary relations, she has recently had a grant proposal funded by NEH which will provide for developing courses on non-Western Literature. Orendi's publications include a biography of Rahel Sanzara, whose novel *Das Verlorene Kind* she re-edited.

Scott Spector is Assistant Professor of History and German at the University of Michigan in Ann Arbor. His research and teaching engage questions of the interplay of ideology and culture in Central Europe from the mid-nineteenth century to the present, focusing on topics including: German-speaking Jewish writers and thinkers, the politics of historiography, nationalism and culture, sexuality and culture, and film studies. He is currently revising his book manuscript entitled "Prague Territories: Culture and Ideology in Franz Kafka's Generation."

Denis M. Sweet completed graduate work in German Studies at Stanford University and the Freie Universität Berlin. He is interested in the function of ideology to provide notions of a social order meant to legitimate some and marginalize others. Having published on Nietzsche and Faust reception in the German Democratic Republic, he is currently at work on a study of gay literature in the former GDR. Denis Sweet teaches German at Bates College in Maine.

Steven Taubeneck is Assistant Professor of Germanic Studies at The University of British Columbia at Vancouver. He received his Ph.D. from the University of Virginia in 1988. Asked about his research interests, Taubeneck reports that "[f]or me, Kafka has always been more than academic. When I was ten years old, it was the truth of his writing that struck. 'Truth' meant the graphic unveiling of family life. Father throwing the apple, Gregor snapping at the coffee, mother fretting, Grete stretching her body: this vision of the family was awful and fantastic. Now it is his edginess that fascinates. His writing cuts like an ax against the frozen lake."

ISBN 0-275-95557-5

9 780275 955571   90000>

EAN

HARDCOVER BAR CODE